Perennial
Reference
Guide

Karleen Shafer
& Nicole Lloyd

Perennial Reference Guide

**Karleen Shafer
& Nicole Lloyd**

ISBN 978-1-58874-682-5

Published by

STIPES PUBLISHING L.L.C.
204 West University Avenue
Champaign, Illinois 61820

Cover photograph by: Keri Shafer

Acknowledgments

A special thank you to the following
people who have given so much to help finish this book.

Your influence, advice & support will never be forgotten.

Angela & Adam Bruckner
Julie & Robert Commet
Gladys & Vernon Fuchs
Jim Jonker
Amanda & Darren Koraleski
Chad Lloyd
Dr. Robert Schutzki
Rus Shafer
Xiola Shafer

Introduction

The Perennial Reference Guide is an all inclusive source for selecting perennials. Drawing on their past work experiences, Nicole and Karleen have collaborated on informative solutions for plant use and site challenges. This book is the result of organizing years of essential information they have gathered in designing gardens and landscapes.

As experienced designers and planners they have put creative and practical lists together to help establish sustainable landscapes. This book provides selections as guidelines for design, site requirements and landscape uses.

Primarily, this book is a source for herbaceous perennial selection, although ephemeral plants, woody groundcovers and vines are listed where appropriate. The plant lists found throughout recommend perennials that can meet client or personal needs and design criteria.

The Perennial Reference Guide presents the information in an immediate and effortless format that will be a useful tool for landscape designers, architects, contractors, as well as horticulturists, consultants, nurseries, students and the garden enthusiast.

The lists are broken into various sections for ease of use. Section formats vary depending on what information is relevant to the list. The lists aid in selecting plants for deer resistance, juglone tolerance, architectural plants, drought tolerance, quick color selection, foliage color choices, flower forms, companion plants, erosion control, nature attracting, aromatherapy, garden themes and many more.

Please keep in mind that growing conditions vary. Plants have distinct requirements in each region. Use it as a general reference and consider that plants react differently based on soil conditions, moisture levels, lighting and weather patterns.

Contents

Where do I find plants for: .... vii- ix
USDA Hardiness Zone Map .... x-xi

Plant Characteristics-Section One 1
    Flower colors 3
    Flower forms 106
    Foliage colors 113
    Chemical 134

Specific Genera-Section Two 137
    Daylilies 139
    Ferns 149
    Grasses 153
    Hostas 159
    Mosses 167
    Vines 168

Site Requirements-Section Three 173
    Soil 175
    Moisture 187
    Environment 197

Landscape Uses-Section Four 203
    Aesthetic 205
    Environmental 219
    Economical 245
    Resistant 251

Plant and Flower Uses-Section Five 263
    Botanical 265
    Nature 293

Theme Gardens-Section Six 309

Glossary 335

Sources of Plant Materials 339

Bibliography 343

vi

Where do I find plants for:

Acidic Soil 175-176
Alkaline Soil 177-178
Architectural Plants 205-208
Aromatherapy 265
Biblical Garden 311-312
Birds 299-300
Bog 187-189
Butterflies 293-298
Children's Garden 313-316
Clay 179-182
Crevices 219-220
Cut Flowers & Foliage 266-271
Deer Resistance 251-261
Dried Flowers & Fruit 272-275
Drought Tolerance 192-196
Dry Shade 190-191
Edible Plants 276-277
Erosion Control 221-223
Evening Garden 317-318
Ferns 149-152
Flower Colors
        Black Flowers 102-103
        Blue Flowers 3-15
        Brown Flowers 104-105
        Green Flowers 84-87
        Lavender Flowers 26-30
        Orange Flowers 68-71
        Pink Flowers 44-67
        Purple Flowers 15-24
        Red Flowers 31-43
        White Flowers 88-101
        Yellow Flowers 72-83

Where do I find plants for:

Flower Forms

      Buttons 106

      Daisies 107-108

      Orbs 106-107

      Plumes. 108-109

      Spires 109-110

      Trumpets 111

      Umbels 111

      Wispy 112

Foliage Colors

      Blue Foliage 124-129

      Chartreuse Foliage 119-123

      Orange Foliage 119-123

      Pink Foliage 113-118

      Purple Foliage 113-118

      Red Foliage 113-118

      Silver Foliage 124-129

      White Foliage 124-129

      Yellow Foliage 119-123

Foot Traffic 223-224

Fragrance 278-284

Grasses 153-158

Healing Garden 329-330

Hemerocallis 139-148

Herbs 285-290

Honeybees 305-308

Hostas 159-166

Hummingbirds 301-304

Japanese Garden 319-320

Juglone Tolerance 197-200

Knot Garden 321-324

Long Bloomers 209-210

Low Pollen 225-232

Where do I find plants for:

Medicinal 291-292
Mosses 167
Native 233-242
Naturalizing 243-244
Poisionous 134-135
Quick Cover 245-246
Rabbit Resistance 251-261
Rock Garden 325-328
Salt Tolerance 201-202
Sand Dune 186
Sandy Soil 183-185
Self Sow 247-250
Sensory Garden 329-330
Trailing 211-212
Tropical Looking 331-333
Vines 168-171
Winter Interest 213-218

USDA Hardiness Zone Map

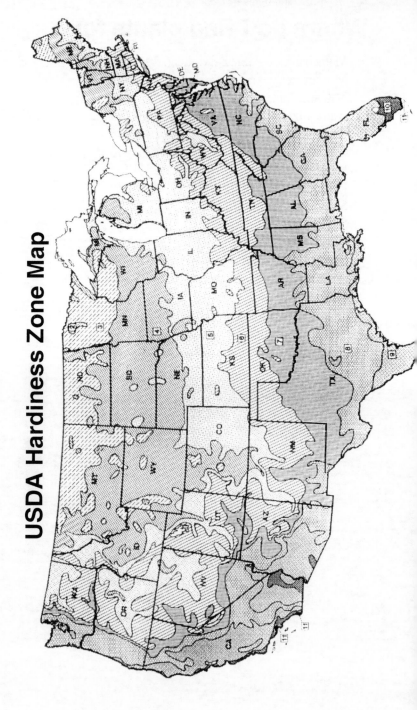

RANGE OF AVERAGE ANNUAL MINIMUM
TEMPERATURES FOR EACH ZONE

ZONE 1	BELOW -50° F
ZONE 2	-50° TO -40°
ZONE 3	-40° TO -30°
ZONE 4	-30° TO -20°
ZONE 5	-20° TO -10°
ZONE 6	-10° TO 0°
ZONE 7	0° TO 10°
ZONE 8	10° TO 20°
ZONE 9	20° TO 30°
ZONE 10	30° TO 40°
ZONE 11	ABOVE 40°

xi

Section One
Plant Characteristics

2

Blue 0-6

Scientific Name	Common Name	Comments	Zone	Lighting	Bloom Season
Ajuga reptans 'Bronze Beauty'	Bugleweed	Evergreen	z3-9	☼ ✹ ●	Sp
Ajuga reptans 'Chocolate Chip'	Bugleweed	Chocolate Green Foilage	z3-9	☼ ✹ ●	Sp
Anemone blanda	Grecian Windflower		z4-7	☼ ✹	Sp
Aster novi-belgii 'Buxton's Blue'	New York Aster		z4-8	☼	Sum Fall
Campanula portenschiagiana	Dalmation Bellflower		z4-8	☼ ✹	Sum Fall
Campanula cochlearifolia	Spiral Bellflower	Blue Violet	z4-7	☼ ✹	Sum
Campanula garganica 'Blue Diamond'	Gargano Bellflower		z5-7	☼ ✹	Sp
Campanula rotundifolia	Harebell		z3-9	☼ ✹	Sum
Chionodoxa luciliae	Glory-of-the-Snow	Corm (Bulb)	z4-8	☼	Sp
Crocus chrysanthus 'Bluebird'	Golden Crocus	Corm (Bulb)	z4-7	☼	Sp
Crocus speciosus 'Conqueror'	Fall Crocus	Corm (Bulb)	z5-7	☼	Fall
Crocus speciosus 'Oxonian'	Fall Crocos	Corm (Bulb)	z5-7	☼	Fall
Gentiana acaulis	Stemless Gentian	Moist Soil	z3-6	☼ ✹	Sp
Gentiana acaulis 'Bevedere'	Stemless Gentian	Moist Soil	z3-6	☼ ✹	Sp
Gentiana x macaulayi 'Wellsii'	Wellsii Gentian		z5-7	☼	Sum Fall
Gentiana sino-ornata	Chinese Gentian	Evergreen	z5-7	☼	Sum Fall
Gentiana verna	Spring Gentian	Evergreen	z4-7	☼	Sp
Ipheion uniflorum	Spring Star Flower		z5-9	☼	Sp
Iris 'Blue Frost'	Bearded Iris		z3-10	☼	Sum

Blue 0-6"

Scientific Name	Common Name	Comments	Zone	Lighting	Bloom Season
Iris 'Butterfly'	Bearded Iris	Lt. Blue Purple Splotches	z3-10	☼	Sum
Iris 'Grandma's Hat'	Bearded Iris		z3-10	☼	Sum
Iris 'Pixie Princess'	Bearded Iris		z3-10	☼	Sum
Iris 'Sky Baby'	Bearded Iris		z3-10	☼	Sum
Iris cristata	Crested Dwarf Iris		z3-8	☼ ☼	Sp
Iris reticulata	Reticulated Iris		z5-8	☼ ☼	Sp
Iris verna	Vernal Iris		z6-10	☼	Sp
Lobelia erinus 'Crystal Palace'	Lobelia		annual	☼ ☼	Sum Fall
Muscari aucheri	Grape Hyacinth	Bulb	z2-9	☼	Sp
Muscari neglectum	Starch Grape Hyacinth	Bulb	z2-9	☼	Sp
Myosotis alpestris	Alpine Forget-me-not		z5-7	☼	Sp
Polygala calcarea	Chalk Milkwort		z5-7	☼	Sp Sum
Polygala calcarea 'Bulley's Variety'	Chalk Milkwort		z5-7	☼	Sp Sum
Puschkinia scilloides	Striped Squill	Bulb	z4-9	☼	Sp
Scilla mischtschenkoana	Tubergen Squill	Bulb	z4-7	☼	Sp
Scilla sibirica	Siberian Squill	Bulb	z2-7	☼	Sp Wtr
Veronica alpina	Alpine Speedwell		z3-8	☼	Sp
Veronica pectinata	Comb Speedwell		z2-7	☼ ☀	Sum
Veronica prostrata	Harebell Speedwell		z5-8	☼	Sum

Blue 0-6"

Scientific Name	Common Name	Comments	Zone	Lighting	Bloom Season
Veronica prostrata 'Blue Sheen'	Harebell Speedwell		z5-8	☼	Sum
Veronica prostrata 'Heavenly Blue'	Harebell Speedwell		z5-8	☼	Sum
Veronica prostrata 'Loddon Blue'	Harebell Speedwell		z5-8	☼	Sum
Veronica spicata 'Waterperry Blue'	Spiked Speedwell	White Eyes	z3-7	☼	Sp
Viola cucullata 'Royal Robe'	Marsh Blue Violet		z4-9	☀	Sp
6-12"					
Agapanthus 'Peter Pan'	African Lily		z7-10	☼	Sum Fall
Ajuga reptans	Bugleweed	Evergreen	z3-9	☼☼☀	Sp
Anchusa capensis 'Blue Angel'	Bugloss		z6-8	☼	Sum
Aster novi-belgii 'Lady in Blue'	New York Aster		z4-8	☼	Sum Fall
Brimeura amethystina	Hyacinth	Bulb	z5-9	☀	Sp
Campanula carpatica	Carpathian Harebell	Likes cool roots	z3-7	☼☼	Sum
Campanula carpatica 'Blueclips'	Carpathian Harebell	Two toned	z3-7	☼☼	Sum
Campanula carpatica 'Chewton Joy'	Carpathian Harebell	Likes cool roots	z3-7	☼☼	Sum
Campanula carpatica 'Kobalt Bell'	Carpathian Harebell	Likes cool roots	z3-7	☼☼	Sum
Campanula poscharskyana	Serbian Bellflower	Blue Lilac	z3-7	☀	Sp
Ceratostigma plumbaginoides	Plumbago	Bronze Green Foliage in fall	z5-8	☼☼	Sum Fall
Dracocephalum grandiflorum	Dragonhead		z3-7	☼	Sum

Blue 6-12"

Scientific Name	Common Name	Comments	Zone	Lighting	Bloom Season
Dracocephalum nutans	Nodding Dragonhead		z3-7	☼	Sum
Gentiana cruciata	Gentian		z3-7	☼ ☀	Sum
Gentiana dahurica	Gentian		z4-7	☼ ☀	Sum
Gentiana septemfida	Crested Gentian	Blue-purple	z3-7	☼ ☀	Sum Fall
Iris 'Rain Dance'	Dwarf Bearded Iris		z3-7	☼	Sp
Iris setosa	Bristle Pointed Iris		z3-9	☼	Sp Sum
Muscari armeniacum	Grape Hyacinth	Bulb	z4-8	☼ ☀	Sp
Muscari armeniacum 'Blue Spike'	Grape Hyacinth	Bulb	z4-8	☼ ☀	Sp
Muscari armeniacum 'Saphir'	Grape Hyacinth	Bulb/White Rim	z4-8	☼ ☀	Sp
Muscari botryoides	Grape Hyacinth	Bulb	z2-8	☼ ☀	Sp
Myosotis scorpioides	True Forget-me-not	Pond Edges	z3-8	☼ ●	Sum Fall
Myosotis sylvatica	Woodland Forget-me-not		z3-7	☼	Sp
Myosotis sylvatica 'Blue Ball'	Woodland Forget-me-not		z3-7	☼	Sp
Myosotis sylvatica 'Royal Blue'	Woodland Forget-me-not		z3-7	☀	Sp
Myosotis sylvatica 'Victoria Blue'	Woodland Forget-me-not		z3-7	☀	Sp
Omphalodes cappadocica	Navel-Seed		z6-8	●	Sp
Omphalodes verna	Blue-Eyed Mary		z6-9	●	Sp
Ophiopogon japonicus	Dwarf Mondo Grass, Dk. Purple Foliage		z6-9	☼ ☀	Sum
Phacelia campanularia	California Bluebell		z3-10	☼	Sum Fall

Blue 6-12"

Scientific Name	Common Name	Comments	Zone	Lighting	Bloom Season
Phlox subulata 'Blue Emerald'	Moss Phlox		z2-8	☼	Sp
Phlox subulata 'Blue Hills'	Moss Phlox		z2-8	☼	Sp
Phlox subulata 'Emerald Cushion Blue'	Moss Phlox		z2-8	☼	Sp
Platycodon g. 'Sentimental Blue'	Balloon Flower	Dislikes Disturbance	z3-7	☼◐	Sum
Pulmonaria angustifolia	Blue Lungwort		z2-7	◐●	Sp
Pulmonaria longifolia	Long-Leafed Lungwort		z3-8	◐●	Sp
Pulmonaria saccharata 'Argentea'	Bethlehem Sage		z3-7	◐●	Sp
Pulmonaria saccharata 'British Sterling'	Bethlehem Sage	Silver White Mottled	z3-7	◐●	Sp
Pulmonaria saccharata 'Excalibur'	Bethlehem Sage	Silver Frosted Foliage	z3-7	◐●	Sp
Pulmonaria saccharata 'Highdown'	Bethlehem Sage		z3-7	◐●	Sp
Pulmonaria saccharata 'Janet Fisk'	Bethlehem Sage	White Marbled Foliage	z3-7	◐●	Sp
Pulsatilla vulgaris	Pasque Flower	Fuzzy Seed Heads	z5-8	☼◐	Sp
Sisyrinchium angustifolium	Blue-Eyed Grass		z3-8	☼◐	Sp
Veronica gentianoides	Gentian Speedwell		z4-7	☼	Sp
Veronica x 'Goodness Grows'	Speedwell		z3-8	☼	Sp
Veronica 'Knallblau'	Speedwell		z4-7	☼	Sp Sum
Veronica 'Shirley Blue'	Speedwell		z4-7	☼◐	Sum
Viola cornuta 'Blaue Schonheit'	Horned Violet		z6-9	☼◐	Sp
Viola cornuta 'Broughton Blue'	Horned Violet		z6-9	☼◐	Sp

Blue 12-18"

Scientific Name	Common Name	Comments	Zone	Lighting	Bloom Season
Agapanthus 'Liliput'	African Lily		z7-10	☼	Sum Fall
Angelonia 'Blue Pacific'	Summer Snapdragon		annual	☼	Sum Fall
Aquilegia x hybrida 'Windswept'	Hybrid Columbine		z3-9	☼ ☼	Sp
Aster dumosus 'Wood's Light Blue'	New York Aster		z3-8	☼	Sum Fall
Brunnera macrophylla	Siberian Bugloss		z3-8	☼ ●	Sp Sum
Campanula glomerata	Clustered Bellflower		z3-8	☼	Sum
Geranium 'Brookside'	Geranium		z4-8	☼ ☼	Sum
Geranium x 'Johnson's Blue'	Geranium		z4-7	☼ ☼	Sum
Iris 'Blue Fragrance'	Bearded Iris		z3-10	☼	Sum
Linum perenne 'Saphir'	Blue Flax		z5-8	☼ ☼	Sp
Mertensia virginica	Virginia Bluebells		z3-8	☼ ●	Sp
Phlox divaricata	Woodland Phlox		z3-8	☼ ●	Sp
Phlox divaricata 'Blue Dreams'	Woodland Phlox		z4-9	☼ ●	Sp
Phlox divaricata 'Clouds of Perfume'	Woodland Phlox		z4-9	☼ ●	Sp
Phlox divaricata 'London Grove Blue'	Woodland Phlox		z4-9	☼ ●	Sp
Platycodon grandiflorus 'Komachi'	Balloon Flower		z3-7	☼ ☼	Sum
Polemonium reptans	Creeping Polemonium		z3-8	☼	Sp
Scabiosa columbaria 'Butterfly Blue'	Pincushion Flower		z3-9	☼ ☼	Sum
Stokesia laevis 'Blue Moon'	Stokes Aster		z5-9	☼	Sum

Blue 12-18"

Scientific Name	Common Name	Comments	Zone	Lighting	Bloom Season
Stokesia laevis 'Wyoming'	Stokes Aster		z5-9	☀	Sum
Veronica austriaca ssp. teucrium	Austrian Speedwell		z4-7	☀	Sum
Veronica spicata	Spiked Speedwell		z3-7	☀ ◑	Sum
Veronica spicata ssp. Incana	Spiked Speedwell		z3-7	☀ ◑	Sum
Veronica 'Crater Lake Blue'	Speedwell		z4-7	☀	Sp Sum
Veronica 'Royal Blue'	Speedwell		z4-7	☀	Sum
Veronica spicata 'Blue Spires'	Spiked Speedwell		z3-7	☀	Sum
Vinca major	Large Periwinkle		z7-9	◑	Sp

18-24"

Scientific Name	Common Name	Comments	Zone	Lighting	Bloom Season
Adenophora lilifolia	Lilyleaf Ladybells		z3-7	☀ ◑	Sp Sum
Allium caeruleum	Blue Globe Onion	Bulb	z2-7	☀	Sp Sum
Amsonia ciliata	Downy Amsonia	Yellow Fall Foliage	z6-10	☀	Sp Sum
Amsonia tabenaemontana	Blue Star	Yellow Fall Foliage	z4-9	☀	Sp Sum
Aquilegia alpina	Alpine Columbine		z3-8	☀ ◑	Sp
Aquilegia vulgaris	Columbine		z3-8	☀ ◑	Sp Sum
Borago laxiflora	Borage		z6-9	☀	Fall
Centaurea montana	Bachelor's Button		z3-8	☀ ◑	Sum
Dracocephalum ruyschianum	Dragonhead		z3-7	☀ ◑	Sum

9

Blue 18-24"

Scientific Name	Common Name	Comments	Zone	Lighting	Bloom Season
Eryngium alpinum	Alpine Sea Holly		z4-7	☼	Sum
Erynigium amethystinum	Amethyst Sea Holly		z2-8	☼	Sum
Eryngium bourgatii	Mediterranean Sea Holly		z5-8	☼	Sum
Eryngium variifolium	Moroccan Sea Holly		z5-9	☼	Sum
Gentiana andrewsii	Bottle Gentian		z3-7	☼☀	Fall
Geranium x magnificum	Showy Geranium		z3-8	☼☀	Sum
Gentiana makinoi	Gentian		z3-7	☼☀	Sum
Platycodon g. 'Hakone Double Blue'	Balloon Flower		z3-7	☼☀	Sum
Platycodon grandiflorus 'Komachi'	Balloon Flower		z3-7	☼☀	Sum
Polemonium caeruleum	Jacob's Ladder		z 2-7	☼☀	Sum
Salvia 'Blue Hill'	Sage		z4-7	☼	Sum
Salvia patens 'Cambridge Blue'	Gentian Sage		z7-9	☼	Sum
Salvia pratensis	Meadow Sage		z3-7	☼	Sum
Scabiosa caucasica 'Moerheim Blue'	Pincushion Flower		z3-7	☼	Sum
Symphytum caucasicum	Caucasian Comfrey		z3-7	☀	Sp
Tradescantia x andersoniana	Spiderwort		z3-9	☼☀	Sum
Veronica perfoliata	Digger's Speedwell		z7-9	☼	Sum
Veronica spicata 'Blue Peter'	Spiked Speedwell		z3-7	☼	Sum

Blue 24-36"

Scientific Name	Common Name	Comments	Zone	Lighting	Bloom Season
24-36"					
Aconitum carmichaelii	Azure Monkshood		z3-7	☼	Sum Fall
Adenophora confusa	Common Ladybells		z3-7	☼☼	Sp Sum
Agapanthus 'Blue Moon'	African Lily		z7-10	☼	Sum
Agapanthus 'Kingston Blue'	African Lily		z7-10	☼	Sum
Amsonia hubrichii	Arkansas Amsonia	Yellow Fall Foliage	z6-9	☼	Sp Sum
Aster azureus	Sky Blue Aster	Blue/Violet	z4-9	☼	Sum
Campanula persicifolia	Peach-leaf Bellflower		z3-8	☼☼	Sum
Catananche caerulea 'Major'	Blue Cupids Dart		z4-7	☼	Sum
Centaurea cyanus	Cornflower		annual	☼	Sum Fall
Cerinthe major	Blue Shrimp Plant		annual	☼☼	Sum
Clematis heracleifolia	Tube Clematis	Non Vining	z3-7	☼	Sum Fall
Clematis integrifolia	Solitary Clematis	Non Vining	z3-7	☼	Sum
Codonopsis clematidea	Bonnet Bellflower		z5-7	☼☼	Sum
Cynoglossum nervosum	Hound's Tongue		z4-8	☼☼	Sum
Echinops ritro 'Blue Glow'	Globe Thistle		z3-9	☼	Sum
Echinops ritro 'Taplow Blue'	Globe Thistle		z5-9	☼	Sum
Eryngium planum	Flat Sea Holly		z5-8	☼	Sum
Gentiana asclepiadea	Willow Gentian		z3-7	☼☼	Sum Fall

11

Blue 24-36"

Scientific Name	Common Name	Comments	Zone	Lighting	Bloom Season
Geranium sylvaticum 'Mayflower'	Wood Cranesbill		z4-8	☀	Sp
Hyssopus officinalis	Hyssop		z3-11	☀ ☽	Sum
Iris ensata 'Blue Beauty'	Japanese Iris		z4-9	☀ ☽	Sum
Iris ensata 'Favorite'	Japanese Iris		z4-9	☀ ☽	Sum
Iris pallida	Sweet Iris		z4-9	☀	Sum
Iris siberica	Siberian Iris		z3-9	☀ ☽	Sp
Iris siberica 'Blue Brilliant'	Siberian Iris		z3-9	☀ ☽	Sp
Iris siberica 'Chartreuse Beauty'	Siberian Iris		z3-9	☀ ☽	Sp
Iris siberica 'Perry's Blue'	Siberian Iris		z3-9	☀ ☽	Sp
Limonium latifolium	Sea Lavender		z3-8	☀	Sum
Linum perenne	Blue Flax		z5-8	☀ ☽	Sp
Lobelia siphilitica	Great Blue Lobelia		z3-9	☀ ☽	Sum
Nepeta x faassenii	Faassen Nepeta		z3-10	☀	Sum
Platycodon grandiflorus	Balloon Flower		z3-7	☀ ☽	Sum

36-48"

Scientific Name	Common Name	Comments	Zone	Lighting	Bloom Season
Aconitum x 'Bressingham Spire'	Bicolor Monkshood		z4-8	☀ ☽	Sp Sum Fall
Aconitum napellus	Monkshood		z3-6	☽	Sum Fall
Aconitum 'Spark's Variety'	Monkshood		z3-7	☀ ☽	Sum Fall

Blue '36-48"

Scientific Name	Common Name	Comments	Zone	Lighting	Bloom Season
Agapanthus sp.	African Lily		z7-10	☼	Sum Fall
Anchusa azurea 'Loddon Royalist'	Alkanet		z3-8	☼ ☀	Sp Sum
Aster novae-angliea 'Fanny's Aster'	New England Aster		z 4-8	☼	Sum Fall
Aster novae-belgii 'Blue Danube'	New York Aster, Yellow maroon centers		z5-8	☼	Sum Fall
Aster tataricus	Tatarian Daisy		z4-8	☼	Fall
Baptisia australis	False Blue Indigo		z3-8	☼ ☀	Sp Sum
Camassia cusickii	Cusick Quamash	Bulb	z3-8	☼	Sum
Camassia leichtinii	Leichtlin Quamash	Bulb	z5-9	☼ ☀	Sum
Delphinium x belladonna	Delphinium		z3-7	☼ ☀	Sum
Delphinium 'Centurion Sky Blue'	Delphinium		z5-7	☼ ☀	Sum
Echinops ritro	Globe Thistle		z3-8	☼	Sum
Echinops ritro 'Veitch's Blue'	Globe Thistle		z3-9	☼	Sum
Eryngium x tripartitum	Sea Holly		z5-8	☼	Sum
Galega officinalis	Common Goat's Rue	Blue Violet	z3-7	☼	Sp Sum
Iris sibirica 'Caesar's Brother'	Siberian Iris		z3-9	☼ ☀	Sp
Lupinus perennis	Sundial Lupine		z3-9	☼	Sp Sum
Meconopsis betonicifolia	Himalayan Blue Poppy, Difficult to grow		z7-8	☀ ☼	Sum
Salvia azurea	Sage		z5-9	☼	Fall
Salvia guaranitica	Blue Anise Sage		z7-10	☼ ☀	Sum

13

Blue 48"+

Scientific Name	Common Name	Comments	Zone	Lighting	Bloom Season
Symphytum x uplandicum	Russian Comfrey		z4-7	☼	Sp
48"+					
Agastache 'Blue Fortune'	Anise Hyssop		z6-9	☼☀	Sum Fall
Ageratum houstonianum 'Blue Horizon'	Floss Flower		annual	☼	Sum Fall
Anchusa azurea	Alkanet		z3-9	☼☀	Sp Sum
Aster cordifolius	Heart-Leaf Aster		z3-8	☼	Sum
Aster ericoides 'Blue Star'	Heath Aster		z5-8	☼	Sum Fall
Aster ericoides 'Blue Wonder'	Heath Aster		z5-8	☼	Sum Fall
Aster laevis 'Bluebird'	Smooth Aster		z4-9	☼	Fall
Aster novae-angliae 'Wild Light Blue'	New England Aster		z4-8	☼	Sum Fall
Clematis-See Vine Section					
Delphinium 'Blue Bird'	Delphinium	White Center	z3-7	☼☀	Sum
Delphinium 'Blue Spires'	Delphinium	Ht. 3-8'	z3-7	☼☀	Sum
Delphinium 'Moody Blues'	Delphinium		z6-8	☼☀	Sum
Delphinium 'Summer Skies'	Delphinium		z3-10	☼☀	Sum
Eryngium giganteum	Miss Wilmot's Ghost	Ht. 3-6'	z4-7	☼	Sum
Eupatorium coelestinum	Mist Flower	Ht. 4-5'	z5-10	☼	Fall
Perovskia atriplicifolia	Russian Sage	Ht. 4-5'	z5-9	☼	Sum

Blue 48''+

Scientific Name	Common Name	Comments	Zone	Lighting	Bloom Season
Perovskia atriplicifolia 'Blue Mist'	Russian Sage	Ht. 4-5'	z5-9	☼	Sum
Perovskia atriplicifolia 'Blue Spire'	Russian Sage	Ht. 4-5'	z5-9	☼	Sum
Perovskia atriplicifolia 'Longin'	Russian Sage	Ht.4-5'	z4-9	☼	Sum
Rosmarinus officinalis 'Arp'	Rosemary		z6-9	☼	Sp Sum
Rosmarinus officinalis 'Tuscan Blue'	Rosemary		z6-9	☼	Sp Sum
Salvia guaranitica 'Black and Blue'	Blue Anise Sage	Ht. 5-6'	z7-10	☼ ☀	Sum
Veronicastrum virginicum sibiricum	Culver's Root	Ht. 4-6'	z4-8	☼	Sum

15

Purple 0-6"

Scientific Name	Common Name	Comments	Zone	Lighting	Bloom Season
Arabis blepharophylla 'Spring Charm'	Fringed Rock Cress	Bright purple	z5-7	☼	Sp
Aubrieta 'Cobalt Violet'	False Rock Cress		z5-7	☼	Sp
Campanula glomerata var. acaulis	Clustered Bellflower		z3-8	☼	Sum
Colchicum autumnale	Autumn Crocus	Corm Purple/Pk	z4-7	☼	Fall
Colchicum speciosum	Showy Colchicum	Corm (Bulb)	z5-7	☼	Fall
Crocus 'Flower Record'	Crocus	Corm (Bulb)	z3-8	☼	Sp
Crocus 'Rememberence'	Crocus	Corm (Bulb)	z3-8	☼	Sp
Crocus tommasinianus	Tommasini's Crocus	Corm (Bulb)	z5-9	☼	Sp
Iris reticulata	Reticulated Iris		z5-8	☼	Sp
Iris reticulata 'Edward'	Reticulated Iris	Deep Purple	z4-8	☼	Sp
Iris reticulata 'Purple Gem'	Reticulated Iris		z5-8	☼	Sp
Lobelia erinus	Lobelia		annual	☼	Sum Fall
Mazus reptans	Mazus	Evergreen	z3-10	☼ ●	Sp
Penstemon fructicosus 'Purple Haze'	Shrubby Penstemon	Evergreen	z4-8	☼	Sum
Prunella grandiflora	Self Heal	Evergreen	z5-8	☼	Sum
Prunella vulgaris	Self Heal		z3-10	☼	Sum
Sedum anacampseros	Sedum		z6-10	☼	Sum
Thymus praecox 'Purple Beauty'	Creeping Thyme	Evergreen	z5-7	☼	Sp
Veronica repens 'Sunshine'	Harebell Speedwell	Yellow Foliage	z5-10	☼	Sum

Purple 0-6"

Scientific Name	Common Name	Comments	Zone	Lighting	Bloom Season
Viola labradorica	Labrador Violet		z3-8	☼ ◐	Sp
Viola missouriensis	Common Violet	Evergreen	z5-9	☼ ◐	Sp
Viola odorata	Sweet Violet		z5-10	☼ ◐	Sp
Viola pedata	Bird's Foot Violet		z4-8	☼ ◐	Sp
Viola sororaria	Wooly Blue Violet	Evergreen	z4-9	☼ ◐	Sp Sum
6-12"					
Ajuga reptans 'Royalty'	Bugleweed	Evergreen	z3-9	☼ ◐ ●	Sp
Allium christophii	Star of Persia	Bulb	z4-8	☼ ◐	Sum
Aubrieta deltoidea 'Carnival'	False Rock Cress		z4-7	☼ ◐	Sp
Aubrieta deltoidea 'Greencourt Purple'	False Rock Cress		z4-7	☼ ◐	Sp
Aubrieta deltoidea 'Whitewall Gem'	False Rock Cress		z4-7	☼ ◐	Sp
Callirhoe involucrata	Poppy Mallow		z4-7	☼	Sum
Crocus sativus	Saffron Crocus	Corm (Bulb)	z6-9	☼	Sum Fall
Erythronium dens-canis	Dog Tooth Violet	Corm (Bulb)	z2-7	◐	Sp
Hosta-See Hosta Section					
Hyacinthus orientalis 'Atlantic'	Hyacinth	Bulb	z3-7	☼	Sp Wtr
Iris pumila 'Banberry Ruffles'	Dwarf Bearded Iris		z4-9	☼	Sp
Phlox x procumbens	Phlox		z3-9	☼	Sp Sum

17

Purple 6-12"

Scientific Name	Common Name	Comments	Zone	Lighting	Bloom Season
Phlox stolonifera 'Frans Purple'	Creeping Phlox		z2-8	☼◐	Sp
Pulmonaria a. 'Mawson's Variety'	Blue Lungwort		z4-8	◐●	Sp
Pulmonaria x 'Berries & Cream'	Pulmonaria	Pink Purple/Variegated	z4-9	◐●	Sp
Pulmonaria longifolia 'Cevennensis'	Long-Leafed Lungwort	Silv./Var iegated	z3-9	◐●	Sp
Pulmonaria saccharata	Bethlehem Sage		z4-8	◐●	Sp
Pulsatilla vulgaris	Pasque Flower	Fuzzy Sead Head	z5-8	☼◐	Sp
Ruellia caroliniensis	Carolina Wild Petunia		z6-10	◐●	Sp Sum Fall
Scaevola aemula	FairyFanflower		annual	☼	Sp Sum Fall
Trillium sessile	Toad Trillium	Spotted Foliage	z4-7	◐●	Sp
Vinca minor 'Atropurpurea'	Myrtle	Evergreen	z4-8	☼◐●	Sp
Vinca minor 'Variegata'	Myrtle	Evergreen/Variegated	z4-8	☼◐●	Sp
Viola cornuta 'Purple Showers'	Horned Violet	Evergreen	z4-8	☼◐	Sp

12-18"

Scientific Name	Common Name	Comments	Zone	Lighting	Bloom Season
Arisaema triphyllum	Jack-in-the-Pulpit		z4-9	◐●	Sp
Aster novae-angliae 'Purple Dome'	New England Aster		z3-8	☼	Sum Fall
Campanula glomerata 'Joan Elliott'	Clustered Bellflower		z3-8	☼◐	Sum
Erysimum linifolium	Flax Wallflower		z5-8	☼	Sp
Geranium 'Philippe Vapelle'	Geranium		z4-8	☼◐	Sum

Purple 12-18"

Scientific Name	Common Name	Comments	Zone	Lighting	Bloom Season
Geranium s. 'New Hampshire Purple'	Cranesbill		z4-8	☼ ●	Sum
Helleborus atrorubens	Red Hellebore	Evergreen	z5-9	●	Wtr
Helleborus orientalis	Lenten Rose	Evergreen	z4-9	●	Sp
Helleborus orientalis 'Dusk'	Lenten Rose	Evergreen	z4-9	●	Sp
Helleborus orientalis 'Pluto'	Lenten Rose	Evergreen	z4-9	●	Sp
Hemerocallis-See Daylily Section					
Hosta-See Hosta Section					
Hyacinthoides hispanica	Spanish Bluebell	Bulb	z4-7	● ☼	Sp
Iris 'Bingo'	Bearded Iris		z3-10	☼	Sum
Iris chrysographes	Beardless Siberian Iris		z6-10	● ☼	Sp Sum
Iris cristata	Crested Dwarf Iris		z3-8	●	Sp
Iris 'Dark Fairy'	Bearded Iris		z3-10	☼	Sum
Iris 'Jewel Baby'	Dwarf Bearded Iris	Reblooms	z4-9	☼	Sp Fall
Iris 'Tarheel Elf'	Dwarf Bearded Iris		z3-8	☼	Sp Wtr
Lamium byzantinum	Lambs Ears		z5-9	☼ ●	Sp Sum
Lavandula angustifolia 'Hidcote Blue'	English Lavender		z6-9	☼	Sp Sum
Lavandula stoechas	French Lavender	Purple w/Red Bracts	z7-10	☼	Sp Sum
Liriope muscari 'Royal Purple'	Lily Turf	Evergreen	z6-10	☼ ●	Sum Fall
Mertensia siberica	Siberian Bluebells		z3-5	☼ ●	Sp

Purple 12-18"

Scientific Name	Common Name	Comments	Zone	Lighting	Bloom Season
Penstemon barrettiae	Barrett's Bearded Tongue		z6-9	☼	Sum
Penstemon x 'Midnight'	Gloxinia Penstemon		z5-7	☼	Sum Fall
Salvia 'East Friesland'	Sage		z4-7	☼	Sum
Salvia verticillata 'Purple Rain'	Lilac Sage		z4-9	☼	Sum Fall
Stachys macrantha 'Superba'	Big Betony		z4-8	☼	Sum
Symphytum grandiflorum	Large-Flowered Comfrey		z3-9	☼☀	Sp
Tradescantia x 'Concord Grape'	Spiderwort		z4-9	☼☀	Sum
Tricyrtis formosana 'Samurai'	Formosa Toad Lily		z6-8	●☀	Sum Fall
Trillium cuneatum	Toad Trillium	Spotted foliage	z6-9	●☀	Sp
Trillium erectum	Stinking Benjamin		z4-9	●☀	Sp
Tulipa	Tulip	Bulb	z4-9	☼	Sp

18-24"

Scientific Name	Common Name	Comments	Zone	Lighting	Bloom Season
Allium sphaerocephalum	Drumstick Chives	Bulb	z4-8	☼	Sp Sum
Allium thunbergii	Japanese Onion	Bulb	z5-8	☼	Fall
Astilbe chinensis 'Purple Glory'	Chinese Astilbe		z4-8	☀	Sum
Aquilegia x *hybrida* 'Musfe'	Hybrid Columbine	White & Purple	z3-9	☼☀	Sp
Bergenia x 'Pugsley's Purple'	Hybrid Bergenia	Evergreen	z4-8	☀	Sp
Campanula x 'Kent Belle'	Bellflower		z5-9	☼	Sum Fall

Purple 18-24"

Scientific Name	Common Name	Comments	Zone	Lighting	Bloom Season
Catananche caerulea 'Cupid's Dart'	Cupid's Dart		z4-9	☼	Sum
Dalea purpurea	Prairie Clover		z3-8	☼ ☀	Sum
Erigeron speciosus 'Dignity'	Daisy Fleabane		z3-9	☼ ☀	Sum
Geranium pratense 'Plenum-Violaceum'	Meadow Cranesbill		z5-9	☼	Sp Sum
Heliotropium arborescens 'Marine'	Heliotrope	Fragrant	annual	☼ ☀	Sp Sum Fall
Hemerocallis-See Daylily Section					
Hosta-See Hosta Section					
Incarvillea delavayi	Hardy Gloxinia	Rose Purple	z5-7	☀	Sum
Iris germanica	Bearded Iris		z3-10	☼ ☀	Sum
Liatris spicata 'Kobold'	Spike Gayfeather		z3-9	☼	Sum
Lobelia 'La Fresco'	Cardinal Flower		z4-9	☼ ☀	Sum Fall
Nepeta x faassenii	Faassen Nepeta		z3-10	☼	Sum
Nepeta subsessilis	Catnip		z3-8	☼ ☀	Sum
Origanum laevigatum 'Herrenhausen'	Oregano		z4-9	☼	Sum
Origanum vulgare	Oregano		z3-7	☼ ☀	Sum
Penstemon barbatus 'Prairie Dusk'	Common Bearded Tongue		z3-8	☼ ☀	Sum
Penstemon 'Purple Passion'	Bearded Tongue		z4-7	☼	Sum
Phlox x arendsii 'Anja'	Eye Catcher Phlox		z3-8	☼ ☀	Sum
Platycodon grandiflorus	Balloon Flower		z3-7	☼ ☀	Sum

21

Purple 18-24"

Scientific Name	Common Name	Comments	Zone	Lighting	Bloom Season
Salvia x superba	Sage		z4-7	☼	Sum
Sedum telephium 'Atropurpureum'	Sedum		z4-9	☼ ☀	Sum Fall
Teucrium chamaedrys	Germander		z4-9	☼	Sum
Tradescantia x a. 'Purple Dome'	Spiderwort		z4-9	☼ ☼	Sum
Verbena rigida	Rigid Verbena		z7-10	☼	Sum
Veronica longifolia	Speedwell		z4-8	☼ ☼	Sum Fall
Tulipa	Tulip	Bulb	z4-9	☼	Sp

24-36"

Scientific Name	Common Name	Comments	Zone	Lighting	Bloom Season
Adenophora stricta	Ladybells		z7-9	☼ ☼	Sum Fall
Agastache foeniculum	Anise Hyssop		z6-9	☼	Sum
Aquilegia atrata	Columbine		z4-8	☼	Sp Sum
Aster dumosus 'Wood's Purple'	New York Aster		z3-9	☼	Sum Fall
Astilbe chinensis 'Purple Candle'	Chinese Astilbe	Rose Purple	z4-8	☼	Sum
Campanula glomerata	Clustered Bellflower	Blue Purple	z3-8	☼ ☼	Sum
Campanula glomerata var. *dahurica*	Clustered Bellflower		z3-8	☼ ☼	Sum
Campanula glomerata 'Superba'	Clustered Bellflower		z3-8	☼ ☼	Sum
Dahlia	Dahlia		z7-10	☼	Sum Fall
Epimedium grandiflorum 'Purple Prince'	Fairy Wings		z4-8	☼	Sp

Purple 24-36"

Scientific Name	Common Name	Comments	Zone	Lighting	Bloom Season
Erigeron x hybridus 'Azure Fairy'	Fleabane		z3-9	☼☀	Sum
Erigeron speciosus	Daisy Fleabane		z2-7	☼	Sum
Fritillaria persica	Persian Fritillary	Bulb	z5-9	☼☀	Sp
Hemerocallis-See Daylily Section					
Hosta-See Hosta Section					
Iris ensata 'Nikiyama'	Japanese Iris	Violet with white viens	z4-9	☼☀	Sum
Iris pallida	Sweet Iris	Lavender Blue	z4-9	☼	Sum
Iris siberica 'Caesar's Brother'	Siberian Iris		z3-9	☼☀	Sp
Lunaria annua 'Munstead Purple'	Money Plant	(biennial)	z4-8	☼☀	Sp
Lupinus 'The Governor'	Lupine		z5-8	☼	Sp Sum
Tricyrtis x 'Empress'	Toad Lily	White w/Purple Spots	z5-9	☀◑	Fall
Tricyrtis hirta 'Miyazaki'	Toad Lily	White w/Purple Spots	z4-8	☀◑	Fall
Penstemon 'Sour Grapes'	Bearded Tongue		z6-11	☼☀	Sum
Platycodon grandiflorus 'Misato Purple'	Balloon Flower		z3-7	☼☀	Sum
Salvia 'May Night'	Meadow Sage		z5-9	☼	Sum
Stokesia laevis 'Omega Skyrocket'	Stokes Aster		z5-9	☼☀	Sum
Thalictrum a. 'Atropurpureum'	Columbine Meadow-Rue		z5-7	☼☀	Sp
Thalictrum aquilegifolium 'Thundercloud'	Columbine Meadow-Rue		z5-7	☼☀	Sp
Veratrum nigrum	False Hellebore		z5-7	☼◑	Sp

Purple 36-48"

36-48"

Scientific Name	Common Name	Comments	Zone	Lighting	Bloom Season
Acanthus mollis	Common Bear's Breeches		z7-9	☀ ☀	Sp
Allium aflatunense	Persian Onion	Bulb	z4-8	☀	Sp Sum
Baptisia 'Purple Smoke'	False Indigo		z4-9	☀	Sp
Camassia leichtlinii 'Atroviolacea'	Leichtlin Quamash	Bulb	z5-9	☀	Sum
Cleome hassleriana 'Purple Queen'	Cleome		annual	☀ ☀	Sum Fall
Dahlia	Dahlia		z7-10	☀	Sum Fall
Delphinium x *belladonna* 'Lamartine'	Delphinium		z3-7	☀ ☀	Sum
Delphinium x *elatum* 'King Arthur'	Delphinium		z3-7	☀ ☀	Sum
Echinops ritro 'Taplow Purple'	Globe Thistle		z3-7	☀	Sum
Galega orientalis	Oriental Goat's Rue		z5-8	☀	Sp Sum
Geranium psilostemon	Armenian Geranium	Evergreen	z5-6	☀ ☀	Sum
Hibiscus x 'Plum Crazy'	Hibiscus		z4-9	☀ ☀	Sum Fall
Lavandula angustifolia 'Hidcote Giant'	English Lavender		z6-9	☀	Sp Sum
Lespedeza thunbergii	Thunburg Bush Clover		z4-7	☀	Fall
Liatris pycnostachya	Kansas Gayfeather		z3-9	☀	Sum
Liatris spicata 'Floristan Violet'	Spike Gayfeather		z3-9	☀	Sum
Lunaria rediviva	Perennial Honesty		z4-8	☀	Sp
Phlox paniculata 'Amythest'	Garden Phlox		z4-8	☀ ☀	Sum

Purple 36-48"

Scientific Name	Common Name	Comments	Zone	Lighting	Bloom Season
Phlox paniculata 'Robert Poore'	Garden Phlox		z4-8	☼ ☀	Sum
Phlox paniculata 'Russian Violet'	Garden Phlox		z4-8	☼ ☀	Sum
Phlox paniculata 'Starlight'	Garden Phlox		z4-8	☼ ☀	Sum
Symphytum officinale	Common Comfrey		z4-7	☼ ☀	Sp
Thalictrum delavayi	Yunnan Meadow-Rue		z5-9	☼ ☀	Sum
Verbena bonariensis	Butterfly Verbena		z6-9	☼	Sum Fall
Veronica longifolia 'Romiley Purple'	Speedwell		z4-8	☼	Sum
48"+					
Allium giganteum	Giant Onion	Bulb	z4-8	☼	Sp Sum
Angelica gigas	Purple Parsnip		z4-8	☼ ☀	Sum Fall
Aster novae-angliae 'Hella Lacy'	New England Aster		z4-8	☼	Sum Fall
Aster tataricus	Tatarian Daisy	Ht. 4-6'	z4-8	☼	Fall
Astilbe chinensis 'Purple Lance'	Chinese Astilbe	Red Purple, Ht. 4-4.6 'z4-8		☀	Sum
Clematis-See Vine Section					
Cynara cardunculu	Cardoon		z7-10	☼ ☀	Sum
Dahlia	Dahlia		z7-10	☼	Sum Fall
Delphinium x elatum 'Black Knight'	Delphinium		z2-7	☼ ☀	Sum
Dierama pulcherrimum	Angel's Fishing Rod	Ht.4-6'	z7-9	☼	Sum

Lavender 6-12"

Scientific Name	Common Name	Comments	Zone	Lighting	Bloom Season
Hepatica acutiloba	Hepatica		z3-9	☼ ●	Sp
Hepatica americana	Round-Lobed Liverleaf		z3-7	☼ ●	Sp
Hosta-See Hosta Section					
Iris cristata	Crested Dwarf Iris		z3-8	☼	Sp
Iris 'Curtsy'	Dwarf Bearded Iris White w/Lav. Falls		z4-9	☼	Sum
Lavandula angustifolia 'Munstead Dwarf'	English Lavender		z6-9	☼	SpSum
Liriope muscari	Blue Lily Turf	Evergreen	z6-9	☼ ●	SumFall
Liriope muscari 'Big Blue'	Blue Lily Turf	Evergreen	z6-9	☼ ●	SumFall
Liriope muscari 'Variegata'	Blue Lily Turf	Evergreen/Varigated	z6-10	☼ ●	SumFall
Liriope spicata	Creeping Liriope	Evergreen	z4-10	☼ ●	Sum
Liriope spicata 'Silver Dragon'	Creeping Liriope	Evergreen/Varigated	z4-10	☼ ●	Sum
Nepeta x faassenii 'Walker's Low'	Faassen Nepeta		z3-8	☼ ●	Sum
Phlox 'Chattahoochee'	Phlox		z4-9	☼ ●	Sp
Phlox divaricata subsp. *Laphamii*	Woodland Phlox		z4-8	●	Sp
Phlox stolonifera 'Sherwood Purple'	Creeping Phlox		z2-8	☼	Sp
Pulsatilla vulgaris	Pasque Flower	Fuzzy Seed Head	z5-8	☼	Sp
Scilla peruviana	Cuban Lily	Bulb	z6-9	☼	Sp
Thymus x citriodorus	Lemon Thyme		z6-10	☼	Fall
Vinca minor 'Bowle's Variety'	Myrtle	Evergreen	z4-8	☼ ●	Sp

Lavender 12-18"

Scientific Name	Common Name	Comments	Zone	Lighting	Bloom Season
Achillea millefolium 'Lilac Beauty'	Yarrow		z3-9	☼	Sum
Achillea millefolium 'Lilac Queen'	Yarrow		z3-9	☼	Sum
Bletilla striata	Hyacinth Bletilla	Bulb/Evergreen	z5-9	☼ ☀	Sp
Campanula x symphiandra	Bellflower		z3-8	☼ ☀	Sum
Geranium himalayense	Lilac Geranium		z4-7	☼	Sum
Hosta-See Hosta Section					
Liriope muscari 'Gold Band'	Lily Turf		z6-10	☼ ☀	Sp Sum Fall
Osteospermum fruticosum	Trailing African Daisy		annual	☼	Sp Sum
Scabiosa caucasica 'Fama'	Pincushion Flower		z3-7	☼	Sum
Sisyrinchium bellum	Blue-Eyed Grass		z5-8	☼ ☀	Sp
Stachys macrantha	Big Betony		z2-8	☼ ☀	Sum
Stokesia laevis 'Klaus Jelitto'	Stokes Aster	Evergreen	z5-9	☼ ☀	Sum
Tulipa	Tulip	Bulb	z4-9	☼	Sp

18-24"

Scientific Name	Common Name	Comments	Zone	Lighting	Bloom Season
Achillea millefolium 'Sawa Sawa'	Yarrow		z3-9	☼	Sum
Allium tanguticum 'Summer Beauty'	Lavender Globe Lily	Bulb/Liliac Pink	z4-7	☼	Sum
Aster tongolensis 'Wartburgstern'	East Indies Aster		z4-8	☼ ☀	Sum
Conoclinium coelestinum	Mistflower		z5-10	☼ ☀	Sum Fall

Lavender 18-24"

Scientific Name	Common Name	Comments	Zone	Lighting	Bloom Season
Hosta-See Hosta Section					
Iris germanica 'River Hawk'	Bearded Iris		z4-10	☼	Sum
Penstemon cobaea	Wild Foxglove		z4-8	☼	Sp
Penstemon smallii	Small's Penstemon		z6-8	☼ ☀	Sp
Platycodon grandiflorus	Balloon Flower		z3-7	☼	Sum
Polemonium pulcherrimum	Skunkleaf Polemonium		z4-8	☼	Sum
Primula capitata	Asiatic Primrose		z4-7	☼ ☀	Sp Sum
Scabiosa caucasica 'Denise'	Pincushion Flower		z3-7	☼	Sum
Stokesia laevis	Stokes Aster		z5-9	☀	Sum
Trandescantia x a.Lilac Frost'	Spiderwort		z5-9	☼ ☀	Sum
Tricyrtis x 'Lightning Strike'	Toad Lily		z4-9	☼ ●	Fall
Tulipa	Tulip	Bulb	z4-9	☼	Sp

24-36"

Scientific Name	Common Name	Comments	Zone	Lighting	Bloom Season
Ageratum houstonianum	Floss Flower		annual	☼	Sum Fall
Allium 'Globemaster'	Hybrid Onion	Bulb	z4-8	☼	Sp Sum
Aster x *frikartii*	Frikart's Aster		z5-8	☼	Sum Fall
Aster x *frikartii* 'Monch'	Frikart's Aster		z5-8	☼	Sum Fall
Asyneuma canescens	Asyneuma		z5-8	☼ ☀	Sum

Lavender 24-36"

Scientific Name	Common Name	Comments	Zone	Lighting	Bloom Season
Boltonia asteroids var. *latisquama* 'Nana'	Boltonia		z4-8	☼	Fall
Hibiscus rosa-sinensis 'Fantasia'	Chinese Hibiscus	Red Eye	z4-9	☼ ☼	Sp Sum Fall
Hosta-See Hosta Section					
Iris ensata 'Anna'	Japanese Iris	Lav. fading to White	z4-9	☼ ☼	Sum
Iris ensata 'Light in Opal'	Japanese Iris		z4-9	☼ ☼	Sum
Iris ensata 'Sapphire Star'	Japanese Iris	Lav. w/White Veins	z4-9	☼ ☼	Sum
Iris sibirica 'Lavender Bounty'	Siberian Iris		z3-9	☼ ☼	Sp
Lavandula angustifolia 'Grey Lady'	English Lavender		z6-9	☼	Sp Sum
Lavandula angustifolia 'Grosso'	English Lavender		z6-9	☼	Sp Sum
Lavandula angustifolia 'Lavender Lady'	English Lavender		z6-9	☼	Sp Sum
Nepeta x faassenii 'Six Hills Giant'	Faassen Nepeta		z3-8	☼	Sum
Papaver 'Lavender Glory'	Poppy		z2-7	☼	Sp
Perovskia atriplicifolia 'Little Spire'	Russian Sage		z4-9	☼	Sum
Phlomis cashmeriana	Kashmir Sage		z8-9	☼	Sum
Phlox paniculata 'Franz Schubert'	Garden Phlox		z4-9	☼ ☼	Sum
Phlox paniculata 'Katherine'	Garden Phlox		z4-8	☼ ☼	Sum
Phlox paniculata 'Sternhimmel'	Garden Phlox		z4-8	☼ ☼	Sum
Tricyrtis x 'Tojen'	Toad Lily		z4-8	◐ ☼	Sum Fall
Veronica spicata 'Blue Charm'	Spiked Speedwell		z4-8	☼	Sum

29

Lavender 36-48"

Scientific Name	Common Name	Comments	Zone	Lighting	Bloom Season
Astilbe chinensis var. taquetii 'Superba'	Chinese Astilbe		z4-8	☀	Sum
Eryngium x tripartitum	Sea Holly		z5-8	☀	Sum
Hibiscus x 'Lohengrin'	Hibiscus	Red Eye	z4-9	☀	Sum Fall
Iris germanica 'Mary Frances'	Bearded Iris		z3-10	☀	Sum
Monarda fistulosa	Wild Bergamot		z3-7	☀	Sum
Perovskia atriplicifolia 'Longin'	Russian Sage		z4-9	☀	Sum
Phlox paniculata 'Ann'	Garden Phlox		z4-8	☀	Sum
Phlox paniculata 'Progress'	Garden Phlox		z4-8	☀	Sum
Thalictrum aquilegifolium	Columbine Meadow-Rue		z5-7	☀	Sp
Verbena bonariensis	Butterfly Verbena	Seeds Everywhere	z6-9	☀	Sum Fall

48"

Scientific Name	Common Name	Comments	Zone	Lighting	Bloom Season
Campanula lactiflora 'Prichard's Variety'	Milky Bellflower	Ht. 4-5'	z4-8	☀	Sum
Delphinium x elatum 'Lanceolot'	Delphinium	White eyes or bee	z2-7	☀	Sum
Eupatorium purpureum	Joe Pye Weed	Ht. 4-7'	z4-8	☀	Fall
Perovskia atriplicifolia	Russian Sage		z5-9	☀	Sum
Thalictrum delavayi 'Hewitt's Double'	Yunnan Meadow-Rue	Ht. 4-5'	z4-7	☀	Sp
Thalictrum r. 'Lavender Mist'	Lavender Mist	Ht. 6-8'	z3-8	☀	Sum
Veronicastrum virginicum var. sibericum	Culver's Root	Ht. 4-7'	z4-9	☀	Sum

Red 0-6"

Scientific Name	Common Name	Comments	Zone	Lighting	Bloom Season
Aubrieta deltoides 'Bressingham Red'	False Rock Cress		z4-7	☼	Sp
Aubrieta deltoides 'Leichtlinii'	False Rock Cress		z4-7	☼	Sp
Begonia Cocktail Series 'Vodka'	Wax Begonia		annual	☼ ◐	Sp Sum Fall
Dianthus deltoides 'Inshriach Dazzler'	Maiden Pinks		z3-8	☼ ◐	Sum
Dianthus deltoides 'Samos'	Maiden Pinks		z3-8	☼ ◐	Sum
Dianthus deltoides 'Zing Rose'	Maiden Pinks	Evergreen	z3-8	☼	Sum
Dianthus 'Frosty Fire'	Pinks	Evergreen	z4-8	☼	Sum
Lewisia 'George Henley'	Lewisia		z6-9	☼	Sp Sum
Phlox x 'Mars'	Phlox		z2-8	☼	Sum
Phlox x 'Scarlet Flame'	Phlox	Scarlet	z2-8	☼	Sum Fall
Phlox subulata 'Atropurpurea'	Moss Phlox	Wine Red	z2-8	☼	Sum
Phlox subulata 'Beauty of Ronsdorf'	Moss Phlox	Rose	z2-8	☼	Sp
Phlox subulata 'Cracker Jack'	Moss Phlox		z2-8	☼	Sp
Phlox subulata 'Crimson Beauty'	Moss Phlox	Rose	z2-8	☼	Sp
Phlox subulata 'Red Wing'	Moss Phlox	Crimson	z2-8	☼	Sp
Primula auricula 'Dale's Red'	Bear's Ears	Evergreen	z3-7	☼ ◐	Sp Sum
Primula auricula 'The Mikado'	Bear's Ears	Evergreen	z3-7	☼ ◐	Sp Sum
Prunella 'Little Red Riding Hood'	Self Heal		z5-9	◐ ☼	Sum
Sedum spurium 'Fuldaglut'	Two Row Stonecrop		z3-8	☼	Sum

Red 6-12"

Scientific Name	Common Name	Comments	Zone	Lighting	Bloom Season
Anemone coronaria 'Governor'	Poppy Anemone		z7-10	☼	Sp
Anemone coronaria 'Mona Lisa Red'	Poppy Anemone		z6-10	☼	Sp
Armeria maritima 'Splendens'	Sea Thrift		z4-8	☼	Sp Sum
Aster novi-belgii 'Alert'	New York Aster		z4-8	☼	Sum Fall
Begonia	Wax Begonia		annual	☼ ◐	Sp Sum Fall
Corydalis solida 'George Baker'	Dracula Corydalis		z5-8	◐	Sp Sum
Dianthus barbatus 'Sooty'	Sweet William		z5-9	☼	Sp
Dianthus deltoides 'Brilliancy'	Maiden Pinks		z3-8	☼ ◐	Sum
Dianthus deltoides 'Brilliant'	Maiden Pinks		z3-8	☼ ◐	Sum
Dianthus deltoides 'Coccineus'	Maiden Pinks		z3-8	☼ ◐	Sum
Dianthus deltoides 'Fanal'	Maiden Pinks		z3-8	☼ ◐	Sum
Dianthus deltoides 'Flashing Light'	Maiden Pinks		z3-8	☼ ◐	Sum
Epimedium x rubrum	Red Barrenwort	Evergreen	z5-8	◐ ☼	Sp
Hemerocalis–See Daylilly Section					
Iris pumila 'Already'	Dwarf Bearded Iris		z3-10	☼	Sp
Iris pumila 'Lena'	Dwarf Bearded Iris		z3-10	☼	Sp
Iris pumila 'Red Gem'	Dwarf Bearded Iris		z3-10	☼	Sp
Iris pumila 'Wee Lad'	Dwarf Bearded Iris		z3-10	☼	Sp
Lathyrus vernus 'Rose Fairy'	Spring Vetchling	Non Vining	z5-7	☼	Sp

Red 6-12"

Scientific Name	Common Name	Comments	Zone	Lighting	Bloom Season
Papaver somniferum 'Pepperbox'	Opium Poppy		annual	☼	Sum
Phelypaea tournefortii (parasitizes on Achillea & Tanacetum available as seed)			z5-8	☼	Sum
Pulsatilla vulgaris 'Rubra'	Pasque Flower	Fuzzy Seed Heads	z5-8	☼ ☼	Sp
Saxifraga x arendsii 'Triumph'	Arend's Saxifrage		z5-7	☼	Sp
Trifolium incarnatum	Clover		annual	☼	Sum

12-18"

Scientific Name	Common Name	Comments	Zone	Lighting	Bloom Season
Achillea millefolium 'Paprika'	Yarrow	Fades	z3-9	☼	Sum
Adonis annua	Pheasant's Eye		annual	☼ ☼	Sp Sum Fall
Begonia tuber hybrida-cultorum	Begonia		annual	☼ ●	Sp Sum Fall
Castilleja coccinea, Paintbrush, parasitizes Schizachyrium Penstemon &Sisyrinchium			z4-8	☼	Sp Sum
Coreopsis 'Limerock Ruby'	Tickseed		z6-9	☼	Sum
Delphinium nuducale	Larkspur		z7-10	☼ ☼	Sp Sum
Dianthus barbatus 'Blood Red'	Sweet William		z3-8	☼ ☼	Sp
Dianthus barbatus 'Homeland'	Sweet William		z3-8	☼ ☼	Sp
Dianthus barbatus 'Nigracans'	Sweet William		z3-8	☼ ☼	Sp
Dianthus barbatus 'Ruby Moon'	Sweet William		z3-8	☼ ☼	Sp
Dianthus barbatus 'Scarlet Beauty'	Sweet William		z3-8	☼ ☼	Sp
Dianthus caryophyllus 'Red Sims'	Clove Pinks		z4-8	☼ ☼	Sum

33

Red 12-18"

Scientific Name	Common Name	Comments	Zone	Lighting	Bloom Season
Dianthus 'Ian'	Pinks		z5-8	☼ ☀	Sum
Dianthus 'Laced Romeo'	Pinks		z4-8	☼ ☀	Sum
Dianthus 'Thomas'	Pinks		z4-8	☼ ☀	Sum
Dianthus superbus 'Crimsonia'	Fringed Pink		z4-8	☼ ☀	Sum
Dichelostemma ida-maia	Fire Cracker Flower	Bulb	z5-8	☼	Sum
Fuchsia	Fuchia		annual	☼ ●	Sp Sum Fall
Pelargonium	Geranium		annual	☼	Sp Sum Fall
Helianthemum n. 'Cerise Queen'	Sunrose		z5-7	☼	Sum
Helianthemum nummularium 'Fireball'	Sunrose		z5-7	☼	Sum
Helianthemum nummularium 'Fire Dragon'	Sunrose		z5-7	☼	Sum
Helianthemum nummularium 'Red Orient'	Sunrose		z5-7	☼	Sum
Helleborus 'Atrorubens'	Hellebore	Evergreen	z5-9	☀	Sp
Helleborus 'Philip Ballard'	Hellebore	Evergreen	z4-9	☀	Sp
Helleborus 'Queen of the Night'	Hellebore	Evergreen	z3-6	☀	Sp
Helleborus 'Red Lady'	Hellebore	Evergreen	z4-8	☀	Sp
Hemerocalis-See Daylilly Section					
Heuchera sanguinea 'Maxima'	Coral Bells		z3-8	☼ ☀	Sp Sum
Heuchera sanguinea 'Splendens'	Coral Bells		z3-8	☼ ☀	Sp Sum
Heuchera 'Crimson Cloud'	Coral Bells		z3-8	☼ ☀	Sp Sum

Red 12-18"

Scientific Name	Common Name	Comments	Zone	Lighting	Bloom Season
Heuchera 'Fairy Cups'	Coral Bells		z3-8	☼ ☼	Sp Sum
Heuchera 'Firefly'	Coral Bells		z3-8	☼ ☼	Sp Sum
Heuchera 'Frosty'	Coral Bells		z3-8	☼ ☼	Sp Sum
Heuchera 'Leuchtkafer'	Coral Bells		z3-8	☼ ☼	Sp Sum
Heuchera 'Mt. St. Helens'	Coral Bells		z3-8	☼ ☼	Sp Sum
Heuchera 'Pluie de Feu'	Coral Bells		z3-8	☼ ☼	Sp Sum
Heuchera 'Rakete'	Coral Bells		z3-8	☼ ☼	Sp Sum
Heuchera 'Raspberry Regal'	Coral Bells		z3-8	☼ ☼	Sp Sum
Heuchera 'Scintillation'	Coral Bells		z3-8	☼ ☼	Sp Sum
Heuchera 'Sioux Falls'	Coral Bells		z3-8	☼ ☼	Sp Sum
Heuchera 'Snowstorm'	Coral Bells		z3-8	☼ ☼	Sp Sum
Heuchera 'Splendour'	Coral Bells		z3-8	☼ ☼	Sp Sum
Iris 'Cherry Garden'	Bearded Iris		z3-10	☼	Sum
Lychnis viscaria	German Catchfly		z3-7	☼	Sum
Lycoris radiata	Spider Lily	Bulb	z7-10	☼	Fall
Lycoris sanguinea	Spider Lily	Bulb	z7-10	☼	Sum
Penstemon barbatus 'Coccineus'	Common Bearded Tongue		z2-8	☼	Sum
Penstemon barbatus 'Torre'	Common Bearded Tongue		z2-8	☼	Sum
Penstemon x 'Port Wine'	Bearded Tongue		z7-9	☼	Sum Fall

35

Red 12-18"

Scientific Name	Common Name	Comments	Zone	Lighting	Bloom Season
Penstemon pinifolius	Pine-Leaf Penstemon		z7-8	☼	Sum
Primula cockburniana	Primrose Red Form		z5-8	☼ ☀	Sp
Primula japonica 'Jim Saunders'	Japanese Primrose		z3-5	☼ ☀	Sp Sum
Pulmonaria rubra 'Bowle's Red'	Red Lungwort		z4-7	☼ ●	Sp
Pulmonaria rubra 'Redstart'	Red Lungwort		z4-7	☼ ●	Sp
Salvia coccinia 'Lady in Red'	Mealy-cup Sage		annual	☼	Sum Fall
Tulipa	Tulip	Bulb	z4-9	☼	Sp

18-24"

Scientific Name	Common Name	Comments	Zone	Lighting	Bloom Season
Achillea millefolium 'Angelique'	Yarrow		z4-8	☼	Sum
Achillea millefolium 'Cerise Queen'	Yarrow		z3-9	☼	Sum
Achillea millefolium 'Fire King'	Yarrow		z3-9	☼	Sum
Achillea millefolium 'Red Beauty'	Yarrow	Crimson	z3-9	☼	Sum
Alstromeria psittacina	Parrot Lily		z7-10	☼	Sum
Alstromeria psittacina 'Variegata'	Parrot Lily		z7-10	☼	Sum
Antirrhinum majus 'Red Rocket'	Snapdragon	Reseeds	annual	☼	Sum Fall
Aquilegia canadensis	Wild Columbine		z3-9	☼ ☀	Sp
Astilbe x arendsii 'Fanal' Hybrid	Astilbe		z4-9	☀	Sum
Astilbe chinensis 'Visions in Red'	Chinese Astilbe		z4-9	☀	Sum
Centranthus var. coccineus	Red Valerian		z5-8	☼ ☀	Sp Sum

Red 18-24"

Scientific Name	Common Name	Comments	Zone	Lighting	Bloom Season
Chrysanthemum coccineum 'Sensation'	Painted Daisy	Double Flower	z3-7	☼	Sp Sum
Cosmos atrosanguineus	Chocolate Cosmos		annual	☼	Sum Fall
Dahlia 'Arabian Night'	Dahlia		z8-10	☼	Sum Fall
Dahlia 'Bishop of Liandaff'	Dahlia		z8-10	☼	Sum Fall
Erysimum x allionii 'Scarlett Bedder'	Siberian Wall Flower	(biennial)	z3-9	☀	Sp Sum
Geum chiloense 'Mrs. Bradshaw'	Chilean Avens		z5-9	☼	Sum
Gladiolus 'Atom'	Gladiolus	Bulb	z7-9	☼	Sum
Hemerocalis-See Daylilly Section					
Kniphofia 'Corallina'	Torchlily		z5-8	☼	Sp Sum
Lilium pumilum	Coral Lily	Bulb	z3-7	☼	Sum
Papaver nudicaule 'Red Sails'	Iceland Poppy		z2-8	☼	Sp
Papaver orientale 'Allegro'	Oriental Poppy		z2-7	☼	Sum
Papaver orientale 'Glowing Embers'	Oriental Poppy		z2-7	☼	Sum
Penstemon x 'Chester Scarlet'	Bearded Tongue		z6-9	☼	Sum
Tulipa	Tulip	Bulb	z4-9	☼	Sp

24-36"

Scientific Name	Common Name	Comments	Zone	Lighting	Bloom Season
Achillea x 'Fanal' or 'The Beacon'	Yarrow		z3-9	☼	Sum
Alstromeria 'Freedom'	Peruvian Lily	Peachy Red	z5-8	☼	Sum

37

Red 24-36"

Scientific Name	Common Name	Comments	Zone	Lighting	Bloom Season
Aquilegi 'Crimson Star'	Columbine	Red sepals/White petals	z3-10	☼ ☀	Sp Sum
Aquilegia vulgaris 'Double Rubies'	Columbine		z3-8	☼ ☀	Sp Sum
Amaranthus tricolor 'Flaming Fountain'	Joseph's Coat		annual	☼ ☀	Sum
Aster novi-belgii 'The Bishop'	New York Aster		z4-8	☼	Sum Fall
Astilbe x arendsii 'Fire'	Hybrid Astilbe		z4-9	☀	Sum
Astilbe x arendsii 'Glow'	Hybrid Astilbe		z4-9	☀	Sum
Astilbe x arendsii 'Montgomery'	Hybrid Astilbe		z4-9	☀	Sum
Astilbe x arendsii 'Red Cattleya'	Hybrid Astilbe		z4-9	☀	Sum
Astilbe x arendsii 'Red Sentinel'	Hybrid Astilbe		z4-9	☀	Sum
Astilbe x arendsii 'Spartan'	Hybrid Astilbe		z4-9	☀	Sum
Astrantia major 'Lars'	Great Masterwort		z5-7	☀	Sp Sum
Chrysanthemum 'Duchess of Edinburgh'	Chysanthemum	Muted Red	z5-9	☼	Sum Fall
Crocosmia x crocosmiiflora 'Lucifer'	Montbretia	Corm (Bulb)	z5-9	☀	Sum
Euphorbia griffithii 'Fireglow'	Griffith's Spurge		z5-7	☼ ☀	Sum
Gaillardia x grandiflora 'Bremen'	Blanket Flower		z3-10	☼	Sum
Gaillardia x grandiflora 'Burgundy'	Blanket Flower		z3-9	☀	Sum
Gaillardia x g. 'Kobold' or 'Goblin'	Blanket Flower		z3-10	☀	Sum
Hemerocalis-See Daylilly Section					
Heuchera 'Torch'	Coral Bells		z3-8	☼ ☀	Sp Sum

Red 24-36'

Scientific Name	Common Name	Comments	Zone	Lighting	Bloom Season
Hibiscus moscheutos 'Disco Rosy Red'	Common Mallow		z5-9	☀	Sum
Iris fulva	Beardless Iris		z6-11	☀☼	Sp Sum
Kniphofia x 'Bressingham Comet'	Torchlily		z5-8	☀	Sp Sum
Kniphofia 'Glow'	Torchlily		z5-8	☀	Sp Sum
Lilium amabile	Lily	Bulb	z5-10	☀☼	Sum
Lilium 'Brenda Watts'	Lily	Bulb	z4-9	☀☼	Sum
Lilium 'Cinnabar'	Lily	Bulb	z4-9	☀☼	Sum
Lilium 'Enchantment'	Lily	Bulb	z4-9	☀☼	Sum
Lilium 'Scarlet Emperor'	Lily	Bulb	z4-9	☀☼	Sum
Lobelia 'Cherry Ripe'	Lobelia		z5-7	☀☼	Sum
Lobelia x *speciosa* 'Dark Crusader'	Lobelia		z4-8	☀☼	Sum
Lychnis chalcedonica	Maltese Cross		z3-7	☀	Sum
Monarda didyma 'Cambridge Scarlet'	Bee Balm		z3-7	☀☼	Sum Fall
Monarda didyma 'Jacob Kline'	Bee Balm		z3-7	☀☼	Sum Fall
Monarda didyma 'Kardinal'	Bee Balm		z3-7	☀☼	Sum Fall
Monarda didyma 'Mahogany'	Bee Balm		z3-7	☀☼	Sum Fall
Paeonia 'America'	Peony		z3-8	☀☼	Sp Sum
Paeonia 'Burma Ruby'	Peony		z3-8	☀☼	Sp Sum
Paeonia 'Scarlet O'hara'	Peony		z3-8	☀☼	Sp Sum

Red 24-36"

Scientific Name	Common Name	Comments	Zone	Lighting	Bloom Season
Papaver orientale 'Avebury Crimson'	Oriental Poppy		z2-7	☼	Sum
Papaver orientale 'Beauty of Livermere'	Oriental Poppy		z2-7	☼	Sum
Papaver orientale 'Big Jim'	Oriental Poppy		z2-7	☼	Sum
Papaver orientale 'Bonfire'	Oriental Poppy		z2-7	☼	Sum
Papaver orientale 'Carmen'	Oriental Poppy		z2-7	☼	Sum
Papaver orientale 'Feverriese'	Oriental Poppy		z3-7	☼	Sum
Penstemon barbatus	Common Bearded Tongue		z2-8	☼	Sum
Penstemon x 'Chester Scarlet'	Bearded Tongue		z6-9	☼	Sum
Penstemon x 'Firebird'	Bearded Tongue		z7-10	☼	Sum Fall
Penstemon x 'Garnet'	Bearded Tongue		z7-9	☼	Sum Fall
Penstemon x 'Rubicundus'	Bearded Tongue		z7-9	☼	Sum
Phlox 'Tenor Tall'	Phlox		z3-9	☼	Sum
Tulipa	Tulip	Bulb	z4-9	☼	Sp

36-48"

Scientific Name	Common Name	Comments	Zone	Lighting	Bloom Season
Achillea millefolium 'Fireland'	Yarrow		z3-9	☼	Sum
Astilbe x *arendsii* 'Red Charm'	Hybrid Astilbe		z4-9	☼ ☽	Sum
Canna 'Black Knight'	Canna		z7-10	☼ ☽	Sum
Fritillaria imperialis 'Rubra'	Crown Imperial	Bulb	z5-8	☼ ☽	Sp

Red 36-48"

Scientific Name	Common Name	Comments	Zone	Lighting	Bloom Season
Gladiolus	Gladiolus	Bulb	z8-10	☼	Sum
Helenium autumnale 'Bruno'	Sneezeweed		z3-8	☼	Sum Fall
Helenium autumnale 'Moerheim Beauty'	Sneezeweed		z3-8	☼	Sum Fall
Hemerocalis-See Daylilly Section					
Kniphofia uvaria	Torchlily		z5-8	☼	Sp Sum
Kniphofia x 'Alcazar'	Torchlily		z5-8	☼	Sp Sum
Kniphofia 'Paramentier'	Torchlily		z5-8	☼	Sp Sum
Lilium 'Burgundy Strain'	Lily	Bulb	z4-9	☼☀	Sum
Lilium 'Conquistador'	Lily	Bulb	z4-9	☼☀	Sum
Lilium 'Monte Negro'	Lily	Bulb	z4-9	☼☀	Sp
Lilium 'Tabasco'	Lily	Bulb	z4-9	☼☀	Sum
Lobelia cardinalis	Cardinal Flower		z2-9	☼☀	Sum
Lobelia x speciosa 'Queen Victoria'	Lobelia		z6-8	☼☀	Sum
Lupinus 'Inverewe Red'	Lupine		z3-6	☼	Sp
Penstemon x 'Cherry Ripe'	Bearded Tongue		z7-10	☼	Sum
Pennisetum setaceum 'Rubrum'	Purple Fountain Grass		z9-10	☼	Sum
Polygonum amplexicaule 'Inverleith'	Mountain Fleece Flower		z5-7	☼	Sum
Ricinus communis 'Carmencita'	Castor Oil Plant		annual	☼	Sum
Ricinus communis 'Impala'	Castor Oil Plant		annual	☼	Sum

41

Red 48"+

Scientific Name	Common Name	Comments	Zone	Lighting	Bloom Season
Rodgersia pinnata var. *rubra*	Featherleaf Rodgersia		z5-8	☀	Sp
Veratrum nigrum	False Hellebore		z5-7	☀☀	Sp
Veratrum woodii	False Hellebore		z6-9	☀☀	Sum Fall
Alcea 'Charters Double's Red'	Hollyhock	(biennial)	z2-10	☀	Sp Sum
Alcea 'Charters Double's Scarlet'	Hollyhock	(biennial)	z2-10	☀	Sp Sum
Alcea rosea 'Negrita'	Hollyhock	(biennial)	z3-7	☀	Sp Sum
Amorphophallus konjac	Voodoo Lily		z6-10	☀●☀	Sp
Canna 'Roi Humbert'	Canna		z7-10	☀	Sum
Clematis-See Vines Section					
Helenium autumnale 'Dunkle Pracht'	Sneezeweed		z3-8	☀	Sum Fall
Helenium autumnale 'Rubrum'	Sneezeweed		z3-8	☀	Sum Fall
Hemerocalis-See Daylilly Section					
Hibiscus coccineus	Swamp Hibiscus		z7-9	☀	Sum
Hibiscus 'Lord Baltimore'	Common Mallow		z5-9	☀	Sum
Hibiscus moscheutos 'Crimson Wonder'	Common Mallow		z5-9	☀☀	Sum
Kniphofia 'Samuel's Sensation'	Torchlily		z5-8	☀	Sp Sum
Papaver bracteatum	Poppy		z2-7	☀	Sum
Papaver orientale 'Goliath'	Oriental Poppy		z2-7	☀	Sum
Polygonum a. 'Atrosanguineum'	Mountain Fleece Flower		z5-7	☀	Sum

Red 48"+

Scientific Name	Common Name	Comments	Zone	Lighting	Bloom Season
Polygonum amplexicaule 'Firetail'	Mountain Fleece Flower		z5-7	☼	Sum
Rheum palmatum 'Hadspen Crimson'	Ornamental Rhubarb		z5-8	☼	Sum
Rheum palmatum var. *Tanguticum*	Ornamental Rhubarb		z5-9	☼	Sum

43

Pink 0-6"

Scientific Name	Common Name	Comments	Zone	Lighting	Bloom Season
Acaena anserinifolia	Goose-Leaf Bur		z7-9	☼	Sp
Acaena buchananii	New Zealand Bur		z7-9	☼	Sum
Acaena microphylla	New Zealand Bur		z7-9	☼	Sum
Ajuga reptans 'Pink Elf'	Bugleweed	Evergreen	z3-9	☼ ◑	Sp
Ajuga reptans 'Pink Surprise'	Bugleweed	Evergreen	z3-9	☼ ●	Sp
Ajuga reptans 'Rosea'	Bugleweed	Evergreen	z3-9	☼ ◑	Sp
Alstroemeria hookeri	Peruvian Lily		z7-9	☼	Sum
Anagallis tenella 'Studland'	Pimpernel		z5-7	☼	Sp
Androsace carnea	Rock Jasmine		z4-7	☼	Sum
Androsace lanuginosa	Rock Jasmine		z4-5	☼	Sum
Antennaria dioica rosea	Rose Pussytoes	Soft Fuzzy Foliage	z3-7	☼	Sp Sum
Arabis blepharophylla	Fringed Rock Cress		z5-7	☼	Sp
Arabis blepharophylla 'Spring Charm'	Fringed Rock Cress		z5-7	☼	Sp
Arabis caucasica 'Rosabella'	Wall Rock Cress		z4-8	☼	Sp
Arenaria purpurascens	Pink Sandwort		z4-7	☼	Sp
Armeria maritima 'Rubrifolia'	Sea Thrift		z4-8	☼ ●	Sp Sum
Armeria maritima 'Vindictive'	Sea Thrift		z4-8	☼ ●	Sp Sum
Chionodoxa 'Pink Giant'	Glory-of-the-Snow	Bulb	z4-8	☼ ◑	Sp
Claytonia megarhiza subsp. nivalis	Claytonia	Evergreen	z5-7	☼	Sp

Pink 0-6"

Scientific Name	Common Name	Comments	Zone	Lighting	Bloom Season
Crocus vernus	Crocus	Corm(Bulb)	z3-8	☼ ☀	Sp
Cyclamen coum subsp. *coum*	Hardy Cyclamen	Corm (Bulb)	z6-9	☀	Sp Wtr
Cyclamen hederifolium	Cyclamen	Corm (Bulb)/Evergreen	z5-10	☀	Fall Wtr
Cyclamen purpurascens	Cyclamen	Corm (Bulb)/Evergreen	z5-9	☀	Sum Fall
Delosperma cooperi	Ice Plant	Florescent Pink	z6-9	☼	Sum
Delosperma 'Mesa Verde'	Ice Plant	Salmon Pink	z4-8	☼ ☀	Sum
Dianthus alpinus	Alpine Pinks		z3-7	☼	Sp
Dianthus 'Annabelle'	Pinks		z4-8	☼	Sum
Dianthus gratianopolitanus	Cheddar Pinks		z3-8	☼	Sp
Dianthus 'Little Jock'	Pinks		z4-8	☼	Sum
Dianthus 'Mars'	Pinks		z3-7	☼	Sum
Dianthus myrtinervius	Pinks	Evergreen	z5-8	☼	Sum
Dianthus plumarius 'Oakington'	Cottage Pinks	Silver Foliage	z3-8	☼	Sum
Dianthus plumarius 'Pike's Pink'	Cottage Pinks	Silver Foliage	z3-8	☼	Sum
Dianthus plumarius 'Randy's Pink'	Cottage Pinks	Silver Foliage	z3-8	☼	Sum
Erinus alpinus	Liver Balsam		z4-7	☼	Sp Sum
Erodium corsicum	Heron's-bill		z4-7	☼	Sp Sum
Erodium reichardii 'Plenum'	Rock Geranium		z3-7	☼	Sp
Erodium reichardii 'Roseum'	Rock Geranium		z3-7	☼	Sp

45

Pink 0-6"

Scientific Name	Common Name	Comments	Zone	Lighting	Bloom Season
Erysimum nivale 'Mountain Magic'	Wallflower		z3-7	☼	Sum
Fragaria x 'Lipstick'	Strawberry		z3-10	☼ ☀	Sp Sum Fall
Geranium cinereum 'Ballerina'	Grayleaf Cranesbill		z4-9	☼ ☀	Sp
Geranium cinereum 'Splendens'	Grayleaf Cranesbill	Deep Rose	z4-8	☼ ☀	Sp
Geranium cinereum var. subcaulescens	Grayleaf Cranesbill		z4-9	☼ ☀	Sp
Geranium dalmaticum	Dalmatian Cranesbill		z4-7	☼	Sp Sum
Geranium sanguineum var. striatum	Cranesbill		z4-8	☼	Sum
Heuchera rubescens	Alpine Heuchera		z3-7	☼	Sp
Lamium maculatum 'Orchid Frost'	Spotted Nettle	Orchid Pink	z3-8	☼ ☀	Sp Sum
Lamium maculatum 'Pink Pewter'	Spotted Nettle		z3-8	☼ ☀	Sp Sum
Leucojum roseum	Snowflake	Bulb	z5-8	☼ ☀	Fall
Lewisia cotyledon	Lewisia		z6-8	☼	Sum
Lewisia rediviva	Bitter Root		z6-7	☼	Sp Sum
Ourisia microphylla	Mountain Foxglove		z5-7	●	Sp Sum
Oxalis acetosella f. rosea	Wood-Sorrel		z5-8	☀	Sp
Oxalis adenophylla	Sauer Klee		z7-10	☼	
Oxalis crassipes 'Rosea'	Strawberry Shamrock		z5-9	☀ ●	Sp Sum
Penstemon hirsutus 'Pygmacus'	Dwarf Hairy Penstemon		z3-8	☼	Sum
Phlox adsurgens 'Wagon Wheel'	Phlox		z4-8	☀	Sp Sum

Pink 0-6"

Scientific Name	Common Name	Comments	Zone	Lighting	Bloom Season
Phlox 'Camla'	Needleleaf Phlox		z5-8	☼	Sum
Phlox douglasii 'Crackerjack'	Iceberg Phlox		z5-7	☼	Sum
Phlox subulata	Moss Phlox		z3-9	☼	Sp
Polygonum affine 'Donald Lowndes'	Fleece Flower		z4-8	☼	Sum Fall
Saponaria caespitosa	Moss Sandwort		z4-7	☼	Sum
Saponaria x olivana	Alpine Soapwort		z4-7	☼	Sum
Saxifraga x arendsii	Arend's Saxifrage		z4-7	☼	Sp
Saxifraga 'Jenkinsiae'	Saxifrage		z4-6	☼	Sp
Saxifraga oppositifolia	Saxifrage		z2-6	☼	Sp
Sedum hispanicum 'Minus'	Tiny Button Sedum	Pale Pink	z4-9	☼ ☼	Sum
Sedum sieboldii	October Daphne	Rose	z3-10	☼ ☼	Sum Fall
Sedum spurium	Two Row Stonecrop		z3-8	☼	Sum
Sedum spurium 'Bronze Carpet'	Two Row Stonecrop		z3-8	☼	Sum
Sedum spurium 'John Creech'	Two Row Stonecrop	Pink Purple	z3-8	☼	Sum
Sedum spurium 'Royal Pink'	Two Row Stonecrop		z3-8	☼	Sum
Sedum spurium 'Tricolor'	Two Row Stonecrop	Varigated Foliage	z3-8	☼	Sum
Shortia soldanelloides	Fringe Bells		z6-8	●	Sp Sum
Silene acaulis	Moss Campion		z2-6	☼	Sp
Silene caroliniana	Carolina Campion		z5-8	☼ ☼	Sp

47

Pink 6-12"

Scientific Name	Common Name	Comments	Zone	Lighting	Bloom Season
Silene polypetala	Fringed Campion		z6-8	☼	Sp
Silene schafta	Schafta Campion		z4-8	☼	Sum
Thlaspi rotundifolium	Round-leafed Penny-cress		z5-7	☼	Sp
Thymus nitens	Thyme		z5-9	☼ ☼	Sum
Thymus pseudolanuginosus	Wooly Thyme	Fuzzy Leaf	z5-8	☼ ☼	Sum
Thymus serpyllum 'Elfin'	Thyme		z4-9	☼ ☼	Sum Fall

6-12"

Scientific Name	Common Name	Comments	Zone	Lighting	Bloom Season
Aethionema armeneum	Turkish Stonecress		z5-7	☼	Sp
Aethionema 'Warley Rose'	Stonecress		z4-8	☼	Sp
Ajuga reptans 'Pink Spire'	Bugleweed	Evergreen	z3-9	☼ ☼ ●	Sp
Allium acuminatum	Tapertip Onion	Bulb	z4-7	☼	Sum
Allium narcissiform	Narcissus Onion	Bulb	z5-8	☼	Sum
Allium oreophilum	Mountain Onion	Bulb	z3-8	☼	Sum
Allium senescens	German Garlic	Bulb/Lilac Pink	z4-7	☼	Sum
Allium senescens 'Glaucum'	German Garlic	Bulb	z4-7	☼	Sum
Andromeda polifolia 'Compacta'	Bog Rosemary	White Undertones	z2-6	☼	Sp
Anemone x 'Charmer'	Hybrid Windflower	Deep Rose	z4-7	☼	Fall
Anemone coronaria	Poppy Anemone		z6-9	☼ ☼	Sp

Pink 6-12"

Scientific Name	Common Name	Comments	Zone	Lighting	Bloom Season
Anemone x 'Pink Star'	Hybrid Windflower		z4-7	☀	Fall
Anemone x 'Radar'	Hybrid Windflower		z4-7	☀	Fall
Anemonella 'Eco Pink'	Rue-Anemone		z4-8	☀	Sp Sum
Anemonella 'Jade Feather'	Rue-Anemone		z4-8	☀	Sp Sum
Anemonella 'Rosea'	Rue-Anemone		z4-8	☀	Sp Sum
Anemonella 'Schoaf's Double Pink'	Rue-Anemone		z4-8	☀	Sp Sum
Arabis blepharophylla	Fringed Rock Cress		z5-7	☼	Sp
Arabis caucasica 'Pink Pearl'	Wall Rock Cress		z4-7	☼	Sp
Armeria maritima	Sea Thrift		z4-8	☼	Sp Sum
Aster alpinus 'Wargrave Pink'	Alpine Aster		z4-7	☼	Sp Sum
Astilbe simplicifolia 'Inshriach Pink'	Star Astilbe		z4-8	☀	Sum
Astilbe simplicifolia 'William Buchanan'	Star Astilbe		z4-8	☀	Sum
Aubrieta deltoidea 'Bressingham Pink'	False Rock Cress		z4-7	☼	Sp
Coreopsis rosea	Pink Coreopsis		z4-7	☼	Sum
Coreopsis rosea 'American Dream'	Pink Coreopsis		z4-7	☼	Sum
Dianthus x allwoodii 'Little Bobby'	Pinks	Maroon Eye	z4-8	☼	Sum
Dianthus barbatus 'Newport Pink'	Sweet William		z3-8	☼	Sp
Dianthus carthusianorum	Pinks		z5-7	☼	Sum
Dianthus chinensis	China Pinks	(biennial)	z7-10	☼	Sum Fall

49

Pink 6-12"

Scientific Name	Common Name	Comments	Zone	Lighting	Bloom Season
Dianthus gratianopolitanus 'Firewitch'	Cheddar Pinks	Magenta	z4-8	☼	Sp
Dianthus gratianopolitanus 'Petite'	Cheddar Pinks	Silver Blue Foliage	z3-8	☼	Sp
Dianthus gratianopolitanus 'Tiny Rubies'	Cheddar Pinks	Evergreen	z3-8	☼	Sp
Dianthus plumarius 'Mountain Mist'	Cottage Pinks		z3-8	☼	Sum
Dianthus plumarius 'Painted Lady'	Cottage Pinks		z3-8	☼	Sum
Dianthus plumarius 'Peppermint Patty'	Cottage Pinks		z3-8	☼	Sum
Diascia barberae	Barber's Twinspur		z7-9	☼ ◐	Sp Sum
Diascia regescens	Rigid Twinspur		z7-9	☼	Sp Sum
Diascia vigilis	Twinspur		z7-9	☼	Sp Sum
Diascia vigilis 'Dark Eyes'	Twinspur	Purple Pink Eyes	z7-9	☼	Sp Sum
Dodecatheon 'Red Wings'	Shooting Star		z5-7	◐	Sp
Epimedium grandiflorum	Longspur Barrenwort	Evergreen	z5-8	◐	Sp
Epimedium grandiflorum 'Rose Queen'	Longspur Barrenwort	Evergreen	z5-9	◐	Sp
Epimedium x rubrum	Red Barrenwort	Evergreen/Pink White	z5-8	◐ ●	Sp
Erythronium dens-canis	Dog Tooth Violet	Corm (Bulb)	z2-7	◐	Sp
Erythronium hendersonii	Fawn Lily	Corm (Bulb)	z3-9	☼	Sp
Fritillaria meleagris	Guinea Hen Flower	Bulb	z3-8	☼ ◐	Sp
Geranium x cantabrigiense	Geranium		z5-7	☼ ◐	Sp Sum
Geranium x cantabrigiense 'Biokovo'	Geranium		z5-7	☼ ◐	Sp Sum

Pink 6-12"

Scientific Name	Common Name	Comments	Zone	Lighting	Bloom Season
Geranium x c. 'Biokovo Karmina'	Geranium		z5-7	☼ ☀	Sp Sum
Geranium orientalitibeticum	Geranium		z6-8	☼	Sum
Geranium sanguineum	Cranesbill		z4-8	☼	Sp
Geum triflorum	Prairie Smoke	Mauve	z1-7	☼	Sum
Helianthemum nummularium 'Annabel'	Sunrose		z6-7	☼	Sum
Heuchera 'Autumn Haze'	Coral Bells		z4-9	☼ ☀	Sum
X *Heuchera* 'Stoplight'	Foamy Bells	Yellow w/ Red Foliage	z4-8	☀	Sp
Impatiens	Impatiens		annual	☀	Sp Sum Fall
Iris	Dwarf Bearded Iris		z3-10	☼	Sp
Lamium maculatum 'Beacon Silver'	Spotted Nettle	Varigated	z3-8	☀ ●	Sp Sum
Lamium maculatum 'Chequers'	Spotted Nettle	Varigated	z3-8	☀ ●	Sp Sum
Lamium maculatum 'Shell Pink'	Spotted Nettle	Varigated	z3-8	☀ ●	Sp Sum
Malcolmia maritima	Stock		annual	☼	Sp Sum Fall
Mimulus 'Andean Nymph'	Monkey Flower		annual	☼	Sum Fall
Ophiopogon planiscapus 'Nigrescens'	Black Mondo Grass, Dark Purple Foliage		z6-9	☀	Sum
Origanum laevigatum	Oregano		z5-9	☼	Sum
Oxalis deppei	Iron Cross Plant		z7-9	☼	Sp Sum
Oxalis violacea	Violet Wood Sorrel		z6-8	☀	Sp Sum Fall
Persicaria vaccinifolia	Fleece Flower		z5-7	☀	Sp

51

Pink 6-12"

Scientific Name	Common Name	Comments	Zone	Lighting	Bloom Season
Petrorhagia saxifraga	Tunic Flower		z4-8	☼	Sum
Petunia	Petunia		annual	☼	Sp Sum Fall
Phlox stolonifera	Creeping Phlox		z4-9	☼ ☼	Sp
Phlox subulata 'Hillview Pink'	Moss Phlox		z2-8	☼	Sp
Phlox subulata 'Perfection'	Moss Phlox		z2-8	☼	Sp
Primula x polyantha	Polyantha Primrose		z3-8	☼	Sp
Saponaria ocymoides	Soapwort		z2-7	☼	Sum
Saponaria ocymoides 'Carnea'	Soapwort		z2-7	☼	Sum
Saponaria ocymoides 'Floribunda'	Soapwort		z2-7	☼	Sum
Saponaria ocymoides 'Splendens'	Soapwort		z2-7	☼	Sum
Sedum x 'Vera Jameson'	Showy Stonecrop	Purple Fall Foliage	z3-9	☼ ☀	Sum Fall
Tiarella 'Pink Bouquet'	Foamflower		z3-8	☀ ●	Sp
Tiarella wherryi	Wherry's Foamflower	Pale Pk & White	z4-8	☀ ●	Sp Sum
Trillium catesbaei	Rose Trillium		z7-9	☀	Sp
Trillium rivale	Trillium		z5-8	☀	Sp
Tulipa	Tulip	Bulb	z4-9	☼	Sp
Verbena 'Sissinghurst'	Garden Verbena		z5-9	☼	Sum Fall
Zinnia	Zinnia		annual	☼	Sp Sum Fall

Pink 12-18"

Scientific Name	Common Name	Comments	Zone	Lighting	Bloom Season
12-18"					
Aethionema grandiflorum	Persian Stonecress	Rose Pink	z5-7	☼	Sum
Allium schoenoprasum 'Forescate'	Chives	Bulb/Rose Pink	z3-7	☼	Sp Sum
Anemonella 'Cameo'	Rue-Anemone		z4-8	☼	Sp Sum
Anemonella thalictroides 'Shoaf's Double'	Rue-Anemone		z4-8	●☼	Sp Sum
Arisaema candidissimum	White Jack-in-the-Pulpit	White & Pink	z7-9	●☼	Sp
Aster dumosus 'Wood's Pink'	New York Aster		z3-8	☼	Sum Fall
Aster novi-belgii 'Little Pink Beauty'	New York Aster		z4-8	☼	Sum Fall
Aster novi-belgii 'Newton Pink'	New York Aster	Semi Double Flowers	z4-8	☼	Sum Fall
Aster novi-belgii 'Pink Bouquet'	New York Aster		z4-8	☼	Sum Fall
Astilbe chinensis 'Serenade'	Chinese Astilbe		z4-8	☼	Sum
Astilbe chinensis 'Visions'	Chinese Astilbe	Pink Purple	z4-8	☼	Sum
Astilbe simplicifolia 'Carnea'	Star Astilbe	Deep Salmon	z4-8	☼	Sum
Astilbe simplicifolia 'Hennie Graafland'	Star Astilbe	Rosy	z4-8	☼	Sum
Astilbe simplicifolia 'Sprite'	Star Astilbe	Rust Colored Seed Heads	z4-8	☼	Sum
Astrantia 'Tickled Pink'	Masterwort	Pale Pink Starry Flowers	z4-7	☼☼	Sum
Begonia grandis	Hardy Begonia		z6-9	☼	Sum
Berginia ciliata	Winter Begonia	Pale Pink, Evergreen	z5-8	☼☼	Sp
Berginia cordifolia	Heart-leafed Bergenia	Evergreen	z4-8	☼	Sp

Pink 12-18"

Scientific Name	Common Name	Comments	Zone	Lighting	Bloom Season
Berginia crassifolia	Leather Begonia	Evergreen	z4-8	☀	Sp
Berginia crassifolia 'Bressingham Ruby'	Leather Begonia	Evergreen	z4-8	☀	Sp
Berginia crassifolia 'Eco Pink Cherub'	Leather Begonia	Evergreen	z4-8	☀	Sp
Berginia purpurascens	Purple Bergenia	Evergreen	z3-8	☼ ☀	Sp
Dianthus x allwoodii	Pinks		z4-8	☼	Sum
Dianthus 'Rachel'	Pinks		z4-8	☼	Sum
Dianthus 'Cranberry Ice'	Pinks	Fuchsia-Purple Eye	z4-8	☼	Sum
Dianthus 'Susan'	Pinks		z4-8	☼ ☀	Sum
Dicentra eximia	Fringed Bleeding Heart		z3-9	☀	Sp Sum
Dicentra 'King of Hearts'	Fringed Bleeding Heart		z4-8	☀ ●	Sp Sum
Dicentra 'Luxuriant'	Fringed Bleeding Heart		z3-9	☀ ●	Sp Sum Fall
Dodecatheon meadia	Shooting Star		z4-8	☀ ●	Sp
Epimedium acuminatum	Pointed Barrenwort	Evergreen	z5-8	☀	Sp
Erysimum asperum	Western Wallflower	(biennial)	z3-7	☼ ☀	Sum
Eschscholzia californica	California Poppy		annual	☼	Sp Sum Fall
Geranium endressii	Endress's Geranium		z4-8	☼ ☀	Sp Sum
Geranium m. 'Ingwersen's Variety'	Bigroot Geranium		z3-8	☼ ☀	Sp
Geranium x oxonianum 'Claridge Druce'	Cranebill		z4-7	☼	Sum
Hemerocallis-See Daylily section					

Pink 12-18"

Scientific Name	Common Name	Comments	Zone	Lighting	Bloom Season
Helianthemum nummularium 'Rose Queen'	Sunrose		z5-7	☼	Sum
Helianthemum nummularium 'Wisley Pink'	Sunrose		z6-8	☼	Sum
Helleborus 'Ballard Hybrid'	Hellebore	Evergreen/Multi-Pink Shades	z4-9	☼◐	Sp
Helleborus 'Ivory Prince'	Hellebore	Pk. Striped w/Rose & Green	z4-9	☼●	Sp
Helleborus 'Pink Lady'	Hellebore	Evergreen	z4-9	◐	Sp
Heuchera 'Frosted Violet'	Coral Bells	Purple Foliage	z4-9	☼◐	Sp Sum
Heuchera sanguinea 'Chatterbox'	Coral Bells		z3-8	☼◐	Sp Sum
Heuchera 'Venus'	Coral Bells	Silver Green Foliage	z4-8	◐	Sp Sum
Heuchera 'Viking Ship'	Foamy Bells	Reblooms	z4-9	◐	Sp Sum
Iris 'Little Rosy Wings'	Dwarf Bearded Iris		z3-10	☼	Sum
Lavandula 'Jean Davis'	English Lavender		z5-9	☼	Sp Sum
Lavandula 'Hidcote Pink'	English Lavender		z5-9	☼	Sp Sum
Lavandula 'Loddon Pink'	English Lavender		z5-9	☼	Sp Sum
Lavandula 'Rosea'	English Lavender		z5-9	☼	Sp Sum
Monarda didyma 'Pink Delight'	Bee Balm		z2-8	☼◐	Sum Fall
Monarda 'Marshall's Delight'	Bee Balm		z4-8	☼◐	Sp Sum Fall
Monarda 'Pink Supreme'	Bee Balm		z4-8	☼◐	Sum
Nepeta subsessilis 'Sweet Dreams'	Catnip		z4-9	☼◐	Sum
Origanum 'Kent Beauty'	Oregano		z5-8	☼	Sum

55

Pink 12-18"

Scientific Name	Common Name	Comments	Zone	Lighting	Bloom Season
Osteospermum jucundum	African Daisy		annual	☼	Sp Sum Fall
Papaver nudicaule 'Coonara Pink'	Iceland Poppy		z2-7	☼	Sp
Pelargonium	Geranium		annual	☼	Sp Sum Fall
Penstemon 'Elfin Pink'	Bearded Tongue		z3-8	☼	Sum
Penstemon 'Pink Endurance'	Bearded Tongue		z5-8	☼	Sum
Physostegia virginiana 'Vivid'	Obedient Plant		z4-8	☼ ☼	Sum
Phuopsis stylosa	Crosswort		z5-8	☼	Sum
Primula japonica 'Rosea'	Japanese Primrose		z5-7	☼	Sp Sum
Pulmonaria saccharata	Bethlehem Sage		z3-7	● ☼	Sp
Pulmonaria saccharata 'Mrs Moon'	Bethlehem Sage	Silver Dotted Foliage	z3-8	● ☼	Sp
Pulmonaria saccharata 'Pink Dawn'	Bethlehem Sage		z3-8	● ☼	Sp
Salvia nemorosa 'Rose Wine'	Meadow Sage		z4-7	☼	Sum
Sanguisorba minor	Salad Burnet		z4-7	☼ ☼	Sum
Scabiosa columbaria 'Pink Mist'	Pincushion Flower		z3-9	☼	Sum
Scabiosa graminifolia	Grassleaf Scabious		z5-7	☼	Sum
Schizanthus 'Hit Parade'	Butterfly Flower		annual	☼	Sp Sum
Sedum 'Purple Emperor'	Sedum	Dusty Pink	z3-7	☼ ☼	Sum Fall
Sedum spectabile 'Neon'	Sedum		z3-9	☼	Sum Fall
Sedum spectabile 'Pink Chabis'	Sedum	Varigated Foliage	z3-9	☼	Sum Fall

Pink 12-18"

Scientific Name	Common Name	Comments	Zone	Lighting	Bloom Season
Silene armeria 'Electra'	Campion		annual	☼	Sum Fall
Thymus vulgaris	Garden Thyme		z4-10	☼	Sum
Tulipa	Tulip	Bulb	z4-9	☼	Sp
18-24"					
Achillea millefolium 'Heidi'	Yarrow		z3-9	☼	Sum
Achillea millefolium 'Borealis'	Yarrow		z3-9	☼	Sum
Achillea millefolium 'Pink Island Form'	Yarrow		z3-9	☼	Sum
Achillea millefolium 'Ortel's Rose'	Yarrow	Rose Pink & White	z3-9	☼	Sum
Agastache cana	Mosquito Plant		z6-9	☼	Sp Sum
Allium schubertii	Tumbleweed Onion	Bulb	z5-9	☼	Sp
Antirrhinum majus	Snapdragon	Reseeds	annual	☼	Sp Sum Fall
Aster novi-belgii 'Patricia Ballard'	New York Aster	Rose Pink	z4-8	☼	Sum Fall
Aster novi-belgii 'Royal Ruby'	New York Aster		z4-8	☼	Sum Fall
Astilbe chinensis var. *davidii*	Chinese Astilbe		z5-9	☼ ☽	Sum
Astilbe chinensis 'Finale'	Chinese Astilbe		z4-8	☽	Sum
Astilbe chinensis 'Veronica Klose'	Chinese Astilbe		z4-8	☽	Sum
Astilbe simplicifolia 'Atro-rosea'	Star Astilbe	Rose Salmon	z4-8	☽	Sum
Astilbe simplicifolia 'Bronze Elegance'	Star Astilbe	Bronze Foliage	z4-8	☽	Sum

57

Pink 18-24"

Scientific Name	Common Name	Comments	Zone	Lighting	Bloom Season
Astilbe simplicifolia 'Dunkellachs'	Star Astilbe	Bronze Foliage	z4-8	☼	Sum
Campanula punctata 'Cherry Bells'	Spotted Bellflower	Cherry-Pink Bells	z3-8	☼☼	Sum
Centranthus ruber var. *roseus*	Jupiter's Beard	Infertile Soil	z5-8	☼☼	Sp Sum
Chrysanthemum c. 'Eileen May Robinson'	Painted Daisy		z3-7	☼	Sp Sum
Chrysanthemum coccineum 'Pink Bouquet'	Painted Daisy		z3-7	☼	Sp Sum
Clarkia 'Brilliant'	Clarkia		annual	☼	Sum Fall
Clematis integrifolia 'Rosea'	Solitary Clematis	Non Vining	z3-7	☼	Sum
Dianthus plumarius 'Spring Beauty'	Cottage Pinks		z3-8	☼	Sum
Dianthus plumarius 'Miss Kyoto'	Cottage Pinks		z3-8	☼	Sum
Echinacea purpurea 'Kim's Knee High'	Purple Coneflower		z3-8	☼	Sum
Echinacea purpurea 'Prairie Frost'	Purple Coneflower	Variegated Foliage	z3-8	☼	Sum
Erigeron hybrids	Fleabane		z2-8	☼	Sum
Erigeron pulchellus	Poor Robin's Plantain		z3-7	☼	Sum
Erigeron speciosus 'Pink Jewel'	Daisy Fleabane		z2-7	☼	Sum
Erodium manescavii	Manescav Erodium		z5-8	☼	Sp
Gypsophila paniculata 'Pink Fairy'	Baby's Breath		z3-7	☼	Sum
Hemerocallis-See Daylilly section					
Heuchera 'Canyon Pink'	Coral Bells		z3-8	☼☼	Sp Sum
Heuchera 'Raspberry Ice'	Coral Bells	Rose Pink w/ Purple Foliage	z4-9	☼☼	Sp Sum

Pink 18-24"

Scientific Name	Common Name	Comments	Zone	Lighting	Bloom Season
Heuchera sanguinea 'Snow Angel'	Coral Bells	Leaves w/White Mottling	z3-9	☼ ☀	Sp Sum
X *Heucherella* 'Bridget Bloom'	Foamy Bells		z4-8	☀	Sp
X *Heucherella* 'Burnished Bronze'	Foamy Bells	Bronze Foliage	z4-8	☀	Sp
X *Heucherella* 'Pink Frost'	Foamy Bells		z3-7	☀	Sp
X *Heucherella tiarelloides*	Foamy Bells		z3-7	☀	Sp
Incarvillea delavayi	Hardy Gloxinia		z5-7	☼	Sum
Iris 'Sweet Allegro'	Bearded Iris		z3-10	☼	Sum
Lavatera thuringiaca 'Shorty'	Tree Mallow		z6-9	☼	Sp
Lilium 'Acapulco'	Oriental Lily	Bulb	z4-8	☼ ☀	Sum
Lychnis flos-cuculi 'Rosea Plena'	Ragged Robin	Pink to Deep Rose	z3-7	☼	Sum
Lycoris squamigera	Autumn Lycoris	Bulb	z5-9	☼ ☀	Sum
Papaver nudicaule	Iceland Poppy		z2-7	☼	Sp
Penstemon 'Apple Blossom'	Bearded Tongue		z4-8	☼	Sum
Persicaria bistorta superba	Snakeweed		z3-7	☀	Sum
Penstemon barbatus	Common Bearded Tongue		z2-8	☼	Sum
Platycodon grandiflorus 'Shell Pink'	Balloon Flower		z3-7	☼ ☀	Sum
Polemonium carneum	Salmon Polemonium		z6-8	☼ ☀	Sum
Potentilla nepalensis	Nepal Cinquefoil		z5-8	☼	Sum
Potentilla nepalensis 'Miss Willmott'	Nepal Cinquefoil		z5-8	☼	Sum

Pink 18-24"

Scientific Name	Common Name	Comments	Zone	Lighting	Bloom Season
Primula japonica	Japanese Primrose		z5-7	☀	Sp Sum
Primula vulgaris	English Primrose		z5-8	☼ ☀	Sp
Sedum x 'Autumn Joy'	Sedum	Dusty Rose	z3-8	☼	Sum Fall
Sedum spectabile 'Brilliant'	Sedum		z4-9	☼	Sum Fall
Tulipa	Tulip	Bulb	z4-9	☼	Sp
24-36"					
Alstroemeria 'Margaret'	Peruvian Lily		z6-10	☼	Sum
Anemone x 'Alice'	Hybrid Windflower		z5-7	☼ ☀	Fall
Anemone x 'Kriemhilde'	Hybrid Windflower		z5-7	☀	Fall
Anemone x 'Margarete'	Hybrid Windflower		z5-7	☀	Fall
Anemone x 'Queen Charlotte'	Hybrid Windflower		z4-8	☼ ☀	Fall
Anemone x 'September Charm'	Hybrid Windflower		z4-8	☼ ☀	Fall
Anemone tomentosa 'Robustissima'	Grapeleaf Anemone		z4-8	☼	Fall
Antirrhinum majus	Snapdragon	Reseeds	annual	☼	Sp Sum Fall
Aquilegia 'Robin'	Columbine		z3-9	☼ ☀	Sp Sum
Aster alpinus 'Abendschein'	Alpine Aster		z4-7	☼	Sp Sum
Aster novae-angliae 'Rose Serenade'	New England Aster		z4-8	☼	Sum Fall
Astilbe x *arendsii* 'Europa'	Hybrid Astilbe		z4-8	☀	Sp Sum

Pink 24-36"

Scientific Name	Common Name	Comments	Zone	Lighting	Bloom Season
Astilbe x arendsii 'Irene'	Hybrid Astilbe		z4-8	☀	Sum
Astilbe x arendsii 'Rheinland'	Hybrid Astilbe		z4-8	☀	Sum
Astilbe chinensis 'Suberba'	Chinese Astilbe	Magenta Pink	z4-8	☀	Sum
Astilbe x rosea	Rose Astilbe		z4-8	☀	Sum
Astrantia major 'Rosea'	Great Masterwort		z5-7	☀	Sp Sum
Astrantia major 'Rose Symphony'	Great Masterwort		z5-7	☀	Sp Sum
Astrantia maxima	Large Masterwort		z5-7	☀	Sp Sum
Centaurea pulcherrima	Pink Bachelor's Button		z3-8	☼	Sum
Chelone lyonii	Turtlehead		z3-7	☀	Sum Fall
Chelone lyonii 'Hot Lips'	Turtlehead		z3-7	☀	Sum Fall
Chelone obliqua	Turtlehead		z5-8	☀	Sum Fall
Delphinium 'Baby Doll'	Delphinium		z2-7	☼	Sum
Echinacea purpurea	Purple Coneflower		z3-8	☼	Sum
Echinacea purpurea 'Bravado'	Purple Coneflower		z3-8	☼	Sum
Echinacea purpurea 'Bright Star'	Purple Coneflower		z3-8	☼	Sum
Echinacea purpurea 'Double Decker'	Purple Coneflower	Double Fl. Head	z3-8	☼	Sum
Echinacea purpurea 'Magnus'	Purple Coneflower		z3-8	☼	Sum
Echinacea purpurea 'Razzamatazz'	Purple Coneflower	Pom Pom Heads	z3-8	☼	Sum
Erigeron 'Charity'	Fleabane		z5-9	☼	Sum

61

Pink 24-36"

Scientific Name	Common Name	Comments	Zone	Lighting	Bloom Season
Filipendula vulgaris	Dropwort		z3-7	☼	Sum
Geranium x *oxonianum* 'Winscombe'	Cranesbill		z5-8	☼	Sum
Gladiolus	Gladiolus	Bulb	z3-7	☼	Sum
Gladiolus communis subsp. *byzantinus*	Gladiolus	Bulb	z5-10	☼	Sum
Gypsophila paniculata 'Festival Pink'	Baby's Breath		z3-7	☼	Sum
Gypsophila paniculata Flamingo'	Baby's Breath	Double Flowers	z3-7	☼	Sum
Hemerocallis-See Daylilly section					
Heuchera 'Carmen'	Coral Bells		z3-8	☼	Sp Sum
Iris	Bearded Iris		z3-10	☼	Sum
Iris siberica 'Strawberry Fair'	Siberian Iris	Crushed Strawberry Color	z3-9	☼	Sum
Lavatera trimestris 'Silver Cup'	Tree Mallow	(biennial)	z6-9	☼	Sum Fall
Liatris spicata	Spike Gayfeather		z3-9	☼	Sum
Linaria purpurea 'Canon Went'	Toadflax		z5-8	☼	Sum
Lobelia cardinalis 'Rosea'	Cardinal Flower	Rose Pink	z2-9	☼	Sum
Lobelia x *speciosa* 'Rose Beacon'	Lobelia		z5-8	☼	Sum
Lunaria annua	Money Plant	(biennial)	z5-9	☼	Sp
Malva alcea 'Fastigiata'	Mallow		z4-7	☼	Sum
Malva moschata	Musk Mallow		z4-8	☼	Sum
Malva sylvestris 'Brave Heart'	Mallow		z4-8	☼	Sp

Pink 24-36"

Scientific Name	Common Name	Comments	Zone	Lighting	Bloom Season
Papaver orientale 'Betty Ann'	Oriental Poppy		z2-7	☀	Sum
Papaver orientale 'Glowing Rose'	Oriental Poppy		z2-7	☀	Sum
Papaver orientale 'Lighthouse'	Oriental Poppy		z2-7	☀	Sum
Papaver rhoeas	Corn Poppy		annual	☀	Sum
Phlox maculata 'Tracy's Treasure'	Spotted Phlox		z3-8	☀ ☀	Sum
Phlox paniculata 'Eva Cullum'	Garden Phlox		z4-8	☀ ☀	Sum
Phlox paniculata 'Fesselballon'	Garden Phlox		z4-8	☀ ☀	Sum
Phlox paniculata 'Laura'	Garden Phlox		z4-8	☀	Sum
Physostegia virginiana	Obedient Plant		z2-9	☀ ☀	Sum
Physostegia virginiana 'Pink Bouquet'	Obedient Plant		z2-9	☀ ☀	Sum
Physostegia virginiana 'Variegata'	Obedient Plant		z4-8	☀ ☀	Sum
Platycodon grandiflorus	Balloon Flower		z3-7	☀ ☀	Sum
Schizostylis coccinea 'Sunrise'	Kaffir Lily		z6-9	☀	Fall
Sidalcea malviflora 'Party Girl'	Checkerbloom		z5-7	☀ ☀	Sum
Thalictrum aquilegifolium	Columbine Meadow-Rue		z5-7	☀ ☀	Sp
Tulipa	Tulip	Bulb	z4-9	☀	Sp

36-48"

Scientific Name	Common Name	Comments	Zone	Lighting	Bloom Season
Acanthus spinosus	Spiny Bear's Breeches	Pink Pur. Bracts	z6-10	☀	Sp

Pink 36-48"

Scientific Name	Common Name	Comments	Zone	Lighting	Bloom Season
Achillea x 'Appleblossom'	Yarrow		z4-8	☼	Sum
Agastache x 'Pink Panther'	Anise Hyssop		z5-8	☼ ☀	Sum
Agastache x 'Tutti Frutti'	Anise Hyssop		z5-8	☼ ☀	Sum Fall
Anemone x 'Elegantissima'	Hybrid Windflower		z5-7	☼ ☀	Sum
Anemone x 'Montrose'	Hybrid Windflower	Deep Rose	z5-7	☀	Sum
Asclepias incarata	Swamp Milkweed		z3-7	☼	Sum
Aster novae-angliae 'Alma Potschke'	New England Aster	Bright Rose	z4-8	☼	Sum Fall
Aster novae-angliae 'Patricia Ballard'	New England Aster		z4-8	☼	Sum Fall
Astilbe x *arendsii* 'Bressingham Beauty'	Hybrid Astilbe		z4-8	☀	Sum
Astilbe x *arendsii* 'Cattleya'	Hybrid Astilbe	Orchid Pink	z4-8	☀	Sum
Astilbe x *japonica* 'Peach Blossom'	Hybrid Astilbe		z4-8	☀	Sum
Canna 'Pink President'	Canna		z7-10	☼	Sum
Centranthus ruber	Red Valerian		z5-10	☼ ☀	Sp Sum
Cleome hassleriana	Cleome		annual	☼	Sum Fall
Cosmos 'Sensation'	Cosmos		annual	☼	Sum Fall
Dahlia	Dahlia		z7-10	☼	Sum Fall
Dicentra spectabilis	Bleeding Heart		z2-8	☀ ●	Sp
Dicentra spectabilis 'Gold Heart'	Bleeding Heart	Gold Foliage	z2-8	☀ ●	Sp
Digitalis x *mertonenesis*	Strawberry Foxglove		z3-8	☼	Sum

Pink 36-48"

Scientific Name	Common Name	Comments	Zone	Lighting	Bloom Season
Dictamnus albus var. purpureus	Gas Plant	Dislikes Disturbance	z3-8	☼	Sp Sum
Filipendula palmata 'Rosea'	Siberian Meadowsweet		z3-7	☼	Sum
Fritillaria imperialis	Crown Imperial	Bulb	z5-8	☼ ◑	Sp
Gaura lindheimeri 'Siskiyou Pink'	Gaura		z5-8	☼	Sum
Hemerocallis-See DaylilySection					
Iris	Bearded Iris		z3-10	☼	Sum
Lavatera thuringiaca 'Candy Floss'	Tree Mallow		z6-9	☼	Sp
Liatris pycnostachya	Kansas Gayfeather		z3-9	☼	Sum
Lobelia x speciosa 'Pink Flamingo'	Lobelia		z5-8	☼ ◑	Sum
Malva alcea	Mallow		z4-8	☼ ◑	Sum
Monarda didyma 'Croftway Pink'	Bee Balm		z4-8	☼ ◑	Sum Fall
Paeonia 'Monsieur Jules Elie'	Peony		z3-8	☼ ◑	Sp Sum
Paeonia obovata	Woodland Peony		z4-7	☼ ◑	Sp Sum
Papaver orientale 'Cedar Hill'	Oriental Poppy		z2-7	☼	Sum
Phlox maculata	Spotted Phlox		z4-8	☼ ◑	Sum
Phlox paniculata 'Harlequin'	Garden Phlox		z4-8	☼	Sum
Phlox paniculata 'Starfire'	Garden Phlox		z4-8	☼ ◑	Sum
Sanguisorba obtusa	Japanese Burnet		z4-7	☼ ◑	Sum
Sidalcea 'Jimmy Whittet'	Checkerbloom		z5-8	☼	Sum

Pink 48"

Scientific Name	Common Name	Comments		Zone	Lighting	Bloom Season
Sidalcea malviflora 'Rose Queen'	Checkerbloom			z5-7	☼ ☼	Sum
48"+						
Alcea rosea 'Barnyard Pink-red'	Hollyhock	(biennial)	Ht. 4-8'	z3-7	☼	Sp Sum
Alcea rosea 'Chaters Pink'	Hollyhock	(biennial)	Ht. 4-8'	z3-7	☼	Sp Sum
Anemone x 'Bressingham Glow'	Hybrid Windflower			z6-8	☼	Fall
Anemone x 'Max Vogel'	Hybrid Windflower			z5-7	☼	Fall
Aster novae-angliae 'Barr's Pink'	New England Aster		Ht. 3-5'	z4-8	☼	Sum Fall
Aster novae-angliae 'Harrington' Pink'	New England Aster			z4-8	☼	Sum Fall
Boltonia asteroides 'Pink Beauty'	False Aster		Ht. 5-6'	z4-8	☼	Fall
Dahlia	Dahlia			z7-10	☼	Sum Fall
Darmera peltata	Umbrella Plant			z5-7	☼	Sp
Delphinium x elatum	Delphinium			z3-7	☼	Sum
Echinacea purpurea 'The King'	Purple Coneflower			z3-8	☼	Sum
Echinacea purpurea 'Robert Bloom'	Purple Coneflower			z4-9	☼	Sum
Epilobium angustifolium	Fireweed			z2-10	☼	Sum Fall
Eremurus robustus	Foxtail Lily		Ht. 7'	z5-8	☼	Sum
Eremurus x shelford 'Rosalind'	Shellford Foxtail Lily		Ht. 5-6'	z5-7	☼	Sum
Eupatorium cannabinum	Hemp Agrimony	Mauve		z5-8	☼	Sum Fall

Pink 48"

Scientific Name	Common Name	Comments	Zone	Lighting	Bloom Season
Eupatorium dubium 'Little Joe'	Joe Pye Weed		z4-8	☼	Sum
Eupatorium fistulosum Hollow	Joe Pye Weed	Ht. 7'	z3-8	☼	Sum Fall
Eupatorium purpureum 'Gateway'	Joe Pye Weed		z4-8	☼	Fall
Filipendula rubra	Queen-of-the-Prairie		z3-7	☼	Sum
Hibiscus moscheutos	Common Mallow	Ht. 3-8'	z5-9	☼	Sum
Hibiscus mutabilis	Confederate Rose	Ht.8-10'	z7-10	☼	Sum Fall
Lavatera cachemiriana	Tree Mallow	Ht. 5-6'	z6-8	☼	Sum
Lavatera thuringiaca 'Bredon Springs'	Tree Mallow	Ht. 5-6'	z6-9	☼	Sp
Lavatera thuringiaca 'Kew Rose'	Tree Mallow	Ht. 8-10'	z6-9	☼	Sp
Lespedeza thunbergii 'Gibralter'	Thunburg Bush Clover	Ht. 4-5'	z4-7	☼	Fall
Lilium henryi 'Pink Perfection'	Henry Lily	Bulb/White & Pink, Ht. 8'	z4-8	☼	Sum Fall
Lupinus 'The Chatelaine'	Lupine		z5-8	☼	Sp Sum
Meconopsis napaulensis	Satin Poppy	Ht. 6'	z6-8	●	Sp Sum
Phlox paniculata 'Brigadier'	Garden Phlox		z4-8	☼	Sum
Rheum palmatum	Ornamental Rhubarb	Ht. 5-8'	z4-7	☼	Sum
Rheum palmatum 'Atrosanguineum'	Ornamental Rhubarb	Purple Foliage	z5-9	☼	Sum
Rodgersia pinnata	Featherleaf Rodgersia	Bronze Foliage	z5-7	☼	Sum
Salvia involucrata 'Bethellii'	Rose Leaf Sage		z7-9	☼	Sum Fall
Spodiopogon sibiricus	Frost Grass		z5-8	☼	FallWtr

67

Orange 6-12"

Scientific Name	Common Name	Comments	Zone	Lighting	Bloom Season
Celosia argentea 'Jewel Box Salmon'	Cockscomb		annual	☼	Sum Fall
Crocus gargaricus	Crocus	Corm(Bulb)	z5-9	☼	Sp
Epimedium x warleyense	Barrenwort		z4-8	☼◐●	Sp
Erigeron aurantiacus	Orange Fleabane		z4-7	☼	Sum
Eriogonum umbellatum	Wooly Sunflower		z6-10	☼	Sum
Gazania rigens 'Daybreak Bright Orange'	Treasure Flower		annual	☼	Sp Sum Fall
Geum x borisii	Boris Avens		z5-7	☼◐	Sum
Helianthemum n. 'Orange Sunrise'	Sunrose		z5-7	☼	Sum
Lychnis x arkwrightii 'Orange Gnome'	Arkwright's Campion		z6-8	☼◐	Sum
Papaver nudicaule 'Wonderland'	Iceland Poppy		z2-7	☼◐	Sp
Tropaeolum majus 'Whirlybird Cream'	Nasturtium	Multicolors	annual	☼	Sum Fall
Tulipa clusiana	Tulip	Bulb	z5-7	☼	Sp

12-18"

Scientific Name	Common Name	Comments	Zone	Lighting	Bloom Season
Begonia sutherlandii	Begonia		annual	◐●	Sum Fall
Cosmos sulphureus 'Cosmic Orange'	Cosmos		annual	☼	Sum Fall
Dianthus x allwoodii 'Danielle Marie'	Pinks		z5-8	☼	Sum
Eschscholzia californica	California Poppy	Yellow Orange	annual	☼	Sp Sum Fall
Geum x borisii 'Werner Arends'	Boris Avens		z5-7	☼◐	Sum

Orange 12-18"

Scientific Name	Common Name	Comments	Zone	Lighting	Bloom Season
Geum reptans	Creeping Avens		z5-10	☀	Sp
Hemerocallis-See Daylily Section					
Meconopsis cambrica 'Aurantiaca'	Orange Welch Poppy		z6-8	☀ ☀	Sum
Papaver nudicaule 'Party Fun'	Iceland Poppy		z2-7	☼	Sp
Papaver nudicaule 'Wonderland Orange'	Iceland Poppy		z2-7	☼	Sp
Sedum rosea var. *heterodontum*	Stonecrop		z2-8	☼	Sp Sum
Tulipa	Tulip	Bulb	z4-9	☼	Sp

18-24"

Scientific Name	Common Name	Comments	Zone	Lighting	Bloom Season
Asclepias tuberosa	Butterfly Weed		z4-9	☼	Sum
Dendranthema 'Bolero'	Garden Mum		z5-9	☼	Sum Fall
Hemerocallis-See Daylily Section					
Inula royleana	Himalayan Elecampane		z3-7	☼	Sum
Tropaeolum majus	Nasturtium	Some Yellow Flowers	annual	☼	Sum Fall
Tulipa	Tulip	Bulb	z4-9	☼	Sp

24-36"

Scientific Name	Common Name	Comments	Zone	Lighting	Bloom Season
Achillea x 'Terra-cotta'	Yarrow	Color Fades to Yellow	z3-8	☼	Sum
Alstromeria aurea	Peruvian Lily		z7-10	☼	Sum

69

Orange 24-36'

Scientific Name	Common Name	Comments	Zone	Lighting	Bloom Season
Canna 'Orange Punch'	Canna		z7-11	☼	Sum
Crocosmia 'Emberglow'	Montbretia	Corm (Bulb)	z6-9	☼	Sum
Crocosmia x c. 'Emily McKenzie'	Montbretia	Corm (Bulb)	z5-8	☼	Sum
Crocosmia x c. 'Lady Hamilton'	Montbretia	Corm (Bulb) Apricot Coral	z5-8	☼	Sum
Echinacea 'Sundown'	Coneflower		z4-8	☼	Sum
Euphorbia griffithii 'Dixter'	Griffith's Spurge		z5-7	✹	Sum
Fritillaria imperialis 'Aurora'	Crown Imperial	Bulb/Orange Scarlet	z5-7	☼	Sp
Fritillaria imperialis 'Orange Brilliant'	Crown Imperial	Bulb	z5-7	☼	Sp
Helenium 'Wyndley'	Sneezeweed		z4-8	☼	Sum Fall
Hemerocallis-See Daylily Section					
Iris 'Rustler'	Bearded Iris	Multi color	z3-10	☼	Sp Sum
Papaver orientale 'Curlilocks'	Oriental Poppy		z3-7	☼	Sum
Papaver orientale 'Harvest Moon'	Oriental Poppy		z3-7	☼	Sum
Papaver orientale 'Prince of Orange'	Oriental Poppy		z3-7	☼	Sum
Phlox paniculata 'Orange Perfection'	Garden Phlox		z4-8	☼ ✹	Sum
Tulipa	Tulip	Bulb	z4-9	☼	Sp
Tulipa 'Blushing Lady'	Tulip	Bulb	z3-7	☼	Sp

Orange 36-48"

36-48"

Scientific Name	Common Name	Comments	Zone	Lighting	Bloom Season
Agastache rupestris	Rock Anise Hyssop	Orange Lavender	z5-8	☼	Sum
Belamcanda chinensis	Blackberry Lily		z5-10	☼☀	Sum
Canna 'Tropicana'	Canna	Variegated foliage	z7-10	☼	Sum
Helenium autumnale 'Brilliant'	Sneezeweed	Bronze Orange	z3-8	☼	Sum Fall
Helenium autumnale 'Coppelia'	Sneezeweed		z3-8	☼	Sum Fall
Kniphofia 'Catherine's Orange'	Torchlily		z5-8	☼	Sp Sum
Leonotis leonurus	Lion's Tail		annual	☼	Sum Fall
Lilium bulbiferum var. croceum	Fire Lily	Bulb	z3-8	☼	Sum
Papaver somniferum 'Burnt Orange'	Opium Poppy		annual	☼	Sp
Phlomis leucophracta	Jerusalem Sage		z5-8	☼	Sum

48"+

Scientific Name	Common Name	Comments	Zone	Lighting	Bloom Season
Canna 'Bengal Tiger'	Canna	Variegated foliage, Ht 6'	z7-10	☼	Sum
Eremurus stenophyllus	Foxtail Lily	Yellow Orange	z5-8	☼	Sum
Hedychium 'Assam Orange'	Ginger Lily	Ht.5'	z7-10	☼☀	Sum Fall
Hedychium coccineum	White Ginger Lily	Ht.6-8'	z8-10	☼☀	Sum Fall
Helenium autumnale 'Rubrum'	Sneezeweed	Red Orange	z3-8	☼	Sum Fall
Lilium henryi	Henry Lily	Bulb	z4-7	☼☀	Sum Fall

Yellow 0-6"

Scientific Name	Common Name	Comments	Zone	Lighting	Bloom Season
Lilium pardalinum	Panther Lily	Bulb/ Ht. up to 8'	z5-9	☼	Sum
Lilium superbum	Turk's Cap Lily	Bulb/Ht up to 8'	z3-10	☼ ☀	Sum Fall
Lilium tigrinum	Tiger Lily	Bulb/ Ht. 6'	z3-9	☼ ☀ ●	Sum Fall
Crocus chrysanthus 'Advance'	Golden Crocus	Bulb	z4-9	☼	Sp
Crocus chrysanthus 'Dorothy'	Golden Crocus	Bulb	z4-9	☼	Sp
Crocus chrysanthus 'Moonlight'	Golden Crocus	Bulb	z4-9	☼	Sp
Crocus x luteus 'Golden Yellow'	Crocus	Bulb	z4-9	☼	Sp
Delosperma congestum 'Gold Nugget'	Ice Plant		z4-8	☼ ☀	Sp Sum
Delosperma nubigena	Ice Plant		z4-8	☼ ☀	Sp
Eranthis hyemalis	Winter Aconite	Bulb	z3-7	☼	Sp
Iris danfordiae	Danford Iris		z5-9	☼	Sp
Limnanthes douglasii	Poached Egg Flower		annual	☼	Sum
Lysimachia lysii	Loosestrife		z6-8	☼ ☀	Sum
Lysimachia nummularia	Creeping Jenny	Tolerates Wet Soil	z3-9	☼ ●	Sum
Lysimachia nummularia 'Aurea'	Creeping Jenny	Tolerates Wet Soil	z3-9	☼ ☀	Sum
Narcissus bulbocodium	Hoop Petticoat Daffodil	Bulb	z5-8	☼ ☀	Sp
Potentilla aurea var. *verna*	Golden Cinquefoil		z5-9	☼	Sum
Primula auricula 'Barnhaven hybrids'	Bear's Ears	Evergreen	z4-7	●	Sp Sum
Primula auricula 'Gold of Ophir'	Bear's Ears	Evergreen	z4-7	☀	Sp Sum

Yellow 0-6"

Scientific Name	Common Name	Comments	Zone	Lighting	Bloom Season
Primula veris	Cowslip		z5-9	☼	Sp
Ranunculus montanus	Mountain Buttercup		z5-8	☼ ☀	Sp
Sedum acre	Goldmoss Sedum		z3-8	☼	Sp
Trollius acaulis	Dwarf Globeflower		z5-7	☀	Sp Sum
Waldsteinia fragarioides	Barren Strawberry		z4-7	☼ ☀	Sp
Waldsteinia ternata	Siberian Barrenwort		z3-9	☼ ☀	Sp Sum

6-12"

Scientific Name	Common Name	Comments	Zone	Lighting	Bloom Season
Achillea x lewisii 'King Edward'	Yarrow	Silver Foliage	z4-9	☼	Sum
Aurinia saxatilis	Basket-of-Gold	Silver Foliage	z3-7	☼	Sp
Belamcanda chinensis 'Nana'	Blackberry Lily		z4-10	☼ ☀	Sum
Belamcanda flabellata 'Halo Yellow'	Blackberry Lily		z5-10	☼ ☀	Sum
Calochortus amabilis	Diogene's Lantern	Bulb/Green Tinged	z7-10	☼	Sp
Chiastophyllum oppositifolium	Lamb's Tail		z5-7	☼	Sp
Chrysogonum virginianum	Goldenstar		z6-9	☼	Sp
Coreopsis auriculata 'Nana'	Tickseed		z4-9	☼	Sp
Coreopsis verticillata 'Zagreb'	Thread Leaf Coreopsis		z5-10	☼	Sum
Corydalis cheilanthifolia	Ferny Corydalis		z3-6	☼ ☀	Sp
Corydalis lutea	Yellow Corydalis		z5-7	☼ ☀	Sp Sum

73

Yellow 6-12"

Scientific Name	Common Name	Comments	Zone	Lighting	Bloom Season
Epimedium x perralchium 'Frohmleiten'	Bishop's Hat	Evergreen	z5-9	☀◐	Sp
Epimedium x versicolor	Barrenwort	Evergreen	z5-9	☀◐	Sp
Epimedium x versicolor 'Sulphurum'	Barrenwort	Evergreen	z5-9	◐	Sp
Erythronium americanum	American Trout Lily	Corm(Bulb)	z3-8	☀◐	Sp
Erythronium tuolumnense	Pagoda Lily	Corm (Bulb)	z5-9	☀◐	Sp
Euphorbia cyparissias	Cypress Spurge		z6-8	☀☀	Sp
Euphorbia myrsinites	Myrtle Euphorbia		z5-10	☀	Sp
Euphorbia polychroma 'First Blush'	Cushion Spurge	Variegated Foliage	z5-9	☀☀	Sp Sum
Fritillaria pudica	Fritillaria	Bulb	z2-9	☀☀	Sp
Gaillardia x grandiflora 'Goblin'	Blanket Flower	Red with Yellow	z2-9	☀	Sum
Helianthemum nummularium 'Goldie Lock'	Sunrose		z5-8	☀	Sum
Hypoxis hirsuta	Star Grass		z4-8	☀☀	Sp Sum
Iris 'Watercolor'	Dwarf Bearded Iris		z3-10	☀	Sp
Lamiastrum galeobdolan 'Herman's Pride'	Dead Nettle	Variegated/ Aggresive	z4-8	☀◐	Sum
Linum flavum 'Compactum'	Gold Toadflax		z5-7	☀	Sum
Oenothera m. 'Greencourt Lemon'	Ozark Sundrops		z4-7	☀	Sum
Oenothera missouriensis	Ozark Sundrops		z4-7	☀	Sum
Osteospermum 'Buttermilk'	African Daisy		annual	☀	Sp Sum Fall
Potentilla tabernaemontani	Cinquefoil		z4-7	☀	Sp

Yellow 6-12"

Scientific Name	Common Name	Comments	Zone	Lighting	Bloom Season
Primula elatior	Oxlip		z5-9	☼ ☼	Sp
Primula vulgaris	English Primrose		z5-8	☼ ☼	Sp
Primula x 'Kewensis'	Primrose		z3-9	☼ ●	Sp
Sedum kamtschaticum 'Diffusum'	Stonecrop		z3-8	☼	Sum Fall
Sedum k. 'Weihenstephaner Gold'	Stonecrop		z3-8	☼	Sum Fall
Sedum kamtschaticum	Stonecrop		z3-8	☼	Sum Fall
Sedum reflexum	Stonecrop		z5-9	☼	Sum
Senecio aureus	Squaw-Weed		z3-8	☼ ☼	Sp
Tricyrtis macrantha ssp. macranthopsis	Yellow Toad Lily		z5-9	● ☼	Sum Fall
Trillium luteum	Yellow Trillium		z4-7	☼ ●	Sp
Trollius pumilus	Dwarf Globeflower		z4-7	☼	Sp
Tulipa	Tulip	Bulb	z4-9	☼	Sp

12-18"

Scientific Name	Common Name	Comments	Zone	Lighting	Bloom Season
Alchemilla mollis	Lady's Mantle		z4-7	☼ ☼	Sp
Allium moly	Golden Onion	Bulb	z3-9	☼	Sp Sum
Ajania pacifica	Chrysanthemum	Variegated Leaf Edge	z6-10	☼ ☼	Sum Fall
Arum creticum	Creton Arum		z7-9	☼	Sp
Baileya multiradiata	Desert Marigold		annual	☼	Sp Sum Fall

Yellow 12-18"

Scientific Name	Common Name	Comments	Zone	Lighting	Bloom Season
Caltha palustris	Marsh Marigold	Moist Soil/ Bog	z3-8	☼	Sp
Coreopsis auriculata	Tickseed		z4-9	☼	Sp
Coreopsis lanceolata	Lanceleaf Coreopsis		z3-9	☼◐	Sp Sum
Euphorbia amygdaloides var. *robbiae*	Wood Spurge		z5-8	☼◐●	Sp Sum
Euphorbia dulcis 'Chameleon'	Spurge	Purple Foliage	z5-7	☼	Sp
Euphorbia polychroma	Cushion Spurge		z6-9	☼	Sp Sum
Gallardia x grandiflora 'The Sun'	Blanket Flower		z4-8	☼	Sum
Hemerocallis-See Daylily Section					
Hypericum calycinum	Aaron's Beard		z5-7	☼	Sum
Inula ensifolia	Swordleaf Inula	Tolerates Boggy Soil	z3-7	☼	Sp Sum
Iris 'Baby Blessed'	Dwarf Bearded Iris	Reblooms	z3-10	☼◐	Sp Fall
Iris bucharica	Juno Iris		z5-9	☼◐	Sp
Iris 'Early Sunshine'	Bearded Iris		z3-10	☼◐	Sum
Iris 'Sunlit Trail'	Dwarf Bearded Iris		z3-10	☼◐	Sp
Linum flavum	Gold Toadflax		z5-7	☼	Sum
Patrina gibbosa	Patrina		z5-8	☼	Sum
Potentilla recta	Sulphur Cinquefoil		z3-7	☼	Sum
Roscoea cautleyoides 'Kew Beauty'	Roscoea		z6-9	☼◐	Sum
Santolina chamaecyparissus	Lavender Cotton	Evergreen & Silver	z6-8	☼	Sum

Yellow 12-18"

Scientific Name	Common Name	Comments	Zone	Lighting	Bloom Season
Sedum aizoon	Aizoon Stonecrop		z4-8	☼	Sum
Sisyrinchium striatum	Yellow-Eyed Grass		z4-8	☼	Sp Sum
Stylophorum diphyllum	Celadine Poppy		z4-8	☼ ◑	Sp
Tulipa	Tulip	Bulb	z4-9	☼	Sp
Uvularia grandiflora	Large Flowered Bellwort		z3-9	●	Sp
Uvularia grandiflora 'Sunbonnet'	Large Flowered Bellwort		z3-9	◑	Sp

18-24"

Scientific Name	Common Name	Comments	Zone	Lighting	Bloom Season
Achillea x 'Moonshine'	Yarrow	Silver Foliage	z3-7	☼	Sum
Aquilegia canadensis 'Corbett'	Columbine		z3-9	☼ ◑	Sp
Asclepias tuberosa 'Hello Yellow'	Butterfly Weed		z4-8	☼	Sum
Buphthalmum salicifolium	Willowleaf Oxeye		z4-9	☼	Sum Fall
Centaurea montana 'Ochroleuca'	Bachelor's Button		z3-9	☼	Sum
Coreopsis grandiflora	Tickseed		z4-9	☼	Sum
Coreopsis grandiflora 'Early Sunrise'	Tickseed		z4-9	☼	Sum
Coreopsis verticillata 'Moonbeam'	Thread Leaf Coreopsis		z5-9	☼	Sum
Crocosmia x 'Norwich Canary'	Montbretia		z5-8	☼	Sum
Disporum flavens	Fairy Bells		z4-8	☼ ◑	Sp Sum
Doronicum orientale	Leopard's Bane		z4-9	☼ ◑	Sp

77

Yellow 18-24"

Scientific Name	Common Name	Comments	Zone	Lighting	Bloom Season
Geum chiloense 'Lady Stratheden'	Chilean Avens		z4-8	☀	Sum
Hemerocallis–See Daylily Section					
Hieracium lanatum	Hawkweed	Likes Poor Soil	z5-9	☼	Sum
Iris 'Butterbit'	Bearded Iris		z3-10	☼ ☀	Sum
Iris foetidissima 'Lutea'	Stinking Gladwin	Decorative Seedhead	z6-9	☀ ☀●	Sum
Iris sibirica 'Butter and Sugar'	Siberian Iris	Moist Soil/Bog	z3-9	☀ ☀	Sp
Kniphofia 'Bressingham Sunbeam'	Torchlily		z5-8	☼	Sp Sum
Kniphofia 'Little Maid'	Torchlily		z5-9	☀	Sp Sum
Lysimachia punctata	Yellow Loosestrife	Aggressive	z4-8	☀	Sum
Lysimachia punctata 'Alexander'	Yellow Loosestrife	Variegated	z4-8	☼ ☀	Sum
Meconopsis cambrica	Welsh Poppy		z6-9	☀ ☀	Sp Sum
Oenothera fruticosa	Common Sundrops	Dry Soil	z4-8	☀	Sum
Penstemon x 'Schooley's Yellow'	Bearded Tongue		z5-7	☼	Sp Sum
Rudbeckia laciniata 'Goldquelle'	Cutleaf Coneflower		z3-9	☀ ☀	Sum
Santolina virens	Green Lavender Cotton		z7-8	☼	Sum
X Solidaster luteus	Golden Aster		z5-9	☼	Sum Fall
Stokesia laevis 'Mary Gregory'	Stokes Aster		z5-9	☼ ☀	Sum
Thalictrum minus var. adiantifolium	Lesser Meadow-Rue		z3-7	☀	Sum
Trollius chinensis 'Golden Queen'	Globeflower		z4-7	☀	Sp

Yellow 18-24"

Scientific Name	Common Name	Comments	Zone	Lighting	Bloom Season
Trollius europaeus 'Superbus'	Globeflower		z4-7	☀	Sp
Tulipa	Tulip	Bulb	z4-9	☼	Sp

24-36"

Scientific Name	Common Name	Comments	Zone	Lighting	Bloom Season
Achillea x 'Coronation Gold'	Yarrow		z3-9	☼	Sum
Anthemis tinictoria	Golden Marguerite		z3-7	☼	Sum
Anthemis tinictoria 'Kelwayi'	Golden Marguerite		z4-7	☼	Sum
Aquilegia x 'McKanas Giant'	Hybrid Columbine		z3-10	☼ ◐	Sp Sum
Aquilegia longissima	Longspur Columbine		z4-8	☼ ◐	Sum
Aquilegia chrysantha	Golden Columbine		z3-10	● ◐	Sp
Artemisia absinthium 'Lambrook Silver'	Wormwood		z4-9	☼	Sum
Baptisia tinctoria	Yellow Wild Indigo		z5-8	☼	Sum
Belamcanda chinensis 'Hello Yellow'	Blackberry Lily		z4-10	☼ ◐	Sum
Chelidonium majus	Greater Celadine	Seeds Everywhere	z6-9	☼ ◐ ●	Sp Sum
Coreopsis tinctoria	Tickseed		annual	☼	Sp Sum Fall
Crocosmia x 'Citronella'	Montbretia	Corm (Bulb)	z5-8	☼	Sum
Crocosmia x 'Walberton Yellow'	Montbretia	Corm (Blub)	z5-8	☼	Sum
Dahlia	Dahlia		z7-10	☼	Sum Fall
Digitalis lutea	Straw Foxglove		z3-8	☼	Sum

Yellow 24-36"

Scientific Name	Common Name	Comments	Zone	Lighting	Bloom Season
Echinacea paradoxa	Yellow Coneflower		z4-7	☼	Sum
Echinacea 'Sunrise'	Coneflower		z4-7	☼	Sum
Fritillaria imperialis 'Lutea'	Crown Imperial	Bulb	z5-7	☼☼	Sp
Fritillaria imperialis 'Lutea Maxima'	Crown Imperial	Bulb	z5-7	☼☼	Sp
Helenium hoopesi	Western Sneezeweed		z3-7	☼	Sum
Heliopsis helianthoides 'Summer Sun'	Sunflower Heliopsis		z3-9	☼	Sum
Hemerocallis-See Daylily Section					
Hypericum androsaemum 'Albury Purple'	St. John's Wort		z5-7	☼	Sum
Hypericum patulum	St. John's Wort		z5-8	☼	Sum
Iris germanica 'Gold Galore'	Bearded Iris		z3-10	☼☼	Sum
Iris germanica 'Treasure Map'	Bearded Iris		z3-10	☼☼	Sum
Iris pseudacorus	Yellow Flag Iris	Moist soil/Bog	z5-9	☼☼	Sum
Iris pseudacorus 'Flore Pleno'	Yellow Flag Iris	Double Flower	z4-9	☼☼	Sum
Iris pseudacorus 'Variegatus'	Yellow Flag Iris	Variegated Foliage	z4-9	☼	Sum
Kirengeshoma palmata	Yellow Waxbells		z5-7	☼●	Sum
Kniphofia 'Sunningdale Yellow'	Torchlily		z5-8	☼	Sp Sum
Lilium x 'Gardenia'	Asiatic Lily	Bulb/Yellow w/Pink Tips	z5-9	☼☼	Sum
Lilium pyrenaicum var. *pyrenaicum*	Yellow Turkscap Lily	Bulb	z3-7	☼☼	Sp Sum
Lupinus x 'Chandelier'	Lupine		z4-9	☼	Sp Sum

Yellow 24-36"

Scientific Name	Common Name	Comments	Zone	Lighting	Bloom Season
Lysichiton americanus	Skunk Cabbage	Moist Soil/ Bog	z5-7	☼	Sp Wtr
Paeonia mlokosewitschii	Golden Peony	Purple emerging Leaves	z5-9	☼	Sp Sum
Patrina scabiosifolia 'Nagoya'	Scabious Patrinia		z5-8	☼	Sum
Phlomis fruticosa	Jerusalem Sage		z4-8	☼☼	Sum
Primula florindae	Florida Primrose	Moist soil	z6-8	☼☼	Sp Sum
Ranunculus acris 'Flore Pleno'	Meadow Buttercup	Aggressive	z3-8	☼	Sp
Ratibida columnifera	Mexican Hat	Red w/Yellow Tipped	z3-7	☼	Sum
Rudbeckia fulgida	Black-eyed Susan		z3-8	☼	Sum
Rudbeckia fulgida 'Goldsturm'	Black-eyed Susan		z3-8	☼	Sum
Rudbeckia triloba	Three Lobed Coneflower		z3-10	☼☼	Sum
Ruta graveolens	Rue		z4-8	☼	Sum
Scabiosa ochroleuca	Cream Scabiosa		z6-10	☼	Sum
Senecio tomentosus	Wooly Ragwort		z3-7	☼	Sp Sum
Solidago 'Baby Gold'	Goldenrod		z4-9	☼	Sum Fall
Solidago 'Crown of Rays'	Goldenrod		z4-9	☼	Sum
Tanacetum vulgare	Tansy		z5-7	☼☼	Sum
Tulipa	Tulip	Bulb	z4-9	☼	Sp
Verbascum chaixii	Mullein		z5-8	☼	Sp Sum

Yellow 36-48"

Scientific Name	Common Name	Comments	Zone	Lighting	Bloom Season
36-48"					
Achillea filipendulina	Fern-Leaf Yarrow		z3-8	☼	Sum
Aconitum lycoctonum ssp. neapolitanum	Yellow Wolfbane		z3-6	☼ ☼	Sum
Argyranthemum 'Jamaica Primrose'	Marguerite Daisy		annual	☼	Sum
Artemisia ludoviciana	White Sage	Silver Foiliage	z4-9	☼	Sum
Artemisia ludoviciana 'Valerie Finnis'	White Sage	Silver Foiliage	z4-10	☼	Sum
Asphodeline lutea	Jacob's Rod		z6-9	☼ ☼	Sum
Centaurea macrocephala	Globe Centaurea		z3-7	☼	Sum
Dahlia	Dahlia		z7-10	☼	Sum Fall
Heliopsis helianthoides	Sunflower Heliopsis		z3-9	☼	Sum
Hypericum x 'Hidcote'	St. John's Wort		z6-9	☼	Sum
Ligularia dentata	Big Leaf Ligularia	Moist soil	z5-8	☼ ●	Sum
Ligularia dentata 'Desdemona'	Big Leaf Ligularia	Moist soil	z5-8	☼ ●	Sum
Ligularia stenocephala 'The Rocket'	Narrow-Spiked Ligularia	Moist soil	z5-9	☼ ●	Sum
Lilium canadense	Canada Lily	Bulb	z4-9	☼ ☼	Sum
Phlomis russelliana	Jerusalem Sage		z5-8	☼ ☼	Sum
Ratibida pinnata	Grayhead Coneflower		z3-7	☼	Sum
Sarracenia flava	Yellow Pitcher Plant	Water/Bog	z6-9	☼ ☼	Sp Sum
Senecio doria	Senecio		z4-7	☼	Sum

Yellow 36-48"

Scientific Name	Common Name	Comments	Zone	Lighting	Bloom Season
Solidago rugosa 'Fireworks'	Rough Stemmed Goldenrod		z4-9	☼	Fall
Thalictrum flavum	Yellow Meadow-Rue		z5-8	☀	Sum
Thermopsis caroliniana	Southern Lupine		z3-9	☼	Sp
Veratrum viride	Indian Poke	Yellow/Green	z3-7	☼ ☀	Sum

48"+

Scientific Name	Common Name	Comments	Zone	Lighting	Bloom Season
Cephalaria gigantea	Tatarian Cephalaria	Ht. 8'	z3-9	☼	Sum
Clematis-See Vine Section					
Eremurus stenophyllus	Foxtail Lily	Ht. 3-5'	z5-8	☼	Sum
Foeniculum vulgare	Fennel		z6-9	☼	Sum
Fritillaria collina	Fritillaria	Bulb	z5-9	☼ ☀	Sp
Helenium autumnale	Sneezeweed		z3-8	☼	Sum Fall
Helenium autumnale 'Butterpat'	Sneezeweed		z3-9	☼	Sum Fall
Helenium autumnale 'Sonnenwunder'	Sneezeweed		z4-8	☼	Sum Fall
Helianthus annuus	Sunflower	Ht. up to 16'	annual	☼	Sum Fall
Helianthus angustifolius	Swamp Sunflower		z6-9	☼	Fall
Helianthus giganteus	Giant Sunflower		z5-9	☼	Fall
Helianthus x multiflorus	Many-Flowered Sunflower	Ht. 6'	z4-8	☼	Sum Fall
Helianthus salicifolius	Willowleaf Sunflower	Ht. 6'	z5-9	☼	Sum Fall

83

Yellow 48+"

Scientific Name	Common Name	Comments	Zone	Lighting	Bloom Season
Lilium auratum	Goldband Lily	Bulb	z4-9	☼◐	Sum
Lilium auratum var. *platyphyllum*	Goldband Lily	Bulb	z4-9	☼◐	Sum
Lilium x *hybridum*	Hybrid Lily	Bulb	z4-7	☼◐	Sum
Patrina scabiosifolia	Scabious Patrinia		z5-8	☼	Sum
Rudbeckia nitida 'Autumn Sun'	Shining Coneflower	Ht.6-7'	z5-9	☼	Sum Fall
Rudbeckia nitida 'Herbstsonne'	Shining Coneflower	Ht. up to 7'	z5-9	☼	Sum Fall
Rudbeckia maxima	Giant Coneflower	Ht. 5-8'	z5-9	☼	Sum
Silphium laciniatum	Silybum	Ht. 7-8'	z3-7	☼	Sum
Telekia speciosa	Telekia	Ht. 4-6'	z3-9	☼◐	Sum

Green 0-6"

Scientific Name	Common Name	Comments	Zone	Lighting	Bloom Season
Galanthus nivalis 'Pusey Green Tip'	Snowdrop	Bulb/Green/White	z3-7	☼☀	Sp
Mitella breweri	Mitrewort		z5-7	☼	Sp
6-12"					
Alchemilla alpina	Mountain Lady's Mantle		z3-7	☼☀●	Sp
Alchemilla conjuncta	Lady's Mantle		z4-8	☼	Sp
Alchemilla erythropoda	Red-Stemmed Lady's Mantle		z3-7	☼☀●	Sp
Fritillaria pallidiflora	Pale Flowered Fritillary	Bulb	z5-8	☼	Sp
Fritillaria pontica	Fritillaria	Bulb	z7-8	☀	Sp
Helleborus viridis	Hellebore	Evergreen	z6-8	☀	Sp
Plantago major 'Rosularis'	Plantain		z4-9	☼☀	Sp Sum Fall
Sarracenia leucophylla	White Top Pitcher	Green & White/Bog	z6-9	☼☀	Sum
Sarracenia purpurea	Pitcher Plant	Green & Red/Bog	z4-9	☼☀	Sum
12-18"					
Arisaema triphyllum	Jack-in-the-Pulpit	Green/White/Purple	z4-9	☀●	Sp
Arum italicum	Italian Arum	Orange-Red Berries/Fall	z6-9	☀●	Sp
Euphorbia cyparissias	Cypress Spurge		z6-8	☼☀	Sp
Fritillaria acmopetala	Fritillaria	Bulb	z7-9	☀	Sp

Green 12-18"

Scientific Name	Common Name	Comments	Zone	Lighting	Bloom Season
Helleborus 'Blackthorn Strain'	Lenten Rose	Kiwi Green/Evergreen	z4-9	☀	Sp
Helleborus foetidus	Stinking Hellebore	Evergreen	z5-9	☀ ◉	Sp
Helleborus torquatus 'Dido'	Hellebore	Purple Green, Evergreen	z6-9	☀	Sp
Tulipa 'Spring Green'	Tulip	Bulb/Green & White	z4-9	☼	Sp

18-24"

Scientific Name	Common Name	Comments	Zone	Lighting	Bloom Season
Arisaema dracontium	Green Dragon		z4-8	☀ ◉	Sp
Astrantia major	Great Masterwort		z5-7	☀	Sp Sum
Disporum sessile 'Variegatum'	Japanese Fairy Bells	Green & White	z4-8	☀ ◉	Sp
Eucomis bicolor	Pineapple Flower	Bulb	z7-10	☀	Sum
Euphorbia amygdaloides var. robbiae	Wood Spurge	Green & Yellow	z5-8	☼ ☀	Sp Sum
Fritillaria cirrhosa	Fritillaria	Bulb	z6-8	☼	Sp
Helleborus argutifolius	Corsican Hellebore	Evergreen	z6-8	☼ ☀	Sp
Heuchera 'Chartreuse'	Coral Bells		z3-8	☼ ☀	Sp Sum
Heuchera cylindrical 'Greenfinch'	Roundleaf Alumroot	Green & White	z4-8	☼ ☀	Sum
Tellima grandiflora	Fringe-Cup		z4-7	☼ ☀	Sp
Zinnia 'Envy'	Zinnia		annual	☼	Sum Fall
Zinnia	Zinnia		annual	☼	Sum Fall

Green 24-36"

24-36"

Scientific Name	Common Name	Comments	Zone	Lighting	Bloom Season
Echinacea purpurea 'Coconut Lime'	Purple Coneflower		z5-9	☼	Sum
Echinacea purpurea 'Green Envy'	Purple Coneflower		z3-7	☼	Sum
Galtonia viridiflora	Summer Hyacinth	Bulb	z8-10	☼ ☀	Sum
Gladiolus 'Green Star'	Gladiolus	Bulb	z8-10	☼	Sum
Kniphofia 'Percy's	Pride Torchlily		z5-9	☼	Sp Sum
Moluccella laevis	Bells of Ireland	Green Bracts	annual	☼	Sum Fall
Nectaroscordum siculum	Sicilian Honey Lily	Bulb	z6-10	☼	Sp Sum
Nicotiana langsdorffii	Flowering Tobacco		annual	☼ ☀	Sum
Nicotiana 'Lime Green'	Flowering Tobacco		annual	☼ ☀	Sum Fall
Zantedeschia aethiopica 'Green Goddess'	Calla Lily	Bulb/Green & White	z8-11	☼	Sum
Zigadenus elegans	Mountain Deathcamas		z4-7	☼	Sum

48"+

Scientific Name	Common Name	Comments	Zone	Lighting	Bloom Season
Amaranthus caudatus var. viridis	Love-lies-bleeding		annual	☼	Sum Fall
Angelica archangelica	Angelica		z5-7	☀	Sum
Ferula communis	Giant Fennel		z6-8	☼	Sum
Gunnera manicata	Giant Rhubarb Greenish Br. Conelike Fl.		z7-10	☼	Sum

87

White 0-6"

Scientific Name	Common Name	Comments	Zone	Lighting	Bloom Season
Antennaria dioica	Pussytoes	Soft Fuzzy White Foliage	z4-9	☼	Sum
Arenaria montana	Mountain Sandwort		z4-8	☼☀	Sp
Armeria maritima 'Alba'	Sea Thrift		z4-8	☼	Sp Sum
Chionodoxa luciliae 'Alba'	Glory-of-the-Snow	Bulb	z4-8	☼	Sp
Claytonia virginica	Spring Beauty	Tinged with Pink	z4-7	☀	Sp
Convallaria majalis	Lily-of-the-Valley		z2-7	☀◗	Sp
Cornus canadensis	Bunchberry	Red Berries	z2-7	☀	Sp Sum
Cyclamen hederifolium 'Album'	Cyclamen	Corm (Bulb)	z5-7	☀	Wtr
Dianthus 'Wink'	Pinks		z4-8	☼	Sum
Galium odoratum	Sweet Woodruff		z4-7	☀	Sp
Galtonia candicans	Summer Hyacinth	Bulb	z6-9	☼	Sum
Glechoma hederacea 'Variegata'	Ground Ivy	Variegated	z5-9	☼	Sum
Gypsophila cerastoides	Creeping Baby's Breath	Purple Veined	z5-8	☼	Sp Sum
Gypsophila repens	Creeping Baby's Breath		z3-7	☼	Sum
Lamium maculatum 'White Nancy'	Spotted Nettle		z3-8	☀◗	Sp
Leontopodium alpinum	Edelweiss		z4-6	☼	Sp Sum
Oxalis regnellii	Purple Shamrock	Purple Foliage	z6-8	☼☀	Sp Sum
Phlox subulata 'Candy Stripe'	Moss Phlox	Pink Center Stripe	z2-8	☼	Sp
Phlox subulata 'White Delight'	Moss Phlox		z2-8	☼	Sp

White 0-6"

Scientific Name	Common Name	Comments	Zone	Lighting	Bloom Season
Potentilla tridentata	Shrubby Fivefingers		z2-8	☼	Sp Sum
Primula 'Craddock White'	Primrose		z5-7	◐	Sp
Sagina subulata	Pearlwort		z4-7	☼◐	Sp
Saxifraga paniculata	Aizoon Saxifrage		z3-6	◐	Sum
Tulipa 'Duc van Tol'	Tulip	Bulb	z3-8	☼	Sp
Viola odorata 'White Queen'	Sweet Violet	Cream Color	z6-8	☼	Sp

6-12"

Scientific Name	Common Name	Comments	Zone	Lighting	Bloom Season
Aethionema iberideum	Iberis Stonecress		z5-7	☼◐	Sp
Ajuga genevensis 'Alba'	Geneva Bugleweed	Evergreen	z4-9	◐	Sum
Ajuga pyramidalis 'Alba'	Bugleweed	Evergreen	z3-9	◐	Sp
Allium neapolitanum	Naples Onion	Bulb	z5-9	☼	Sp
Allium triquetrum	Three Cornered Onion	Bulb	z5-9	☼	Sum
Anemone magellanica	Magellan Anemone		z2-7	☼◐	Sp
Anemone nemorosa	Wood Anemone		z4-8	☼●	Sp
Anthemis cupaniana	Marquerite Daisy		z5-7	☼	Sum
Aquilegia flabellata 'Alba'	Fan Columbine		z3-9	◐	Sp
Arabis caucasica	Wall Rock Cress		z4-7	☼	Sp
Aruncus aesthusifolius	Dwarf Goat's Beard		z3-7	☼◐	Sum

White 6-12"

Scientific Name	Common Name	Comments	Zone	Lighting	Bloom Season
Begonia	Begonia		annual	☼☼●	Sum
Campanula carpatica 'White Clips'	Carpathian Harebell		z3-7	◐	Sum
Cerastium tomentosum	Snow-In-Summer	Fuzzy White Foliage	z2-7	☼	
Clintonia umbellulata	Bride's Bonnet		z4-7	◐	Sp
Dianthus deltoides 'Artic Fire'	Maiden Pinks		z3-7	☼	Sum
Dicentra cucullaria	Dutchman's Breeches		z3-7	◐	Sp
Epimedium grandiflorum 'Album'	Longspur Barrenwort	Evergreen	z5-8	◐	Sp
Epimedium x youngianum 'Niveum'	Bishop's Hat	Evergreen	z5-9	◐	Sp
Erythronium albidum	White Trout Lily	Corm (Bulb)	z4-8	◐	Sp
Galanthus elwesii	Giant Snowdrop	Bulb	z4-7	☼	Sp
Galanthus nivalis	Snowdrop	Bulb	z3-7	☼	Sp
Iberis sempervirens	Candytuft	Evergreen	z3-8	◐	Sp
Iberis sempervirens 'Snow Cushion'	Candytuft	Evergreen	z4-8	☼◐●	Sp
Lamium maculatum 'Album'	Spotted Nettle	Variegated	z4-8	☼	Sp
Leucojum vernum	Spring Snowflake	Bulb	z4-8	◐	Sp
Lithophragma parviflorum	Smallflower Fringecup		z4-6	◐	Sp
Ornithogalum umbellatum	Star of Bethlehem	Bulb	z4-9	☼	Sp
Pachysandra terminalis	Japanese Spurge	Evergreen	z5-9	◐●	Sum
Penstemon hirsutus 'Pygmaeus'	Dwarf Hairy Penstemon		z4-8	☼	Sum

White 6-12"

Scientific Name	Common Name	Comments	Zone	Lighting	Bloom Season
Phlox divaricata 'Fuller's White'	Woodland Phlox		z3-8	☼☀	Sp
Primula vulgaris 'Gigha White'	English Primrose	Yellow Eye	z3-8	☼	Sp
Pulmonaria saccharata 'Alba'	Bethlehem Sage		z3-8	☼☀	Sp
Shortia galacifolia	Oconee Bells		z4-8	☼●	Sp
Tiarella 'Candystriper'	Foamflower		z3-8	☼●	Sp
Tiarella cordifolia	Allegheny Foamflower		z3-8	☼☀	Sp
Tiarella trifoliata	3 Leaved Foamflower	White/Pale Pink	z5-7	☼	Sp
Trillium ovatum	Wake Robin		z5-9	●	Sp
Tulipa	Tulip	Bulb	z4-9	☼	Sp
Tulipa kaufmanniana	Tulip	Bulb	z3-8	☼	Sp
Tulipa tarda	Tulip	Bulb	z3-8	☼	Sp

12-18"

Scientific Name	Common Name	Comments	Zone	Lighting	Bloom Season
Anemone sylvestris	Snowdrop Anemone		z4-7	☼	Sp Sum
Berginia 'Silberlicht'	Hybrid Bergenia	Evergreen	z3-8	☼☀	Sp
Calochortus albus	White Fairy Lantern		z4-10	☼	Sp
Campanula rotundifolia 'White Gem'	Harebell		z2-7	☼☀	Sum
Dianthus x allwoodii 'Alba'	Pinks		z4-8	☼	Sum
Dianthus x 'First Love'	Pinks		z3-7	☼	Sum

White 12-18"

Scientific Name	Common Name	Comments	Zone	Lighting	Bloom Season
Dianthus 'Musgrave's Pink'	Pinks	White w/Green Eye	z5-9	☼	Sum
Dianthus 'Mrs. Sinkins'	Pinks		z5-9	☼	Sum
Dicentra eximia 'Alba'	Fringed Bleeding Heart		z3-9	☼	Sp Sum
Dicentra 'Margery Fish'	Fringed Bleeding Heart	Blue Foliage	z3-9	☼	Sp Sum
Geranium renardii	Cranesbill	Purple veined	z6-8	☼	Sum
Helleborus niger	Christmas Rose	Evergreen	z3-8	☼	Sp Wtr
Helleborus niger 'Potter's Wheel'	Christmas Rose	Evergreen/Green eye	z4-8	☼	Sp Wtr
Heuchera x 'Lime Rickey'	Coral Bells	Lime Green Foliage	z4-9	☼ ☼	Sp Sum
Heucherella x alba 'Birthday Cake'	Foamy Bells		z3-7	☼	Sp
Hosta-See Hosta Section					
Leucanthemum x superbum 'Aglaia'	Shasta Daisy		z4-9	☼	Sum
Leucanthemum x superbum 'Snowcap'	Shasta Daisy		z4-9	☼	Sum
Melittis melissophyllum	Bastard Balm		z6-9	☼	Sum
Oenothera speciosa	Showy Evening Primrose		z3-9	☼	Sum
Phlox x 'Minnie Pearl'	Phlox		z5-9	☼ ☼ ●	Sp Sum
Podophyllum hexandrum	Himalayan Mayapple	Brown Mottle lvs	z5-8	☼	Sp
Podophyllum peltatum	Mayapple		z4-8	☼	Sp
Primula denticulata alba	Drumstick Primrose		z6-8	☼	Sp
Primula japonica 'Postford White'	Japanese Primrose		z6-8	☼	Sp Sum

White 12-18"

Scientific Name	Common Name	Comments	Zone	Lighting	Bloom Season
Pulmonaria s. 'Sissinghurst White'	Bethlehem Sage		z3-8	☼☀	Sp
Spiranthes odorata 'Chadd's Ford'	Ladies Tresses		z5-8	☼	Sum Fall
Trillium cernuum f. *album*	Nodding Trillium	Maroon Center	z5-9	●	Sp
Trillium chloropetalum	Giant Wake Robin	Gray Marbled Lvs	z4-9	●	Sp
Trillium grandiflorum	Great White Trillium		z4-9	☼●	Sp
Tulipa	Tulip	Bulb	z4-9	☼	Sp
18-24"					
Anthericum ramosum	Spider Plant		z4-8	☼	Sum
Astilbe x *arendsii* 'Deutschland'	Hybrid Astilbe		z4-9	☼	Sum
Astilbe x *arendsii* 'Irrlicht'	Hybrid Astilbe		z5-9	☼	Sum
Chrysanthemum parthenium	Feverfew		z5-7	☼	Sum
Dianthus 'Haytor'	Pinks		z5-9	☼	Sum
Dicentra spectabilis 'Pantaloons'	Bleeding Heart		z2-8	☼	Sp
Epimedium pubigerum	Bishop's Hat	Evergreen	z5-9	☼	Sp Sum
Erigeron philadelphicus	Common Fleabane	Whitish Pink	z3-8	☼	Sum
Geranium clarkei 'Kashmir White'	Clarke's Geranium		z4-8	☼	Sp
Gypsophila paniculata 'Compacta Plena'	Baby's Breath		z3-7	☼	Sum
Helleborus orientalis	Lenten Rose	Evergreen	z4-9	☼	Sp

93

White 18-24"

Scientific Name	Common Name	Comments	Zone	Lighting	Bloom Season
Heuchera cylindrica 'Greenfinch'	Roundleaf Alumroot	Green & White	z4-8	☼	Sum
Heuchera 'Palace Purple'	American Alumroot	Purple Foliage	z4-8	☼ ☼	Sum
Hosta-See Hosta Section					
Leucanthemum x superbum 'White Knight'	Shasta Daisy		z4-9	☼	Sum
Linum perenne 'Album'	Flax		z5-8	☼ ☼	Sp
Luzula nivea	Snowy Woodrush		z4-9	● ☼	Sum
Penstemon barbatus 'Alba'	Common Bearded Tongue		z3-8	☼	Sum
Penstemon 'White Bedder'	Bearded Tongue		z7-8	☼	Sum
Primula denticulata	Drumstick Primrose		z4-7	☼	Sp
Salvia nemerosa 'Snow Hill'	Meadow Sage		z5-9	☼	Sum
Salvia pratensis 'Swan Lake'	Meadow Sage		z3-7	☼	Sum
Sedum spectabile 'Stardust'	Sedum		z3-8	☼ ●	Sum Fall
Tricyrtis hirta alba	Toad Lily		z4-9	☼ ●	Fall
Tulipa	Tulip	Bulb	z4-9	☼	Sp

24-36"

Scientific Name	Common Name	Comments	Zone	Lighting	Bloom Season
Achillea millefolium	Common Yarrow		z2-9	☼	Sum
Achillea ptarmica 'The Pearl'	Sneezewort		z2-9	☼	Sum
Actaea alba	White Baneberry	White Berries	z3-7	☼ ●	Sp

White 24-36"

Scientific Name	Common Name	Comments	Zone	Lighting	Bloom Season
Actaea rubra	Red Baneberry	Red Berries	z3-7	☼ ◑	Sp
Agapanthus 'Albus'	African Lily		z7-10	☼	Sum Fall
Agapanthus 'Alice Gloucester'	African Lily	Purple Buds open White	z7-10	☼	Sum Fall
Agapanthus 'Getty White'	African Lily		z7-10	☼	Sum Fall
Agastache rugosa 'Alba'	Anise Hyssop		z5-8	☼	Sum
Allium nigrum	Black Onion	Bulb/Black Center	z5-8	☼	Sp
Anaphalis margaritacea	Pearly Everlasting		z4-7	☼ ◑	Sum Fall
Anemone tomentosa	Grapeleaf Anemone		z5-8	☼ ◑	Fall
Anthericum liliago	St. Bernard's Lily		z4-9	☼	Sum
Aruncus dioicus 'Kneiffii'	Goat's Beard		z4-9	☼	Sum
Aster ericoides 'White Heather'	Heath Aster		z5-8	☼	Sum Fall
Aster novae-angliae 'Herisstschnee'	New England Aster		z4-8	☼	Sum Fall
Astilbe x arendsii 'Diamond'	Hybrid Astilbe		z4-8	◑	Sum
Astilbe x arendsii 'Ellie'	Hybrid Astilbe		z4-8	◑	Sum
Astilbe x arendsii 'White Gloria'	Hybrid Astilbe		z4-8	◑	Sum
Astrantia major 'Alba'	Great Masterwort		z4-7	☼	Sp Sum
Baptisia alba	White Wild Indigo		z5-8	☼ ◑	Sp Sum
Begonia	Wax Begonia		annual	☼ ◑ ●	Sp Sum Fall
Campanula alliarifolia	Spurred Bellflower		z4-8	☼	Sum

95

White 24-36"

Scientific Name	Common Name	Comments	Zone	Lighting	Bloom Season
Campanula persicifolia 'Alba'	Peach-leaf Bellflower		z3-7	☼☼	Sum
Chelone glabra	Turtlehead		z3-7	☼	Sum Fall
Chrysanthemum nipponicum	Nippon Daisy		z5-9	☼	Fall
Crambe maritima	Sea Kale		z6-9	☼	Sp Sum
Dianthus 'Eva Humphries'	Pinks		z5-9	☼	Sum
Dicentra spectabilis 'Alba'	Bleeding Heart		z4-8	◐	Sp
Dictamnus albus 'Albiflorus'	Gas Plant	Dislikes Disturbance	z3-8	☼	Sp Sum
Digitalis lanata 'Cafe Creme'	Foxglove	(Usually biennial) Cream	z4-9	☼	Sum
Echinacea purpurea 'White Swan'	Purple Coneflower		z3-8	☼	Sum
Echinops sphaerocephalus 'Arctic Glow'	Globe Thistle		z3-8	☼	Sum Fall
Erigeron 'White Quakeress'	Fleabane		z5-8	☼	Sum
Filipendula vulgaris	Dropwort		z3-7	☼☼	Sum
Gaura lindheimeri 'Whirling Butterflies'	Guara		z5-8	☼	Sum
Geranium phaeum 'Album'	Mourning Widow		z4-8	☼	Sum
Gillenia trifoliata	Bowman's Root		z4-7	☼	Sum
Gypsophila paniculata 'Bristol Fairy'	Baby's Breath		z4-9	☼	Sum
Hesperis matronalis	Dame's Rocket	(biennial)	z3-8	☼	Sp Sum
Hosta-See Hosta Section					
Leucanthemum maximum 'Crazy Daisy'	Pyrenees Chrysanthemum		z4-9	☼	Sum

White 24-36"

Scientific Name	Common Name	Comments	Zone	Lighting	Bloom Season
Leucanthemum x superbum 'Alaska'	Shasta Daisy		z4-9	☼	Sum
Leucanthemum x superbum 'Elizabeth's'	Shasta Daisy		z4-8	☼	Sum
Liatris scariosa 'White Spires'	Devil's Bite		z3-9	☼◐	Sum Fall
Lychnis coronaria 'Angel Blush'	Rose Campion	(biennial) Pink Eye	z4-7	☼	Sp
Lysimachia clethroides	Gooseneck Loosestrife	Vigorous	z3-8	☼	Sum
Monarda didyma 'Alba'	Bee Balm		z3-7	☼◐	Sum
Myrrhis odorata	Sweet Cicily		z4-10	☼	Sum
Nicotiana alata	Flowering Tobacco		annual	☼	Sp Sum Fall
Osteospermum 'Whirlgig'	African Daisy	irridescent blue eye	annual	☼	Sp Sum Fall
Paeonia lactiflora 'Duchesse de Nemours'	Peony		z4-8	☼	SpSum
Paeonia officinalis 'Alba plena'	Common Peony		z5-8	☼	Sum
Papaver orientale 'Perry's White'	Oriental Poppy	Purple Center	z4-9	☼	Sum
Penstemon digitalis 'Husker Red'	Smooth White Penstemon		z3-8	☼	Sum
Petasites japonicus	Japanese Butterbur		z5-9	☼◐●	Sp
Phlox carolina 'Miss Lingard'	Wedding Phlox		z3-8	☼	Sum
Physostegia virginiana 'Crown of Snow'	Obedient Plant		z2-9	☼◐	Sum
Polygonatum odoratum 'Variegatum'	Fragrant Solomon's Seal		z3-9	☼◐●	Sp
Ranunculus aconitifolius	Aconite Buttercup		z5-8	☼◐	Sp
Ranunculus aconitifolius 'Flore Pleno'	Aconite Buttercup		z5-9	☼◐	Sp

White 24-36"

Scientific Name	Common Name	Comments	Zone	Lighting	Bloom Season
Salvia argentea	Silver Sage		z5-8	☼	Sum
Salvia sciarea t. 'Vatican White'	Clary Sage		z4-8	☼ ☼	Sum
Tulipa	Tulip	Bulb	z4-9	☼	Sp
Tradescantia 'Osprey'	Spiderwort		z5-9	☼ ☼	Sum
Yucca filamentosa	Adam's Needle		z5-10	☼	Sum

36-48"

Scientific Name	Common Name	Comments	Zone	Lighting	Bloom Season
Acanthus mollis var. latifolius	Bear's Breeches		z7-9	☼	Sp
Acanthus spinosus	Spiny Bear's Breeches	Purplish Bracts	z6-10	☼	Sp
Anemone x 'Honorine Jobert'	Hybrid Windflower		z4-8	☼	Fall
Asclepias incarnata 'Ice Ballet'	Swamp Milkweed		z3-7	☼ ☼	Sum
Chelone glabra 'Black Ace'	Turtlehead		z3-7	☼	Sum Fall
Cimicifuga simplex 'White Pearl'	Kamchatka Bugbane		z3-8	☼	Fall
Clematis recta	Ground Clematis	None Vining	z3-7	☼	Sum
Delphinium x belladonna 'Casa Blanca'	Delphinium		z3-7	☼	Sum
Digitalis ferruginea	Rusty Foxglove (biennial) w/Orange-Br		z4-8	☼	Sum
Filipendula palmata 'Alba'	Siberian Meadowsweet		z3-7	☼	Sum
Filipendula ulmaria 'Variegata'	Meadowsweet	Variegated	z3-7	☼	Sum
Gaura lindheimeri	Gaura		z5-8	☼	Sum

White 36-48"

Scientific Name	Common Name	Comments	Zone	Lighting	Bloom Season
Hosta-See Hosta Section					
Iris ensata 'Cascade Spice'	Japanese Iris	Bordered/Flecked Purple	z4-9	☼☀	Sum
Iris ensata 'Picotee Wonder'	Japanese Iris	Magenta Picotee Edge	z4-9	☼☀	Sum
Iris sibirica 'White Swirl'	Siberian Iris		z3-9	☼☀	Sp
Leucanthemum x superbum 'Becky'	Shasta Daisy		z4-9	☼	Sum
Liatris spicata 'Floristan White'	Spike Gayfeather		z3-9	☼	Sum
Lysimachia ephemerum	Loosestrife		z3-8	☼☀	Sum
Monarda 'Snow Maiden'	Bee Balm		z3-7	☼☀	Sum
Paeonia lactiflora 'Alice Harding'	Peony		z4-8	☼	Sp Sum
Paeonia lactiflora 'Baroness'	Peony		z4-8	☼	Sp Sum
Paeonia lactiflora 'Dutchess de Nemours'	Peony	Flushed Pale Yellow	z4-8	☼	Sp Sum
Paeonia lactiflora 'Emodi'	Peony		z5-8	☼	Sp Sum
Paeonia lactiflora 'Krinkled White'	Peony		z4-8	☼	Sp Sum
Paeonia lactiflora 'Schroederii'	Peony		z4-8	☼	Sp Sum
Paeonia lactiflora 'White Wings'	Peony		z4-8	☼	Sp Sum
Paeonia lactiflora 'Whitleyi Major'	Peony		z4-8	☼	Sp Sum
Papaver orientale 'Checkers'	Oriental Poppy	Black Cross Inside	z2-7	☼	Sum
Phlox maculata 'Omega'	Spotted Phlox	Lilac Eye	z3-8	☼	Sum
Phlox paniculata 'David'	Garden Phlox		z4-8	☼☀	Sum

White 36-48"

Scientific Name	Common Name	Comments	Zone	Lighting	Bloom Season
Phlox paniculata 'Fujiyama'	Garden Phlox		z4-8	☼	Sum
Phlox paniculata 'Graf Zeppelin'	Garden Phlox		z4-8	☼	Sum
Phlox paniculata 'White Admiral'	Garden Phlox		z4-8	☼	Sum
Polygonatum commutatum	Great Solomon's Seal		z3-7	☼●	Sp
Rodgersia aesculifolia	Fingerleaf Rodgersia		z5-7	☼	Sp
Rodgersia sambucifolia	Rodgersia		z5-8	☼	Sum
Rodgersia tabularis	Shieldleaf Roger's Flower		z5-7	☀	Sp Sum
Smilacina racemosa	False Solomon's Seal		z3-7	●☼	Sp
Thalictrum aquilegiifolium 'White Cloud'	Columbine Meadow-Rue		z5-9	☼●	Sp
Valeriana officinalis	Valerian		z4-9	☼	Sum

48+

Scientific Name	Common Name	Comments	Zone	Lighting	Bloom Season
Anemone x 'Whirlwind'	Hybrid Windflower, Semi Double Flower		z5-7	☀	Fall
Angelica archangelica	Angelica	Monocarpic, Ht. 5-6'	z5-7	☀	Sum
Aruncus dioicus	Goat's Beard		z3-7	☼	Sum
Aster lateriflorus 'Delight'	Calico Aster	Needs Staking	z4-8	☀	Sum Fall
Aster novi-belgii 'White Swan'	New York Aster		z4-8	☼	Sum Fall
Boltonia asteroides	White Boltonia	Ht. 5-6'	z4-8	☼	Fall
Cimicifuga americana	American Bugbane		z3-7	☀	Fall

White 48+

Scientific Name	Common Name	Comments	Zone	Lighting	Bloom Season
Cimicifuga racemosa	Black Cohosh		z3-7	☀	Sum
Cimicifuga ramosa 'Brunette'	Bugbane	Tinged Pink, Purple Foliage	z3-7	☀	Fall
Cimicifuga ramosa 'Hillside Black Beauty'	Branched Bugbane	Purple Foliage	z3-7	☀	Fall
Crambe cordifolia	Colewort		z6-9	☼	Sp Sum
Delphinium 'Butterball'	Delphinium		z2-7	☼	Sum
Delphinium 'Galahad'	Delphinium		z2-7	☼	Sum
Delphinium 'Olive Poppleton'	Delphinium	Tan Eye	z2-7	☼	Sum
Delphinium 'Sandpiper'	Delphinium	Brown Eye	z2-7	☼	Sum
Digitalis purpurea 'Alba'	Foxglove		z4-8	☀	Sp
Epilobium angustifolium 'Album'	Fireweed		z3-7	☼	Sum Fall
Eremurus himalaicus	Himalayan Foxtail Lily		z5-8	☼	Sum
Eremurus x shelford 'White Beauty'	Shelford Foxtail Lily	Ht. 4-8'	z5-7	☼	Sum
Eryngium eburneum	Sea Holly		z7-9	☼	Sp Sum Fall
Kniphofia 'Ice Queen'	Torchlily		z6-9	☼	Sp Sum
Leucanthemella serotina	Giant Daisy		z4-9	☼	Fall
Macleaya cordata	Plume Poppy	Ht. 5-8'	z3-8	☼ ☀	Sum
Nicotiana sylestris	Woodland Tobacco		annual	☼	Sum Fall
Rodgersia podophylla	Rodgersia	Bronze Foliage in Summer	z5-8	☼	Sum
Sanguisorba canadensis	Canadian Burnet		z3-7	☼ ☀	Sum

Black 0-6"

Scientific Name	Common Name	Comments	Zone	Lighting	Bloom Season
Veronicastrum virginicum	Culver's Root		z4-8	☼☼	Sum
Viola cornuta	Black Viola		z6-9	☼	Sp
Viola 'Molly Sanderson'	Violet		z5-8	☼☼	Sp
6-12"					
Aquilegia 'Chocolate Soldier'	Columbine	Green Sepals	z3-8	☼☼	Sp
Tropaeolum minus 'Black Velvet'	Nasturtium		annual	☼	Sum Fall
12-18"					
Dianthus barbatus (Nigrescens Group)	Sweet William		z4-10	☼	Sum
Fritillaria camschatcensis	Fritillaria	Bulb	z4-9	☼☼	Sp Sum
Fritillaria nigra	Fritillaria	Bulb	z5-7	☼☼	Sp
Helleborus 'Ashwood Black Hybrids'	Hellebore	Evergreen	z6-9	●☼	Sp
18-24"					
Aquilegia vulgaris 'Black Barlow'	Columbine		z3-8	☼☼	Sp Sum
Dianthus barbatus nigrescens 'Sooty'	Sweet William	(biennial)	z4-10	☼	Sum
Dianthus c. 'King of the Blacks'	Clove Pinks		z6-10	☼☼	Sum
Helleborus x hyb. 'Metallic Blue Lady'	Hellebore		z5-9	●☼	Sp

Black 18-24"

Scientific Name	Common Name	Comments	Zone	Lighting	Bloom Season
Iris chrysographes	Beardless Siberian Iris		z6-10	☼	Sp Sum
Tulipa 'Queen of Night'	Tulip	Bulb	z5-9	☼	Sp
Zantedeschia 'Schwarzwalder'	Calla Lily	Bulb	z8-9	☼ ☼	Sp Sum
24-36"					
Centaurea cyanus 'Black Ball'	Cornflower		annual	☼	Sum
Rudbeckia fulgida 'Green Wizard'	Black Eyed Susan	3-5" Black Cone	z3-9	☼	Sp Sum
Scabiosa atropurpurea 'Ace of Spades'	Pincushion Flower		annual	☼	Sum Fall
Scabiosa atropurpurea 'Chile Black'	Pincushion Flower		annual	☼	Sum Fall
36-48"					
Cosmos atrosanguineus	Chocolate Cosmos		annual	☼	Sum Fall
Iris 'Before the Storm'	Bearded Iris		z3-9	☼	Sp Sum
Iris 'Blackout'	Bearded Iris		z3-8	☼	Sp Sum
Iris 'Hello Darkness'	Bearded Iris		z3-8	☼	Sp
Papaver somniferum 'Black Paeony'	Peony Poppy		annual	☼	Sp
48"+					
Alcea rosea 'Nigra'	Hollyhock	Ht. 5-6'	z3-7	☼	Sp Sum

103

Brown 0-6"

Scientific Name	Common Name	Comments	Zone	Lighting	Bloom Season
Asarum shuttleworthii 'Callaway'	Shuttleworth Ginger		z5-8	☼☀	Sp
Iris 'Gingerbreadman'	Dwarf Iris	Blue Beard/Ginger Falls	z3-10	☼	Sp
6-12"					
Asarum canadense	Canadian Ginger		z3-7	☀☼	Sp
Asarum shuttleworthii	Shuttleworth Ginger		z5-8	☀☀	Sp
Calceolaria 'Walter Shrimpton'	Calceolaria		z7-8	☼	Sp Sum
Isotria verticillata	Whorled Pogonia		z5-8	☀	Sp
12-18"					
Arisaema fargesii	Chinese Dragon Arum		z5-8	☼☀	Sp
Aristolochia serpentaria	Virginia Snakeroot		z8-10	☀☀	Sp Sum
18-24"					
Tipularia discolor	Crippled Cranefly		z5-9	☀☀	Sum
24-36"					
Digitalis parviflora	Foxglove		z4-10	☼	24-36" Sp Sum
Fritillaria lanceolata	Chocolate Lily	Bulb	z5-9	☼☀	Sp Sum

Brown 48"+

Scientific Name	Common Name	Zone	Light	Height	Bloom Season
Hibiscus rosa-sinensis 'Black Cherry'	Chinese Hibiscus	Ht. 5'	annual	☼	Sp SumFall
Hibiscus rosa-sinensis 'Chocolate Mousse'	Chinese Hibiscus	Ht. 6'	annual	☼	Sp Sum Fall
Hibiscus rosa-sinensis 'Handsome Stranger'	Chinese Hibiscus	Ht. 6'	annual	☼	Sp Sum Fall
Hibiscus rosa-sinensis 'Al Schlueter'	Chinese Hibiscus	Ht. 6'	annual	☼	Sp Sum Fall
Hibiscus rosa-sinensis 'Key Largo'	Chinese Hibiscus	Ht. 6'	annual	☼	Sp Sum Fall

Flower Forms

Flower forms are classified into 8 forms, buttons, orbs, daisies, plumes, spires, umbels, trumpets, and wispy. These forms are arranged in their **categories by heights.**

Flower Forms–Buttons

Scientific Name	Common Name	Zone	Light	Height	Bloom Season
Scabiosa columbaria	Pincushion Flower	z3-7	☼ ☼	12-18"	Sum
Astrantia 'Moulin Rouge'	Masterwort	z4-7	☼	16-18"	Sp Sum
Knautia macedonica 'Mars Midget'	Knautia	z6-7	☼	16-18"	Sum Fall
Knautia macedonica	Knautia	z4-7	☼	18-24"	Sum Fall
Astrantia major	Great Masterwort	z5-7	☼	24-36"	Sp Sum
Centaurea cyanus	Cornflower	annual	☼	24-36"	Sum Fall
Eryngium yuccifolium	Rattlesnake Master	z4-8	☼	36-48"	Sum Fall

Flower Forms–Orbs

Scientific Name	Common Name	Zone	Light	Height	Bloom Season
Allium 'Beauregard'	Hybrid Onion	z4-8	☼	6-12"	Sp Sum
Allium christophii	Star of Persia	z4-8	☼ ☼	6-12"	Sp Sum
Anemonella t. 'Schoaf's Double Pink'	Rue Anemone	z4-8	☼ ●	6-12"	Sp Sum
Armeria maritima	Sea Thrift	z4-8	☼	6-12"	Sp Sum
Gomphrena globosa	Globe Amaranth	annual	☼	12-24"	Sum Fall
Allium sphaerocephalum	Drumstick Chives	z4-8	☼	18-24"	Sp Sum

Flower Form-Orbs...continued

Scientific Name	Common Name	Zone	Light	Height	Bloom Season
Trifolium rubens	Red Feather Clover	z3-8	☼	18-24"	Sp Sum
Allium 'Globemaster'	Hybrid Onion	z4-8	☼	24-36"	Sp Sum
Echinops ritro	Globe Thistle	z3-9	☼	24-36"	Sum
Monarda didyma	Bee Balm	z3-7	☼	24-36"	Sum Fall
Sanguisorba officinalis	Great Burnet	z4-8	☼	24-36"	Sp Sum
Centaurea macrocephala	Globe Centaurea	z3-7	☼	36-48"	Sum
Phlomis russeliana	Jerusalem Sage	z5-8	☼ ☀	36-48"	Sum
Allium giganteum	Giant Onion	z4-8	☼	48"	Sp Sum
Phlomis tuberosa 'Amazone'	Purple Phlomis	z5-8	☼	up to 5'	Sp Sum

Flower Forms-Daisies

Scientific Name	Common Name	Zone	Light	Height	Bloom Season
Anemone blanda	Grecian Windflower	z4-7	☼ ☀	0-6"	Sp
Aster dumosus	Bushy Aster	z3-8	☼	12-15"	Sum Fall
Gaillardia x grandiflora	Blanket Flower	z4-8	☼	12-18"	Sum
Aster tongolensis	Aster	z4-8	☼	18-24"	Sum
Coreopsis grandiflora	Tickseed	z4-9	☼	18-24"	Sum
Leucanthemum x superbum	Shasta Daisy	z4-9	☼	18-24"	Sum
Catananche caerulea	Cupid's Dart	z4-7	☼ ☀	24-36"	Sum
Echinacea purpurea	Purple Coneflower	z3-8	☼	24-36"	Sum

107

Flower Forms-Daisies ...continued

108

Scientific Name	Common Name	Zone	Light	Height	Bloom Season
Rudbeckia fulgida 'Goldsturm'	Black-eyed Susan	z3-8	☼	24-36"	Sum
Aster laevis	Smooth Aster	z4-9	☼	48"+	Fall
Helenium autumnale	Sneezeweed	z3-8	☼	48"+	Sum Fall
Helianthus giganteus	Giant Sunflower	z5-9	☼	48"+	Fall
Helianthus salicifolius	Willowleaf Sunflower	z5-9	☼	48"+	Sum Fall
Silphium perfoliatum	Cup Plant	z3-7	☼	48"+	Sum Fall

Flower Forms-Plumes

Scientific Name	Common Name	Zone	Light	Height	Bloom Season
Astilbe chinensis	Chinese Astilbe	z4-8	☼	18-24"	Sum
Solidago canadensis	Goldenrod	z3-9	☼	18-24"	Sum Fall
Aruncus dioicus	Goat's Beard	z3-7	☼☼	24-36"	Sum
Astilbe x arendsii	Hybrid Astilbe	z4-8	☼	24-36"	Sum
Thalictrum aquilegiifolium	Columbine Meadow-Rue	z5-7	☼☼	24-36"	Sp
Calamagrostis brachytricha	Feather Reed Grass	z4-9	☼☼●	36-48"	Fall
Persicaria polymorpha	White Fleece Flower	z4-9	☼☼	36-48"	Sum Fall
Rodgersia sambucifolia	Rodgersia	z5-8	☼	36-48"	Sum
Filipendula rubra	Queen-of-the-Prairie	z3-7	☼☼	48"	Sum
Rodgersia pinnata	Featherleaf Rodgersia	z5-7	☼	48"	Sp
Thalictrum lucidum	Shining Meadow-Rue	z4-7	☼☼	5'	Sum

Flower Forms-Plumes...continued

Scientific Name	Common Name	Zone	Light	Height	Bloom Season
Aralia californica	Elk Clover	z3-8	☀☀	6-8'	Sum
Cortaderia selloana 'Pumila'	Dwarf Pampas Grass	z6-10	☀	8-12'	Sum Fall
Cortaderia selloana	Pampas Grass	z6-9	☀	8-15'	Sum Fall

Flower Forms-Spires

Scientific Name	Common Name	Zone	Light	Height	Bloom Season
Galax urceolata	Wandflower	z5-8	☀◐	6-9"	Sp Sum
Tiarella wherryi	Wherry's Foamflower	z4-8	☀●	6-12"	Sp Sum
Stachys monieri 'Hummelo'	Lamb's Ear	z4-8	☀☀	18-20"	Sum
Antirrhinum	Snapdragon	annual	☀	18-24"	Sum Fall
Salvia x sylvestris	Hybrid Sage	z4-7	☀	24-30"	Sp Sum
Aconitum carmichaelii	Azure Monkshood	z3-7	☀	24-36"	Sum Fall
Adenophora lilifolia	Lilyleaf Ladybells	z3-7	☀☀	24-36"	Sp Sum
Baptisia alba	White Wild Indigo	z5-8	☀☀	24-36"	Sp Sum
Digitalis lutea	Straw Foxglove	z3-8	☀	24-36"	Sum
Digitalis parviflora	Foxglove	z4-10	☀	24-36"	Sp Sum
Physostegia virginiana	Obedient Plant	z2-9	☀	24-36"	Sum
Verbascum hybrids	Mullein	z5-8	☀	24-36"	Sp Sum
Kniphofia uvaria	Torchlily	z5-8	☀	24-48"	Sp Sum
Lobelia x speciosa	Lobelia	z4-8	☀☀	24-48"	Sum

Flower Forms-Spires...continued

Scientific Name	Common Name	Zone	Light	Height	Bloom Season
Digitalis grandiflora	Yellow Foxglove	z3-8	☀	36"	Sum
Acanthus mollis	Common Bear's Breeches	z7-9	☼☀	36-48"	Sp
Acanthus spinosus	Spiny Bear's Breeches	z6-10	☀	36-48"	Sp
Aconitum napellus	Monkshood	z3-6	☀	36-48"	SumFall
Baptisia australis	False Blue Indigo	z3-8	☼☀	36-48"	Sp Sum
Ligularia stenocephala 'The Rocket'	Narrow Spiked Ligularia	z5-9	☀ ✳	36-48"	Sum
Lobelia cardinalis	Cardinal Flower	z2-9	☀	36-48"	Sum
Lupinus perennis	Sundial Lupine	z3-9	☼	36-48"	Sp Sum
Thermopsis caroliniana	Southern Lupine	z3-9	☼	36-48"	Sp
Veronica longifolia	Speedwell	z4-8	☼☀	36-48"	SumFall
Eremurus stenophyllus	Foxtail Lily	z5-8	☼	36-60"	Sum
Agastache spp.	Anise Hyssop	z6-9	☼☀	48"	SumFall
Cimicifuga spp.	Bugbane	z3-7	☀	48"	Sum
Digitalis purpurea	Foxglove	z4-8	☀	48"	Sp
Veronicastrum virginicum	Culver's Root	z4-8	☼☀	48"	Sum
Calamagrostis x 'Karl Foerster'	Feather Reed Grass	z5-9	☼	4-5'	Sum Fall
Baptisia lactea	False White Indigo	z4-8	☼	4-6'	Sp Sum
Salvia guaranitica	Blue Anise Sage	z7-10	☼☀	5-6'	Sum

Flower Forms-Trumpets

Scientific Name	Common Name	Zone	Light	Height	Bloom Season
Arisaema triphyllum	Jack-in-the-Pulpit	z4-9	☀ ●	12-18"	Sp
Arisaema candidissimum	White Jack-in-the-Pulpit	z7-9	☀ ●	12-18"	Sp
Hemerocallis	Daylily	z3-9	☀ ☀	18-36"	Sum
Lilium hybrids	Hybrid Lily	z4-7	☀ ☀	24-48"	Sum
Lilium candidum	Madonna Lily	z4-9	☀	2-6'	Sum
Lilium formosanum	Formosan Lily	z5-10	☀ ☀	2-8'	Sum Fall
Lilium regale	Regal Lily	z3-8	☀ ☀	36-48"	Sum
Zantedeschia aethiopica	Calla Lily	z8-11	☀	36-48"	Sum

Flower Forms-Umbels

Scientific Name	Common Name	Zone	Light	Height	Bloom Season
Sedum spectabile	Stonecrop	z3-8	☀	18-24"	Sum Fall
Achillea millefolium	Common Yarrow	z2-9	☀	24-36"	Sum
Ammi visagna	Green Mist	annual	☀	24-36"	Sum
Lychnis chalcedonica	Maltese Cross	z3-7	☀	24-36"	Sum
Achillea filipendulina	Fern-Leaf Yarrow	z3-8	☀	36-48"	Sum
Foeniculum vulgare	Fennel	z6-9	☀	48"	Sum
Patrina scabiosifolia	Scabious Patrinia	z5-8	☀	48"	Sum
Eupatorium maculatum	Spotted Joe Pye Weed	z3-8	☀	4-7'	Sum Fall
Angelica gigas	Purple Parsnip	z4-8	☀ ☀	5-6'	Sum Fall
Eupatorium p. 'Atropurpureum'	Joe Pye Weed	z4-8	☀ ☀	6-9'	Sum Fall

Flower Forms-Wispy

Scientific Name	Common Name	Zone	Light	Height	Bloom Season
Heuchera spp.	Coral Bells	z3-8	☼	12-24"	Sp Sum
Molinia caerulea 'Transparent'	Purple Moor Grass	z4-9	☼	12-30"	Sum Fall
Chasmanthium latifolium	Northern Sea Oats	z4-7	☼-☀	24-36"	Sum
Verbena bonariensis	Butterfly Vervain	z6-9	☼	24-36"	Sum Fall
Muhlenbergia capillaris	Pink Muhly	z7-10	☼	36"	Sum
Gaura lindheimeri	Gaura	z5-8	☼	36-48"	Sum
Eryngium eburneum	Sea Holly	z7-9	☼	48"	Sp Sum Fall
Perovskia atriplicifolia	Russian Sage	z5-9	☼	48"	Sum
Thalictrum r. 'Lavender Mist'	Lavender Mist	z3-8	☼-☀	48"	Sum
Miscanthus sinensis 'Nippon'	Maiden Grass	z5-9	☼-☀	4-5'	Sum
Thalictrum delavayi	Yunnan Meadow-Rue	z5-9	☼-☀	4-5'	Sum
Macleaya cordata	Plume Poppy	z3-8	☼-☀	4-6'	Sum
Sanguisorba tenuifolia 'Alba'	Burnet	z4-7	☼-☀	5'	Fall
Miscanthus sinensis 'Graziella'	Maiden Grass	z5-9	☼-☀	5-7'	Fall
Stipa gigantea	Giant Feather Grass	z7-9	☼	6-8'	Sum Fall
Thalictrum pubescens	Tall Meadow-Rue	z3-8	☀	3-8'	Sum Fall
Molinia arundinacea 'Skyracer'	Tall Moor Grass	z5-7	☼-☀	7-9'	Sum

Foliage Colors-Purple, Pink or Red 0-6"

Heights are of the foliage. Texture is listed by F=fine, M=medium, C=coarse. V=variegated, F=frosted

Scientific Name	Common Name	Zone	Light	Textures	Color	V	F
Ajuga pyramidalis 'Metallica Crispa'	Bugle Weed	z3-9	☼●☼	M	Purple		
Ajuga reptans 'Atropurpurea'	Bugle Weed	z3-9	☼●☼	M	Purple		
Ajuga reptans 'Burgundy Glow'	Bugle Weed	z3-10	☼●☼	M	Purple	V	
Ajuga reptans 'Mahogany'	Bugle Weed	z3-9	☼●☼	M	Purple		
Geranium pratense 'Midnight Reiter'	Meadow Cranesbill	z5-9	☼	M	Purple		
Nymphaea 'Evelyn Randig'	Water Lily	z3-11	☼	C	Red	V	
Phlox divaricata 'Montrose'	Woodland Phlox	z4-9	☼●	M	Pink	V	
Ranunculus ficaria 'Brazen Hussy'	Lesser Celadine	z4-7	☼	M	Purple		
Sedum 'Bertram Anderson'	Sedum	z3-9	☼	F	Purple		
Sedum cyaneum 'Rosenteppich'	Stonecrop	z3-9	☼●	F	Pink	V	
Sedum x 'Red Chalk'	Sedum	z3-9	☼●	F	Pink	V	
Sedum spurium 'Fulda Glow'	Two Row Stonecrop	z3-9	☼	F	Red		
Sedum spurium 'Red Carpet'	Two Row Stonecrop	z3-9	☼	F	Red		
Sempervivum calcareum 'Mrs. Giuseppi'	Hens & Chicks	z5-10	☼	F	Red	V	
Sempervivum x 'Raspberry Ice'	Hens & Chicks	z5-9	☼	F	Purple	V	
Sempervivum 'Red Beauty'	Hens & Chicks	z3-8	☼	F	Red	V	
Sempervivum 'Sanford Hybrids'	Hens & Chicks	z3-8	☼	F	Purple	Red	V
Sempervivum 'Silverine'	Hens & Chicks	z3-8	☼	F	Purple	Red	V

Foliage Colors-Purple, Pink or Red 6-12"

Heights are of the foliage.   Texture is listed by F=fine, M=medium, C=coarse.   V=variegated, F=frosted

Scientific Name	Common Name	Zone	Light	Textures	Color	V	F
Begonia semperflorens 'Vodka'	Wax Begonia	annual	☼☀	M	Purple		
Brassica oleracea 'Red Peacock'	Flowering Kale	annual	☼☀	F		V	
Coleus	Coleus	annual	☀	M	Purple Pink Red	V	
Euphorbia epithymoides 'First Blush'	Cushion Spurge	z4-7	☼☀	F	Pink	V	
Heuchera 'Amethyst Myst'	Coral Bells	z4-9	☀	M	Purple		F
Heuchera 'Black Beauty'	Coral Bells	z4-9	☀	M	Purple		
Heuchera 'Chocolate Ruffles'	Coral Bells	z4-9	☀	M	Purple		
Heuchera 'Guardian Angel'	Coral Bells	z4-9	☀	M	Purple	V	F
Heuchera 'Jade Gloss'	Coral Bells	z4-9	☀	M	Purple Pink Red	V	F
Heuchera 'Mystic Angel'	Coral Bells	z4-9	☀	M	Purple Pink	V	F
Heuchera 'Obsidian'	Coral Bells	z3-8	☀	M	Purple		
Heuchera 'Silver Scrolls'	Coral Bells	z4-9	☀	M	Purple	V	F
Heuchera 'Sparkling Burgundy'	Coral Bells	z4-9	☀	M	Purple		
Heucherella 'Burnished Bronze'	Foamy Bells	z4-9	☀	M	Purple		
Ophiopogon planiscapus 'Arabicus'	Black Mondo Grass	z6-9	☼☀	F	Purple		
Ophiopogon planiscapus 'Nigrescens'	Black Mondo Grass	z6-9	☼☀	F	Purple		
Podophyllum delavayi	Chinese Mayapple	z7-9	●	C	Purple	V	
Salvia lyrata 'Burgundy Bliss'	Lyreleaf Sage	z4-9	☼	M	Purple		

Foliage Colors-Purple, Pink or Red 6-12" ...continued

Heights are of the foliage.   Texture is listed by F=fine, M=medium, C=coarse.   V=variegated, F=frosted

Scientific Name	Common Name	Zone	Light	Textures	Color	V	F
Sedum 'Vera Jameson'	Showy Stonecrop	z3-9	☀	M	Purple		
Sedum telephium 'Atropurpureum'	Sedum	z4-9	☀☀	M	Purple		
Sedum 'Xenox'	Stonecrop	z3-9	☀	F	Purple Pink		
12-18"							
Athyrium nipponicum 'Burgundy Lace'	Japanese Painted Fern	z3-8	☀☀	F	Purple	V	F
Coleus	Coleus	annual	☀	M	Purple Pink Red	V	
Corydalis q. 'Chocolate Stars'	Corydalis	z5-7	☀☀	M	Purple		
Euphorbia dulcis 'Chameleon'	Spurge	z5-7	☀	M	Purple Pink	V	
Euphorbia polychroma 'Bonfire'	Cushion Spurge	z5-9	☀☀	F	Purple Red	V	
Geranium 'Katherine Adele'	Cranesbill	z4-8	☀☀	M	Purple	V	
Heuchera 'Bressingham Bronze'	Coral Bells	z4-9	☀☀	M	Purple		
Heuchera 'Plum Pudding'	Coral Bells	z4-9	☀	M	Purple	V	F
Heuchera 'Purple Petticoats'	Coral Bells	z4-9	☀	M	Purple		
Heuchera 'Vesuvius'	Coral Bells	z4-9	☀	M	Purple		
Heuchera villosa 'Night Watch'	Coral Bells	z6-9	☀☀	M	Purple		
Imperata cylindrical 'Red Baron'	Japanese Blood Grass	z5-9	☀☀	F	Red	V	
Ocimum basilicum 'Purple Ruffles'	Basil	annual	☀	M	Purple		
Rodgersia pinnata 'Chocolate Wings'	Featherleaf Rodgersia	z6-9	☀☀	C	Purple		
Rumex sanguineus	Bloody Dock	z6-8	☀☀	M	Purple Red	V	

115

Foliage Colors-Purple, Pink or Red 12-18"...continued

Heights are of the foliage.   Texture is listed by F=fine, M=medium, C=coarse.   V=variegated, F=frosted

Scientific Name	Common Name	Zone	Light	Textures	Color	V	F
Salvia officinalis 'Tricolor'	Garden Sage	z5-9	☼	F	Purple Pink	V	
Sedum x 'Mohrchen'	Sedum	z3-9	☼☼	M	Purple		
Sedum 'Purple Emperor'	Sedum	z3-9	☼	M	Purple		
Tulipa x 'Johann Strauss'	Tulip	z3-8	☼☼	M	Purple	V	
18-24"							
Amaranthus tricolor 'Flaming Fountain'	Joseph's Coat	annual	☼	M	Purple	V	
Begonia rex-cultorum 'Connie Boswell'	Rex Begonia	annual	☼☼	C	Purple	V	F
Begonia rex-cultorum 'Fireworks'	Rex Begonia	annual	☼☼	C	Purple	V	F
Cimicifuga x 'Black Negligee'	Bugbane	z5-9	☼	M	Purple		
Cimicifuga ramosa 'James Compton'	Black Snakeroot	z4-8	☼	M	Purple		
Coleus 'Fire Dragon'	Coleus	annual	☼	M	Red	V	
Dahlia 'Bishop of Llandaff'	Dahlia	annual	☼	M	Purple		
Euphorbia x 'Blackbird'	Euphorbia	z5-9	☼	F	Purple		
Hypericum x *moserianum* 'Tricolor'	St. Johns Wort	z6-9	☼☼	M	Pink	V	
Loropetalum chinensis 'Shang-lo'	Loropetalum	z7-9	☼☼	M	Purple		
Ocimum basilicum 'Red Rubin'	Basil	annual	☼	M	Purple		
Pennisetum setaceum 'Rubrum'	Purple Fountain Grass	annual	☼	F	Purple		
Penstemon digitalis 'Husker's Red'	Bearded Tongue	z3-9	☼	M	Purple		

Foliage Colors-Purple, Pink or Red 18-24"...continued

Heights are of the foliage.   Texture is listed by F=fine, M=medium, C=coarse.   V=variegated, F=frosted

Scientific Name	Common Name	Zone	Light	Textures	Color	V	F
Phormium cookianum 'Flamingo'	New Zealand Flax	z8-11	☼	M	Pink	V	
Ricinus communis	Caster Oil Plant	annual	☼	C	Purple		
Salvia officinalis 'Purpurascens'	Garden Sage	z5-9	☼	M	Purple		
Salvia officinalis 'Purpurea'	Garden Sage	z5-9	☼	M	Purple	V	
Sedum 'Postman's Pride'	Sedum	z4-9	☼	M	Purple		
24-36"							
Amaranthus tricolor 'Early Splendor'	Joseph's Coat	annual	☼☀	M	Purple		
Colocasia antiquorum 'Illustris'	Elephant Ear	z7-10	☀	C	Purple	V	
Canna x generalis 'Ambassador'	Canna	z7-10	☼	C	Purple	V	
Cimicifuga r. var. atropurpurea	Black Snakeroot	z3-8	☀	M	Purple		
Cimicifuga racemosa 'Brunette'	Black Cohosh	z3-7	☼☀	M	Purple		
Ligularia d. 'Britt-Marie Crawford'	Big Leaf Ligularia	z4-9	☀	C	Purple		
Panicum virgatum 'Rostrahlbusch'	Red Switch Grass	z4-9	☼	F.	Red	V	
Pennisetum setaceum 'Princess'	Purple Fountain Grass	annual	☼	F	Purple		
Phormium 'Evening Glow'	New Zealand Flax	z8-11	☼	M	Pink	V	
Phormium 'Platt's Black'	New Zealand Flax	z8-10	☼☀	M	Purple		
Phormium 'Rainbow Maiden'	New Zealand Flax	z8-11	☼	F	Red	V	
Phormium 'Rainbow Warrior'	New Zealand Flax	z8-11	☼	M	Pink	V	

Foliage Colors-Purple, Pink or Red 24-36"...continued

Heights are of the foliage.	Texture is listed by F=fine, M=medium, C=coarse.				V=variegated, F=frosted		
Scientific Name	Common Name	Zone	Light	Textures	Color	V	F
Phormium 'Red Heart'	New Zealand Flax	z8-11	☼	M	Pink	V	
Phormium tenax 'Amazing Red'	New Zealand Flax	z8-10	☼☀	M	Purple		
Rodgersia pinnata	Featherleaf Rodgersia	z5-7	☼☀	C	Purple		
Rodgersia podophylla	Rodgersia	z5-8	☼	C	Purple		
Sedum 'Black Jack'	Sedum	z3-9	☼	M	Purple		
Tricyrtis affinis 'Tricolor'	Toad Lily	z5-9	☼☀	M	Pink	V	
36-48"							
Canna 'Durban'	Canna	z7-10	☼	C	Red	V	
Panicum virgatum 'RR1'	Switch Grass	z4-9	☼	F	Purple		
48"							
Actinidia kolomikta	Kiwi Vine	z4-8	☼☀	M	Pink	V	
Colocasia esculenta 'Black Magic'	Elephant Ear	z7-10	☀	C	Purple		
Cimicifuga r. 'Hillside Black Beauty'	Black Snakeroot	z4-8	☀	M	Purple		
Foeniculum vulgare 'Bronze'	Fennel	z6-9	☼	F	Purple		
Ipomoea batatas 'Blackie'	Black Sweet Potato	annual	☼☀	M	Purple		
Ipomoea batatas 'Tricolor'	Sweet Potato Vine	annual	☼	M	Pink	V	
Lobelia 'Bee's Flame'	Cardinal Flower	z2-9	☼☀	F	Purple		
Phormium tenax 'Bronze'	New Zealand Flax	z8-10	☼☀	M	Purple		
Rheum palmatum 'Atrosanguineum'	Ornamental Rhubarb	z4-7	☼	C	Purple		

Foliage Colors-Yellow, Chartreuse or Orange 0-6"

Heights are of the foliage.   Texture is listed by F=fine, M=medium, C=coarse.   V=variegated, F=frosted

Scientific Name	Common Name	Zone	Light	Textures	Color	V	F
Arabis ferdinandi-coburgi 'Old Gold'	Rockcress	z6-9	☼☀	F	Yellow	V	
Heuchera villosa 'Caramel'	Coral Bells	z4-9	☀	M	Orange		
Lamium maculatum 'Aureum'	Spotted Nettle	z3-8	☀●	F	Yellow	V	
Lamium maculatum 'Beedham's White'	Spotted Nettle	z3-8	☀●	F	Char	V	
Lysimachia nummularia 'Aurea'	Creeping Jenny	z3-9	☀●	F	Yellow		
Sedum makinoi 'Ogon'	Japanese Stonecrop	z7-9	☀	F	Char		
Sedum repestre 'Angelina'	Sedum	z3-11	☼☀	F	Yellow		
Sedum sieboldii 'Mediovariegatum'	Stonecrop	z5-9	☀	F	Yellow	V	
Sedum spurium 'Tricolor'	Two Row Stonecrop	z3-8	☼	F	Yellow	V	
Tiarella x 'Heronswood Mist'	Foamflower	z4-9	☀●	M	Yellow	V	
Veronica repens 'Sunshine'	Creeping Speedwell	z5-10	☼	F	Yellow		
Veronica prostrata 'Aztec Gold'	Veronica	z4-8	☀	F	Char		
6-12"							
Astilbe x arendsii 'Beauty of Lisse'	Lime Astilbe	z4-8	☀	M	Char		
Carex ciliatomarginata 'Island Brocade'	Sedge	z6-9	☼	F	Yellow	V	
Carex dolichostachya 'Kaga-nishiki'	Gold Fountain Sedge	z5-9	☼☀●	F	Char	V	
Carex firma	Sedge	z5-9	☼☀●	F	Yellow		
Carex hachijoensis 'Evergold'	Japanese Forest Grass	z5-9	☀●	F	Yellow	V	
Convallaria majalis 'Aureo-variegata'	Lily-of-the-Valley	z2-7	☀●	M	Yellow	V	

Foliage Colors-Yellow, Chartreuse or Orange 6-12"...continued

Heights are of the foliage.	Texture is listed by F=fine, M=medium, C=coarse.				V=variegated, F=frosted		
Scientific Name	Common Name	Zone	Light	Textures	Color	V	F
Heuchera x 'Lime Rickey'	Coral Bells	z4-9	☀	M	Char		
Heuchera 'Marmalade'	Coral Bells	z4-9	☀	M	Orange		
X Heucherella 'Stoplight'	Foamy Bells	z4-8	☀	M	Char	V	
Heucherella 'Sunspot'	Foamy Bells	z3-7	☀	M	Yellow		
Liriope muscari 'Gold Band'	Lily Turf	z6-10	☀	F	Yellow	V	
Myosotis scorpioides 'Maytime'	Forget-Me-Not	z4-8	☀	F	Yellow	V	
Ranunculus repens 'Buttered Popcorn'	Creeping Buttercup	z3-8	☀●	M	Yellow	V	
Thymus x citriodorus 'Aureus'	Lemon Thyme	z6-10	☀	F	Yellow		
Tradescantia 'Sweet Kate'	Spiderwort	z3-9	☀☀	F	Char		
12-18"							
Astilbe 'Color Flash Lime'	Astilbe	z4-8	☀	M	Char	V	
Carex dolichostachya 'Gold Fountains'	Birdfoot Sedge	z5-9	☀☀	F	Yellow	V	
Carex morrowii 'Aurea-variegata'	Japanese Sedge	z5-9	☀	F	Yellow	V	
Centaurea montana 'Gold Bullion'	Mountain Bluet	z3-8	☀☀	M	Yellow		
Coleus 'Rustic Orange'	Coleus	annual		M	Orange	V	
Deschampsia c.'Northern Lights'	Hair Grass	z5-9	☀☀	F	Yellow	V	
Geranium 'Ann Folkard'	Geranium	z5-8	☀☀	M	Yellow Char		
Hakonechloa macra 'All Gold'	Japanese Forest Grass	z5-9	☀●	F	Yellow		

Foliage Colors-Yellow, Chartreuse or Orange 12-18"...continued

Heights are of the foliage.   Texture is listed by F=fine, M=medium, C=coarse.   V=variegated, F=frosted

Scientific Name	Common Name	Zone	Light	Textures	Color	V	F
Hakonechloa macra 'Aureola'	Japanese Forest Grass	z5-9	☼☼	F	Yellow	V	
Hosta - See Hosta Section							
Kalimeris x 'Shogun'	Japanese Aster	z3-8	☼☼☼	F	Yellow	V	
Liriope muscari 'John Burch'	Lily Turf	z6-10	☼☼☼	F	Yellow	V	
18-24"							
Aquilegia vulgaris 'Woodside Gold'	Columbine	z3-7	☼	M	Yellow		
Aquilegia vulgaris 'Woodside Variegata'	Columbine	z3-7	☼	M	Yellow	V	
Astrantia m. 'Sunningdale'	Masterwort	z4-7	☼	M	Yellow	V	
Carex elata 'Bowles Golden'	Tufted Sedge	z6-8	☼☼	F	Yellow		
Coleus x *hybridus* 'Lime Green'	Coleus	annual	☼☼	M	Char	V	
Coleus 'Peach Torque'	Coleus	annual	☼	M	Char		
Coleus 'Sedona'	Coleus	annual	☼	M	Orange	V	
Dryopteris erythrosora 'Brilliance'	Autumn Fern	z5-9	☼	F	Orange	V	
Hosta - See Hosta Section							
Melissa officinalis 'Aurea'	Lemon Balm	z4-8	☼☼	M	Yellow	V	
Polemonium caeruleum 'Brise d'Anjou'	Jacob's Ladder	z2-7	☼☼	F	Yellow	V	
Salvia officinalis 'Icterina'	Garden Sage		☼	M	Yellow	V	
Sanguisorba obtusa 'Lemon Splash'	Japanese Burnet	z4-9	☼☼	F	Yellow	V	

Foliage Colors-Yellow, Chartreuse or Orange 18-24"...continued

Heights are of the foliage. Texture is listed by F=fine, M=medium, C=coarse.   V=variegated, F=frosted

Scientific Name	Common Name	Zone	Light	Textures	Color	V	F
Tricyrtis x 'Lightning Strike'	Toad Lily	z4-9	☀●☀	M	Yellow	V	
Tricyrtis x 'Shining Light'	Toad Lily	z4-9	☀●☀	M	Yellow	V	
Yucca filamentosa 'Bright Edge'	Adam's Needle	z4-10	☀	M	Yellow	V	
Yucca filamentosa 'Color Guard'	Adam's Needle	z4-10	☀	M	Yellow	V	
Yucca filamentosa 'Golden Sword'	Adam's Needle	z6-10	☀☀	M	Yellow	V	
24-36"							
Caryopteris x 'Worcester Gold'	Blue Mist Spirea	z5-9	☀	M	Char		
Dicentra x 'Gold Heart'	Bleeding Heart	z2-8	☀	M	Yellow		
Hosta - See Hosta Section							
Iris pallida 'Aurea-variegata'	Sweet Iris	z4-8	☀	M	Yellow	V	
Iris pallida 'Variegata'	Sweet Iris	z3-10	☀	M	Yellow	V	
Petasites japonicus 'Variegatus'	Butterbur	z4-9	☀●☀	C	Yellow	V	
Phormium 'Yellow Wave'	New Zealand Flax	z8-10	☀●☀	M	Yellow	V	
Physostegia virginiana 'Variegata'	Obedient Plant	z4-8	☀●	F	Yellow	V	
Tanacetum vulgare 'Isla Gold'	Tansy	z4-8	☀	F	Yellow		
36-48"							
Acuba japonica 'Variegata'	Gold Dust Plant	z6-10	☀●☀	M	Yellow	V	
Canna 'Bengal Tiger'	Canna	z7-10	☀	C	Char	V	

Foliage Colors-Yellow, Chartreuse or Orange 48"+

Heights are of the foliage.   Texture is listed by F=fine, M=medium, C=coarse.   V=variegated, F=frosted

Scientific Name	Common Name	Zone	Light	Textures	Color	V	F
Humulus lupulus 'Aureus'	Hops	z5-9	☼ ☀	M	Yellow		
Ipomoea 'Ivory Jewel'	Sweet Potato Vine	annual	☀	M	Yellow	V	
Ipomoea batatas 'Margarita'	Sweet Potato Vine	annual	☀	M	Char		
Miscanthus sinensis 'Cabaret'	Japanese Silver Grass	z6-9	☼ ☀	F	Yellow	V	

Foliage Colors-Blue, Silver or White 0- 6"

Heights are of the foliage.   Texture is listed by F=fine, M=medium, C=coarse.   V=variegated, F=frosted

Scientific Name	Common Name	Zone	Light	Textures	Color	V	F
Lamium maculatum 'Beacon's Silver'	Spotted Nettle	z4-9	☀	F	White	V	F
Sedum cauticola	Sedum	z3-9	☀☀	F	Blue		
Sedum dasyphyllum 'Major'	Sedum	z3-9	☀	F	Blue		
Sedum fosterianum	Sedum	z5-7	☀	F	Blue		
Sedum hispanicum 'Minus'	Tiny Buttons Sedum	z4-9	☀☀	F	Blue		
Sedum reflexum	Stonecrop	z5-9	☀	F	Blue		
Sedum reflexum 'Blue Lagoon'	Stonecrop	z4-7	☀	F	Blue	V	
Sedum sieboldii	October Daphne	z3-10	☀☀	F	Blue		
Veronica gentianoides 'Variegata'	Speedwell	z4-7	☀	F	White	V	
6-12"							
Achillea x lewisii 'King Edward'	Yarrow	z4-9	☀	F	Silver		
Acorus gramineus 'Variegatus'	Sweet Flag	z5-8	☀☀	F	White	V	
Allium senescens 'Glaucum'	German Garlic	z4-7	☀	F	Blue		
Andromeda polifolia 'Blue Ice'	Bog Rosemary	z2-6	☀☀	F	Blue		
Arabis ferdinandi-coburgi 'Variegata'	Rock Cress	z6-9	☀☀	F	White	V	
Artemisia schmidtiana 'Silver Mound'	Wormwood	z3-7	☀	F	Silver		
Artemisia stelleriana 'Silver Brocade'	Dusty Miller	annual	☀	F	Silver		
Asarum splendens 'Quick Silver'	Wild Ginger	z6-9	☀☀	M	White	V	
Athyrium x 'Wildwood Twist'	Painted Fern	z4-9	☀☀	F	Silver		

Foliage Colors-Blue, Silver or White 6-12"...continued

Heights are of the foliage.   Texture is listed by F=fine, M=medium, C=coarse   V=variegated, F=frosted

Scientific Name	Common Name	Zone	Light	Textures	Color	V	F
Brunnera macrophylla 'Variegata'	Siberian Bugloss	z4-9	☀☼	M	White	V	
Carex glauca	Blue Sedge	z5-9	☼☀	F	Blue		
Cerastium tomentosum	Snow-in-Summer	z2-7	☼	F	Silver		
Dianthus caryophyllus	Clove Pinks	z8-10	☼	F	Silver		
Dianthus gratianopolitanus	Cheddar Pink	z3-8	☼☀	F	Blue		
Euphorbia cyparissias 'Fens Ruby'	Cypress Spurge	z6-8	☼☀	F	Blue		
Euphorbia myrsinites	Myrtle Euphorbia	z5-10	☼	F	Silver		
Festuca glauca 'Boulder Blue'	Fescue	z4-8	☼	F	Blue		
Festuca glauca 'Elijah Blue'	Fescue	z4-8	☼	F	Blue		
Geranium macrorrhizum 'Variegata'	Big Root Geranium	z5-8	☼☀	M	White	V	
Heuchera 'Venus'	Coral Bells	z4-8	☀	M	Silver	V	F
Hosta - See Hosta Section							
Juncus inflexus 'Lovesick Blues'	Hard Rush	z4-9	☼	F	Blue		
Liriope spicata 'Silver Dragon'	Creeping Liriope	z4-10	☼☀☀	F	White	V	
Pachysandra terminalis 'Silver Edge'	Pachysandra	z4-8	☀☀	F	White	V	
Pulmonaria l. 'Bertram Anderson'	Long Leafed Lungwort z3-8		☀☀	M	White	V	
Pulmonaria longifolia 'Diana Clare'	Long Leafed Lungwort z3-8		☀☀	M	Silver	V	F
Pulmonaria longifolia 'Excalibur'	Long Leafed Lungwort z4-9		☀☀	F	Silver	V	F
Pulmonaria 'Majeste'	Lungwort	z4-8	☀☀	M	Silver	V	F

Foliage Colors-Blue, Silver or White 6-12"...continued

Heights are of the foliage.   Texture is listed by F=fine, M=medium, C=coarse   V=variegated, F=frosted

Scientific Name	Common Name	Zone	Light	Textures	Color	V	F
Pulmonaria x 'Milky Way'	Lungwort	z4-9	◐☀	M	White	V	
Pulmonaria 'Samourai'	Lungwort	z4-8	◐☀	M	Silver	V	F
Stachys byzantina 'Silver Carpet'	Lamb's Ears	z4-8	☼	M	Silver		
Thymus vulgaris 'Silver Posie'	Garden Thyme	z5-8	☼	F	White	V	
12-18"							
Artemisia alba 'Canescens'	Wormwood	z4-9	☼	F	Silver		
Athyrium 'Ghost'	Ghost Fern	z3-8	☼☀	F	Silver	V	F
Athyrium n. var. pictum 'Pewter Lace'	Japanese Painted Fern	z3-8	◐☀	F	Silver	V	F
Athyrium nipponicum 'Pictum'	Japanese Painted Fern	z3-8	◐☀	F	Silver	V	F
Athyrium nipponicum 'Silver Falls'	Japanese Painted Fern	z3-8	◐☀	F	Silver	V	F
Aurinia saxatilis	Basket-of-Gold	z3-7	☼	F	Silver		
Brunnera 'Dawson's White'	Siberian Bugloss	z3-8	☀	M	White	V	
Brunnera macrophylla 'Jack Frost'	Siberian Bugloss	z3-8	☀	M	White		F
Brunnera macrophylla 'Looking Glass'	Siberian Bugloss	z3-8	☀	M	White		F
Helichrysum petiolare	Licorice Plant	annual	☼	F	Silver		
Hosta - See Hosta Section							
Lamium galeobdolon 'Variegatum'	Dead Nettle	z4-8	◐☀	F	White	V	
Leymus secalinus	Blue Wild Rye Grass	z6-10	☼	F	Blue		

Foliage Colors-Blue, Silver or White 12-18"...continued

Heights are of the foliage.   Texture is listed by F=fine, M=medium, C=coarse.   V=variegated, F=frosted

Scientific Name	Common Name	Zone	Light	Textures	Color	V	F
Helictotrichon sempervirens	Blue Oat Grass	z3-8	☼ ☀	F	Blue		
Helictotrichon sempervirens 'Sapphire'	Blue Oat Grass	z3-8	☼ ☀	F	Blue		
Hosta – See Hosta Section							
Santolina chamaecyparissus	Lavender Cotton	z6-8	☼	F	Silver		
Schizachyrium scoparium	Little Bluestem	z4-8	☼	F	Blue		
Schizachyrium scoparium 'The Blues'	Little Bluestem	z4-8	☼	F	Blue		
Sedum 'Frosty Morn'	Sedum	z4-8	☼ ☀	M	White	V	
Seseli gummiferum	Moon Carrot	z6-9	☼	F	Blue		
Stachys byzantina 'Helene von Stein'	Lamb's Ears	z4-8	☼	C	Silver		
18-24"							
Achillea x 'Moonshine'	Yarrow	z3-7	☼	F	Silver		
Anaphalis margaritacea	Pearly Everlasting	z4-7	☼ ☀	F	Silver		
Artemisia ludoviciana 'Valerie Finnis'	White Sage	z5-8	☼	F	Silver		
Athyrium nipponicum 'Branford Beauty'	Japanese Painted Fern	z3-8	☀ ●	F	Silver	V	F
Euphorbia marginata	Ghost Spurge	annual	☼ ☀	M	White	V	
Hosta - See Hosta Section							
Lysmachia punctata 'Alexander'	Yellow Loosestrife	z4-8	☼ ☀	M	White	V	
Plectranthus argentatus	Swedish Ivy	annual	☼ ☀ ●	M	Silver		
Salvia officinalis	Sage	z4-7	☼	M	Silver		

Foliage Colors-Blue, Silver or White 18-24"...continued

Heights are of the foliage.   Texture is listed by F=fine, M=medium, C=coarse.   V=variegated, F=frosted

Scientific Name	Common Name	Zone	Light	Textures	Color	V	F
Tropaeolum majus 'Alaska'	Nasturtium	annual	☼	M	White	V	
Veronica incana	Silver Speedwell	z3-7	☼ ☼	F	Silver		
24-36"							
Amoracia rusticana 'Variegata'	Horseradish	z3-9	☼	C	White	V	
Artemisia ludoviciana 'Silver King'	White Sage	z5-10	☼	F	Silver		
Artemisia ludoviciana 'Silver Queen'	White Sage	z4-9	☼	F	Silver		
Artemisia x 'Powis Castle'	Wormwood	z6-8	☼	F	Silver		
Caryopteris x 'Longwood Blue'	Blue Mist Spirea	z6-9	☼	F	Silver		
Caryopteris divaricata 'Snow Fairy'	Blue Mist Spirea	z6-9	☼	M	White	V	
Helichrysum petiolare 'Variegatum'	Licorice Plant	annual	☼	F	White	V	
Heliopsis h. 'Loraine Sunshine'	False Sunflower	z3-9	☼	M	White	V	
Hosta - See Hosta Section							
Iris pallida 'Alba-variegata'	Sweet Iris	z4-10	☼	F	White	V	
Lavandula angustifolia	English Lavender	z5-9	☼	F	Silver		
Lychnis coronaria 'Dancing Ladies'	Rose Campion	z4-10	☼	M	Silver		
Nepeta x faassenii 'Six Hills Giant'	Faassen Nepeta	z3-8	☼	F	Silver		
Polemonium caeruleum 'White Ghost'	Jacob's Ladder	z4-8	☼ ●	F	White	V	
Polygonatum odoratum 'Variegatum'	Solomon's Seal	z3-9	☼ ●	F	White	V	
Polygonatum odoratum var. thunbergii	Solomon's Seal	z5-10	☼ ●	F	White	V	

Foliage Colors-Blue, Silver or White 24-36' ...continued

Heights are of the foliage. Texture is listed by F=fine, M=medium, C=coarse. V=variegated, F=frosted

Scientific Name	Common Name	Zone	Light	Textures	Color	V	F
Ruta graveolens	Rue	z4-8	☼	F	Blue		
Salvia argentea	Silver Sage	z5-8	☼	C	Silver		
36-48"							
Caryopteris x 'Longwood Blue'	Blue Mist Spirea	z6-9	☼	F	Silver		
Hosta - See Hosta Section							
Thalictrum flavum ssp. glaucum	Dusty Meadow Rue	z4-8	☀	M	Blue		
Verbascum bombyciferum	Mullien	z6-10	☼	C	Silver		
48"+							
Artemisia dracunculus 'Sativa'	Tarragon	z5-8	☼	F	Silver		
Arundo donax 'Versicolor'	Giant Reed Grass	z6-9	☼☀	M	White	V	
Canna 'Stuttgardt'	Canna	z7-10	☀	C	White	V	
Miscanthus sinensis 'Cosmopolitan'	Japanese Silver Grass	z4-9	☼☀	F	White	V	
Miscanthus sinensis 'Morning Light'	Japanese Silver Grass	z4-9	☼	F	Silver	V	
Miscanthus sinensis 'Variegatus'	Japanese Silver Grass	z5-9	☼☀	F	White	V	
Panicum virgatum 'Heavy Metal'	Switch Grass	z5-9	☼	F	Blue		
Perovskia atriplicifolia	Russian Sage	z5-9	☼	F	Silver		
Schizophragma hydr. 'Moonlight'	Climbing Hydrangea	z5-8	☼☀	M	Blue	V	F

129

Fall Foliage Colors 0-6"

Heights are of the foliage. Texture is listed by F=fine, M=medium, C=coarse.

Scientific Name	Common Name	Zone	Light	Textures	Color
Cornus canadensis	Bunchberry	z2-7	☀	M	Reddish-Purple
Delosperma congestum	Ice Plant	z6-9	☼	F	Purple Tones
Delosperma cooperi	Ice Plant	z6-9	☼	F	Red
Gaultheria procumbens	Wintergreen	z4-9	●☀	F	Reddish-Purple
Geranium sanguineum 'Striatum'	Cranesbill	z4-8	☼☀	F	Purple
Sedum floriferum	Sedum	z3-7	☼	F	Red
Sedum middendorffianum var. diffusum	Sedum	z3-9	☼☀	F	Purple Hues
Sedum repestre 'Angelina'	Stonecrop	z3-11	☼	F	Reddish-Orange
Sedum sieboldii	October Daphne	z3-10	☼	F	Red
Sedum stefco	Sedum	z5-9	☼	F	Red
Thymus praecox 'Coccineus'	Creeping Thyme	z3-8	☼	F	Bronze
Tiarella wherryi	Wherry's Foamflower	z4-9	☀●	M	Reddish
Waldsteinia ternata	Barren Strawberry	z3-9	☼☀	M	Bronze-Purple

6-12"

Scientific Name	Common Name	Zone	Light	Textures	Color
Bergenia purpurascens	Purple Bergenia	z3-8	☼☀	M	Reddish-Purple
Ceratostigma plumbaginoides	Plumbago	z5-8	☼☀	F	Bronzy-Red
Dianthus deltoides 'Arctic Fire'	Maiden Pinks	z3-7	☼	F	Purplish-Red
Dianthus deltoides 'Zing Rose'	Maiden Pinks	z3-8	☼	F	Purplish-Red
Epimedium x perralchicum 'Frohnleiten'	Bishop's Hat	z5-9	☀●	F	Bronze

Fall Foliage Colors 12-18"

Heights are of the foliage. Texture is listed by F=fine, M=medium, C=coarse.

Scientific Name	Common Name	Zone	Light	Textures	Color
Epimedium x rubrum	Red Barrenwort	z5-8	☀ ●	F	Reddish-Bronze
Geranium cantabrigiense 'Biokovo'	Cranesbill	z5-7	☀ ☀	M	Reddish Tints
Geranium cantabrigiense 'Karmina'	Cranesbill	z5-7	☀ ☀	M	Reddish Tints
Geranium x magnificum	Showy Geranium	z3-8	☀ ☀	F	Red-Yellow
Geranium sanguineum 'Album'	Cranesbill	z3-8	☀ ☀	F	Burgundy
Geranium sanguineum 'Alpenglow'	Cranesbill	Z3-8	☀ ☀	F	Red-Yellow
Sedum x 'Vera Jameson'	Showy Stonecrop	z3-9	☀ ☀	F	Purple
Tiarella 'Crow Feather'	Foamflower	z4-9	● ☀	M	Pink-Red-Purple
Tiarella 'Iron Butterfly'	Foamflower	z4-9	☀ ●	M	Purplish-Bronze
Aruncus aesthusifolius	Dwarf Goat's Beard	z3-7	☀ ☀	F	Red
Bergenia cordifolia 'Winter Glow'	Heart-Leaved Bergenia	z3-8	☀ ☀ ●	C	Reddish Bronze
Euphorbia polychroma	Cushion Spurge	z6-9	☀	F	Red
Euphorbia polychroma 'Bonfire'	Cushion Spurge	z5-9	☀ ☀	F	Orange-Red/Purple
Geranium s. 'New Hampshire Purple'	Cranesbill	z4-8	☀ ☀	F	Crimson-Red
Hakonechloa macra 'Aureola'	Japanese Forest Grass	z5-9	☀ ☀	F	Reddish Pink

18-24"

Scientific Name	Common Name	Zone	Light	Textures	Color
Bergenia cordifolia 'Bressingham Ruby'	Heart-Leaved Bergenia	z3-8	☀ ☀	C	Burgundy
Dryopteris erythrosora	Autumn Fern	z5-9	☀ ☀	F	Red

131

Fall Foliage Colors 18-24"...continued

Heights are of the foliage.   Texture is listed by F=fine, M=medium, C=coarse.

Scientific Name	Common Name	Zone	Light	Textures	Color
Dryopteris erythrosora 'Brilliance'	Autumn Fern	z5-9	☀☀	F	Red-Orange
Geranium 'Brookside'	Cranesbill	z4-8	☼☀	F	Red-Orange
Geranium 'Orion'	Cranesbill	z4-8	☼☀	F	Red
Polygonum odoratum 'Variegatum'	Solomon's Seal	z3-9	☼☀	M	Gold, Varigated
24-36"					
Amsonia hubrichtii	Arkansas Amsonia	z6-9	☼	F	Gold-Orange
Amsonia tabernaemontana	Blue Star	z4-9	☼	F	Yellow
Lysimachia clethroides	Gooseneck Loosestrife	z3-8	☼	M	Copper-Orange-Yellow
Panicum virgatum 'Hanse Herms'	Switch Grass	z4-9	☼	F	Purple-Red
Panicum virgatum 'Shenandoah'	Switch Grass	z4-9	☼	F	Red
Pennisetum alopecuroides 'Cassian'	Dwarf Fountain Grass	z5-9	☼	F	Orange-Red
Schizachrium scoparium	Little Bluestem	z4-10	☼	F	Copper-Red
Sporobolus heterolepis	Prairie Dropseed	z3-9	☼☀	F	Deep Orange
36-48"					
Matteuccia struthiopteris	Ostrich Fern	z3-7	☼☀●	F	Greenish-Bronze
Osmunda regalis	Royal Fern	z3-10	☼☀●	F	Yellow-Brown
Osmunda regalis 'Purpurascens'	Royal Fern	z3-10	☼☀●	F	Gold
Panicum virgatum 'Heavy Metal'	Blue Switch Grass	z4-9	☼	F	Yellow
Sorghastrum nutans	Indian Grass	z4-9	☼	F	Yellow-Orange

Fall Foliage Colors 36-48"...continued

Heights are of the foliage. Texture is listed by F=fine, M=medium, C=coarse.

Scientific Name	Common Name	Zone	Light	Textures	Color
Sorghastrum nutans 'Sioux Blue'	Indian Grass	z4-9	☼	F	Burnt Orange
Spodiopogon sibiricus	Frost Grass	z5-8	☼-❋	F	Burgundy
Sporobolus heterolepis	Prairie Dropseed	z3-9	☼-❋	F	Deep Orange
48"+					
Andropogon gerardii	Big Blue Stem	z3-7	☼	F	Purplish Red
Darmera peltata	Umbrella Plant	z5-7	❋	C	Red
Erianthus ravennae	Ravenna Grass	z5-9	☼-❋	F	Bronze-Orange
Euphorbia epithymoides	Cushion Spurge	z4-10	☼	F	Red
Miscanthus 'Purpurascens'	Flame Grass	z4-9	☼-❋	F	Copper-Red-Orange
Miscanthus sinensis 'Autumn Light'	Maiden Grass	z5-9	☼-❋	F	Yellow
Miscanthus sinensis 'Graziella'	Maiden Grass	z5-9	☼-❋	F	Copper-Red
Miscanthus sinensis 'Little Silver Spider'	Maiden Grass	z5-9	☼-❋	F	Reddish-Bronze
Molinia caerulea 'Skyracer'	Tall Moor Grass	z5-7	☼-❋	F	Yellow
Parthenocissus tricuspidata 'Robusta'	Boston Ivy	z3-9	☼-❋	M	Red-Orange
Patrinia scabiosifolia	Scabiosa Patrina	z5-8	☼	F	Yellow

133

Chemical-Poisonous

This list of poisonous plants is only meant to be informative. There are many plants and shrubs not represented here that are considered poisonous. A plant's absence from the list does not mean that it is harmless. Some plants are safe for animals but not for humans and vice versa.

Scientific Name	Common Name	Scientific Name	Common Name
Aconitum spp.	Monkshood	*Digitalis spp.*	Foxglove
Actaea spp.	Doll's Eyes	*Eupatorium rugosum*	White Snakeroot
Aegopodium spp.	Bishop's Weed	*Euphorbia spp.*	Spurge
Amaranthus	Love-lies-Bleeding	*Glechoma hederacea*	Ground Ivy
Arisaema spp.	Jack-in-the-Pulpit	*Hedera helix*	English Ivy
Asclepias spp.	Milkweed	*Helenium hoopsii*	Sneezeweed
Caladium	Caladium	*Helleborus spp.*	Hellebore
Caltha palustris	Marsh Marigold	*Hyacinthus spp.*	Hyacinth
Chelidonium majus	Greater Celadine	*Hypericum spp.*	St. John's Wort
Colchicum	Autumn Crocus	*Iris spp.*	Iris
Convallaria majalis	Lily of the Valley	*Lantana camara*	Lantana
Cycas revoluta	Cycad	*Lathyrus spp.*	Sweet Pea
Datura spp.	Jimsonweed	*Linum*	Flax
Delphineum spp.	Delphineum	*Lobelia cardinalis*	Cardinal Flower
Dicentra cucullaria	Dutchman's Breeches	*Lobelia spp.*	Lobelia
Dicentra spp.	Bleeding Heart	*Lupinus spp.*	Lupine
Mirabilis jalapa	Four O'Clock	*Narcissus*	Daffodil
Nicotiana spp.	Flowering Tobacco	*Onoclea sensibilis*	Sensitive Fern

Chemical-Poisonous

Scientific Name	Common Name	Scientific Name	Common Name
Ornithogalum umbellatum	Star-of-Bethlehem	*Rumex spp.*	Rhubarb
Papaver spp.	Poppy	*Sanquinaria canadensis*	Bloodroot
Podophyllum peltatum	Mayapple	*Saponaria spp.*	Soapwort
Pteridium aquilinum	Bracken Fern	*Senecio spp.*	Tansy
Ranunculus spp.	Buttercup	*Symplocarpus foetidus*	Skunk Cabbage
Rheum rhaponticum	Rhubarb	*Trifolium spp.*	Clover
Rhus radicans	Poison Ivy	*Veronicastrum virginianum*	Culver's Root
Ricinus communis	Castor plant	*Zigadenus spp.*	Death Camas

135

Section Two
Specific Genera

Daylilies 6-12"

Hemerocallis

Cultivar or Species	Zone	Light	Early Summer	Mid Summer	Late Summer	Rebloomer	Fragrant	Comments
6-12"								
Yellow								
'Eenie Weenie'	z2-6	☼ ☀	x			x	x	Yellow with green throat
Purple								
'Little Grapette'	z3-8	☼ ☀	x	x				Purple with deep purple band green throat
12-18"								
Red								
'Little Red Warbler'	z3-10	☼ ☀	x	x		x		Red with yellow center
'Pardon Me'	z4-9	☀		x		x	x	Purple red with yellow eye
'Petite Rouge'	z2-6	☼ ☀	x	x				Red with yellow eye, yellow stripe on petals
'Siloam Red Ruby'	z3-10	☼ ☀		x				Deep pink red with yellow center
Orange								
'Mauna Loa'	z3-9	☼ ☀		x				Copper orange
'Apricot Sparkles'	z3-9	☼ ☀	x			x		Apricot orange
Yellow								
'Happy Returns'	z4-9	☼ ☀	x			x	x	Pure yellow
'Lightning Bug'	z2-6	☼ ☀	x	x				Yellow with deep red eye

Daylilies 12-18"...continued

Hemerocallis

Cultivar or Species	Zone	Light	Early Summer	Mid Summer	Late Summer	Rebloomer	Fragrant	Comments
Lavender								
'Little Wart'	z4-9	☼		x			x	Lavender with yellow center outlined in purple
White								
'Siloam Peewee'	z2-6	☼☼	x	x				White with yellow/Purple eye
'Siloam Ralph Henry'	z3-10	☼☼	x	x				White with yellow center
Pink								
'Jolyene Nichole'	z3-9	☼☼	x	x				Pink with rose veining yellow eye
'Little Business'	z4-9	☼☼	x	x	x		x	Hot pink with green throat
18-24"								
Red								
'Allegiance'	z4-10	☼☼	x		.			Red with yellow center and yellow stripe on petals
'Bama Bound'	z3-10	☼☼		x		x		Dark red with yellow center
'Bertrand Farr'	z4-10	☼☼		x	x			Red w/yellow center &stripe down center of petals
'Black Cherry'	z4-10	☼☼		x				Red with yellow center
'Chicago Firecracker'	z4-10	☼☼		x				Red with yellow center
'Chipper Cherry'	z4-10	☼☼	x		x			Red with yellow center
'Crimson Glory'	z4-10	☼☼	x	x	x			Red with yellow center
'Sir Modred'	z3-9	☼☼		x			x	Dark black-red with yellow throat

Daylilies 18-24" Red...continued

Hemerocallis

Cultivar or Species	Zone	Light	Early Summer	Mid Summer	Late Summer	Rebloomer	Fragrant	Comments
'Wine Bold'	z4-10	☼ ☼	x					Dark red with yellow center
Orange								
'August Pioneer'	z4-10	☼ ☼	x	x				Pale orange
'Bertie Ferris'	z2-6	☼ ☼	x					Peachy orange
'Painted Lady'	z4-10	☼ ☼	x		x			Pinkish orange
Yellow								
'Aristocrat'	z4-10	☼ ☼	x					Thin yellow petals with orange marks toward center
'August Bright'	z4-10	☼ ☼		x				Clear yellow flowers
'Beauty to Behold'	z3-10	☼ ☼	x					Bright yellow
'Bejeweled'	z4-10	☼ ☼	x		x			Yellow
'Betty Woods'	z3-9	☼ ☼	x		x	x		Ruffly yellow, Double
'Black Eyed Stella'	z3-10	☼ ☼	x		x			Yellow with red eye
'Caballero'	z4-10	☼ ☼	x		x			Yellow with 3 petals tipped in red
'Carolyn Criswell'	z3-10	☼ ☼	x		x			Clear yellow with three ruffled petals
'Custard Candy'	z3-9	☼ ☼	x		x			Pale yellow with maroon band/green eye
'Double Charm'	z2-6	☼ ☼	x					Bright yellow with double form
'Fond Caress'	z4-10	☼ ☼	x		x			Cream with green eye
'Going Bananas'	z3-9	☼ ☼	x	x				Pure yellow

Daylilies 18-24" Yellow...continued

Hemerocallis

Cultivar or Species	Zone	Light	Early Summer	Mid Summer	Late Summer	Rebloomer	Fragrant	Comments
'Goliath'	z4-10	☼ ☀		x		x		Yellow
'Green Flutter'	z3-10	☼ ☀			x	x		Bright yellow with green eye
'Hesperus'	z4-10	☼ ☀		x	x			Pale clear yellow
'Ophir'	z4-10	☼ ☀		x		x	x	Yellow with subtle ruffles
'Siloam June Bug'	z2-6	☼ ☀	x	x				Yellow with dark red eye
'So Lovely'	z4-10	☼ ☀		x				Nearly white with yellow eye
'Stella D'Oro'	z4-10	☼ ☀	x	x		x	x	Deep yellow
Purple								
'Grape Velvet'	z4-10	☼ ☀		x		x		Purple with yellow eye + ruffles
'Raspberry Pixie'	z3-8	☼ ☀		x		x		Purple with yellow center w/deep purple/red outline
'Siloam Plum Tree'	z3-10	☼ ☀	x	x				Dark purple with yellow eye
Lavender								
'Siloam Lilac Magic'	z3-10	☼ ☀	x	x			x	Lavender with yellow-green eye
'Silver Ice'	z4-10	☼ ☀	x	x		x		Lavender with yellow center
Pink								
'Always Afternoon',	z3-9	☼ ☀	x			x		Rose with purple eye/green throat
'Barbara Mitchell'	z3-10	☼ ☀		x		x	x	Soft pink with green throat

142

Daylilies 18-24" Pink ...continued

Hemerocallis

Cultivar or Species	Zone	Light	Early Summer	Mid Summer	Late Summer	Rebloomer	Fragrant	Comments
'Daring Deception'	z3-9	☼ ☼	x	x		x		Light pink with dark purple eye
'Evelyn Claar'	z4-10	☼ ☼	x	x				Pink with orange-yellow throat
'Fairytail Pink'	z3-9	☼ ☼	x		x			Pale pink green throat
'Janice Brown'	z3-9	☼ ☼	x	x				Light pink with dark pink eye/green throat
'Rose Emily'	z3-9	☼ ☼	x	x				Rose pink with yellow eye/green throat
'Strawberry Candy'	z3-9	☼ ☼	x	x	x			Pink with rose eye/gold center
'Sue Rothbauer'	z3-9	☼ ☼	x	x	x	x		Rose pink with yellowgreenthroat
'Wineberry Candy'	z3-9	☼ ☼	x	x	x	x		Pink with wine purple eye

24-36"

Red

Cultivar or Species	Zone	Light	Early Summer	Mid Summer	Late Summer	Rebloomer	Fragrant	Comments
'Anzac'	z2-6	☼ ☼	x	x		x		Red with yellow center
'Baja'	z3-10	☼ ☼	x	x		x		Red with yellow center & midribs
'Baltimore Oriole'	z3-10	☼ ☼	x	x	x			Red with yellow center stripe and yellow picotee
'Carey Quinn'	z2-6	☼ ☼	x	x				Red with yellow center
'Chicago Apache'	z3-10	☼ ☼	x	x	x			Red
'Christmas Carol'	z2-6	☼ ☼	x	x				Deep red with greenish yellow center
'Gordon Biggs'	z3-10	☼ ☼	x					Orangy red

Daylilies 24-36" Red ...continued

Hemerocallis

Cultivar or Species	Zone	Light	Early Summer	Mid Summer	Late Summer	Rebloomer	Fragrant	Comments
'Hot Lips'	z4-8	☼☀	x	x		x		Fall bloom, pinkish red with yellow eye
'Hot Town'	z4-8	☼☀		x	x	x		Deep orange-red
'Mallard'	z4-8	☼☀		x		x		Deep red with darker black-red eye
'Oriental Ruby'	z4-8	☼☀		x	x	x		Red red
'Poin Set'	z3-8	☼☀	x	x	x			Red with yellow eye
'Ruby Throat'	z2-6	☼☀		x	x			Red with yellow center
'Ruffled Ruby'	z3-10	☼☀	x					Red with yellow center/ruffled petals

Orange

Cultivar or Species	Zone	Light	Early Summer	Mid Summer	Late Summer	Rebloomer	Fragrant	Comments
'Spanish Glow'	z3-9	☼☀			x	x		Peach with gold throat
'Bold Tiger'	z3-9	☼☀		x			x	Orange with red eye/yellow throat
'Frans Hals'	z4-8	☼☀		x	x		x	Alternating yellow& red petals with yellow stripe
'Alabama Jubilee'	z3-9	☼☀		x			x	Red-orange with gold throat
'Rocket City'	z2-6	☼☀		x				Orange with darker orange eye
'South Seas'	z3-9	☼☀		x		x		Coral pink tones yellow throat
'Spellbinder'	z3-9	☼☀	x	x		x	x	Pure orange

Yellow

Cultivar or Species	Zone	Light	Early Summer	Mid Summer	Late Summer	Rebloomer	Fragrant	Comments
'Atlanta Moonlight'	z3-10	☼☀		x		x		Pale yellow with paler stripe on petals
'Buttered Popcorn'	z2-6	☼☀		x	x		x	Clear yellow

Daylilies 24-36" Yellow ...continued

Hemerocallis

Cultivar or Species	Zone	Light	Early Summer	Mid Summer	Late Summer	Rebloomer	Fragrant	Comments
'Cragmoor Sweetheart'	z3-10	☼ ◐	x				x	Clear yellow with green eye
'Erin Prairie'	z4-9	☼ ◐	x	x				Deep yellow
'Frans Hals'	z4-8	☼ ◐	x	x			x	Alternating yellow & red petals with yellow stripe
'Golden Gate'	z3-10	☼ ◐	x					Narrow petals bright yellow
'Honest Pleasure'	z4-8	☼ ◐	x				x	Yellow with green eye
'Kindly Light'	z4-8	☼ ◐	x				x	Fall bloom, Yellow with very thin petals
'Limited Edition'	z4-10	☼ ◐		x				Yellow with green center
'Mary Todd'	z3-10	☼ ◐		x				Pure yellow
'Marci'	z3-10	☼	x					Light yellow with green throat
'Prairie Moonlight'	z3-10	☼ ◐	x					Yellow with white stripe on petals
'Siloam Sunday Best'	z2-6	☼ ◐	x	x				Pale yellow with deep yellow eye
'Texas Sunlight'	z3-10	☼ ◐	x					Yellow with reflexed curved petals
citrina	z3-8	☼ ◐	x				x	Yellow
middendorffii	z4-8	☼ ◐			x			Yellow, blooms into Fall
'Siloam Amazing Grace'	z3-9	☼ ◐	x	x			x	Bright yellow with green throat
'Omomuki'	z3-9	☼ ◐	x	x			x	Clear yellow with green throat
'Mary's Gold'	z3-9	☼ ◐	x					Bright gold
'Cleo'	z4-10	☼ ◐	x	x				Yellow w/green center and pinkish red tips on petals

Daylilies 24-36" Lavender ...continued

Hemerocallis

Cultivar or Species	Zone	Light	Early Summer	Mid Summer	Late Summer	Rebloomer	Fragrant	Comments
Lavender								
'Lavender Aristocrat'	z3-10	☼☀	x					Lav with yellow center outlined in deeper lav/purple
'Lavender Blush'	z4-10	☼☀	x		x	x		Lavender with yellow eye, with white stripe on petals
'Mardi Gras Parade'	z2-6	☼☀	x					Lavender with big red eye
'Prairie Blue Eyes'	z3-10	☼☀	x					Dark lavender with yellow eye
White								
'Gentle Shepherd'	z4-9	☼☀	x					White with green throat
'Ice Carnival'	z2-6	☼☀	x		x	x		White with yellow-green throat
'Joan Senior'	z6-9	☼☀	x		x			Cream with yellow-green throat
'Lime Frost'	z3-9	☼☀		x		x		White with green throat
'Pandoras Box'	z3-10	☼☀	x		x	x		White with purple eye
'Siloam Shocker'	z2-6	☼☀	x					White with big red eye
'Siloam Ury Winniford'	z2-6	☼☀	x					Cream with dark purple eye green throat
'Sunday Gloves'	z3-9	☼☀	x		x	x		Near white with pale yellow eye
'White Temptation'	z4-8	☼☀	x			x		White with green-yellow center Fall
Pink								
'Advance Party'	z3-9	☼☀	x	x				Lavender-pink with yellow throat
'Bama Music'	z3-9	☼☀		x				Pink with yellow eye/green throat

Hemerocallis

Cultivar or Species	Zone	Light	Early Summer	Mid Summer	Late Summer	Rebloomer	Fragrant	Comments
'Carlotta'	z3-9	☀☀	x	x	x			Raspberry with cream midribs/yellow throat
'Cherry Cheeks'	z4-8	☀☀	x	x				Hot pink with yellow throat, Fall bloom
'Chorus Line'	z3-9	☀☀			x	x	x	Pink with rose band yellow/green throat
'Country Melody'	z3-9	☀☀	x				x	Pink with green throat
'Dorthy Lambert'	z3-9	☀	x	x				Medium pink with apricot-gold throat
'Dragon's Eye'	z3-9	☀☀	x	x	x			Pink with large rose red eye
'Jedi Free Spirit'	z3-9	☀☀	x				x	Pink with yellow eye/green throat
'Selma Rose'	z3-9	☀☀	x	x			x	Pink with yellow/green throat
'Siloam Double Classic'	z3-9	☀☀	x	x			x	Double pink with yellow halo
Purple								
'Bela Lugosi'	z3-9	☀☀	x					Dark purple with lime green throat
'Catherine Neal'	z2-6	☀☀		x	x			Deep purple with green throat
'Chicago Arnies Choice'	z3-10	☀☀	x					Pale lavender purple with yellow eye
'Strutter's Ball'	z3-9	☀☀	x					Deep purple with yellow green throat
36-48"								
Orange								
'Bright Sunset'	z3-10	☀☀	x				x	Orangy red with yellow center and stripes on petals
fulva 'Kwanso'	z3-11	☀☀		x	x			Orange & yellow double form

Daylilies 36-48" ...continued

Hemerocallis

Cultivar or Species	Zone	Light	Early Summer	Mid Summer	Late Summer	Rebloomer	Fragrant	Comments
Yellow								
'Hyperion'	z4-8	☼ ☀		x		x	x	Clear yellow with green throat
Pink								
'Chosen Love'	z3-9	☼	x	x		x		Lavender pink with light pink-white midribs
'Lilting Belle'	z3-9	☼	x	x	x			Lavender pink with large yellow throat
'Pretty in Pink'	z3-9	☼ ☀	x	x			x	Lavender pink with green throat

Ferns 0-12"

The fern is a much underutilized group of perennials. Ferns lack flowers but still have diversity in shape, size, texture and color. Living in a wide range of ecosystems, ferns are very versatile. Benefits are that some varieties survive the dense shade and create dense root systems, screening out other weeds. Most ferns are deer resistant, require little care and group nicely making a great background plant.

Scientific Name	Common Name	Zone	Light	Specimen	Mass	Creeping	Erosion	Crevices	Evergreen	Drought	Sandy	Wet	Moist/Well Drained
Asplenium ebenoides	Dragon Tail Fern	z5-8	◐					x					x
Asplenium platyneuron	Ebony Spleenwort	z3-9	◐				x	x	x				
Asplenium trichomanes	Maidenhair spleenwort	z2-9	◐				x	x	x				
Athyrium filix-femina 'Encourage'	Lady Fern	z4-8	◐	x									
Athyrium filix-femina 'Frizelliae'	Tatting Fern	z4-8	◐	x									
Athyrium n. 'Burgundy Lace'	Japanese Painted Fern	z5-8	◐	x									
Athyrium n. 'Pewter Lace'	Japanese Painted Fern	z5-8	◐	x	x								
Blechnum penna marina	Alpine Water Fern	z7-9	◐		x							x	
Cheilanthes argentea	Silver Cloak Fern	z5-9	☀		x				x				
Cheilanthes lanosa	Hairy Lip Fern	z5-9	☀						x				
Cystopteris bulbifera	Bulbet Bladder Fern	z3-8	◐			x					x	x	
Dryopteris filix-mas 'Parsley'	Male Fern	z5-9	◐	x									
12-24"													
Adiantum pedatum	Maidenhair Fern	z2-8	◐	x	x	x							x
Athyrium 'Ghost'	Ghost Lady Fern	z4-8	◐	x	x							x	

149

Ferns 12-24" ...continued

Scientific Name	Common Name	Zone	Light	Specimen	Mass	Creeping/Erosion	Crevices	Evergreen	Sandy/Drought	Wet	Moist/Well Drained
Athyrium f.'Vernoniae Cristatum'	Crested Lady Fern	z3-9	☼◐	x							x
Athyrium n. 'Red Beauty'	Japanese Painted Fern	z4-9	☼◐	x							x
Athyrium nipponicum 'Pictum'	Japanese Painted Fern	z4-8	☼◐	x							x
Athyrium n. 'Silver Falls'	Japanese Painted Fern	z3-8	☼◐	x							x
Athyrium otophorum	Eared Lady Fern	z5-9	☼◐	x				x			
Athyrium thelypteroides	Silver Glade Fern	z4-9	☼◐								x
Athyrium x 'Branford Beauty'	Lady Fern	z4-8	☼◐	x							
Dennstaedtia punctilobula	Hayscented Fern	z3-8	☼◐	x	x			x			x
Dryopteris a. 'Angustata Crispa'	Narrow Crested Fern	z4-9	☼◐				x				
Dryopteris atrata	Black Wood Fern	z5-8	☼◐	x			x	x			
Dryopteris d.'Crispa Whiteside'	Buckler Fern	z5-9	☼◐	x							
Dryopteris e. 'Brilliance'	Autumn Fern	z5-9	☼◐	x	x		x	x	x		
Dryopteris erythrosora	Autumn Fern	z5-9	☼◐	x	x		x	x	x		x
Dryopteris 'Linearis Polydactyla'	Lace leaved Wood Fern	z5-9	☼◐	x				x			
Nephrolepis 'Rita's Gold'	Boston Fern	z9-10	☼◐	x		x					
Onoclea sensibilis	Sensitive Fern	z3-8	☼◐☽	x	x	x			x		x
Thelypteris decursive-pinnata	Japanese Beech Fern	z4-10	◐	x	x		x		x		
Thelypteris novaboracensis	New York Fern	z4-9	◐	x	x			x		x	
Thelypteris palustris	Marsh Fern	z2-9	☼◐	x	x					x	x

Ferns 24-36"

Scientific Name	Common Name	Zone	Light	Specimen	Mass	Creeping	Erosion	Crevices	Evergreen	Drought	Sandy	Wet	Moist/Well Drained
Athyrium angustum 'Lady in Red'	Lady Fern	z2-9	☼☀	x	x								x
Athyrium f. 'Lady in Red'	Northern Lady Fern	z2-8	☼☀	x	x								x
Athyrium filix-femina 'Victoriae'	Victoriae Lady Fern	z4-8	☼☀	x	x								
Athyrium filix-femina	Lady Fern	z3-9	☼☀	x	x				x	x			x
Blechnum spicant	Deer Fern	z5-8	☼☀	x					x	x			x
Dryopteris affinis 'The King'	Male Fern	z4-8	☼☀	x	x			x	x	x			
Dryopteris affinis	Male Fern	z4-8	☼☀	x	x								
Dryopteris crassirhizoma	Wood Fern	z5-8	☼☀	x	x			x					x
Dryopteris cristata	Crested Shield Fern	z4-9	☼☀								x	x	x
Dryopteris d. 'Jimmy Dyce'	Jimmy Dyce Fern	z4-7	☀	x	x			x					
Dryopteris f. 'Undulata Robusta'	Robust Male Fern	z4-8	☼☀	x	x								
Dryopteris goldiana	Goldies Wood Fern	z3-7	☼☀										x
Dryopteris intermedia	Intermediate Wood Fern	z3-8	☼☀	x	x			x	x				x
Dryopteris marginalis	Marginal Wood Fern	z2-8	☼☀	x	x	x			x	x	x		x
Dryoptris pseudofilix-mas	Mexican Male Fern	z5-8	☼☀	x						x	x		
Matteuccia struthiopteris	Ostrich Fern	z2-10	☼☀	x	x	x	x						x
Osmunda cinnamomea	Cinnamon Fern	z3-8	☼☀	x	x	x							x
Osmunda claytoniana	Interupted Fern	z3-8	☼☀	x	x	x							x

Fern 24-36" ...continued

Scientific Name	Common Name	Zone	Light	Specimen	Mass	Creeping	Erosion	Crevices	Evergreen	Drought	Sandy	Wet	Moist/Well Drained
Osmunda regalis	Royal Fern	z3-9	☼ ●	x	x		x					x	
Polystichum acrostichoides	Christmas Fern	z3-9	◐ ●	x	x		x	x	x	x	x	x	
Polystichum polyblepharum	Tassel Fern	z6-8	◐ ●					x				x	
48"													
Matteuccia s. 'The King'	King Ostrich Fern	z2-8	☼ ●	x	x							x	

Grasses 0-6"

Scientific Name	Common Name	Zone	Light	Bloom	Comments
Acorus g. 'Pusillus Minimus Aurens'	Golden Sweet Flag	z5-10	☀·☀	Sp	Gold edged, Evergreen
Carex caryophyllea 'Beatlemania'	Spring Sedge	z5-7		Sp	
Festuca scoparia 'Hobbitt' 6-12"	Bearskin Fescue	z4-8	☀ ☀	Sum	Hedgehog look
Acorus gramineus 'Oborozuki'	Sweet Flag	z5-8	☀·☀	Sp	Fragrant, Leaves fan shaped
Carex conica 'Snowline'	Miniature Sedge	z5-8	☀	Sp	Snow white edge, edger
Carex dolichostachya 'Kaga Nishiki '	Gold Fountains Sedge	z5-9	☀·☀	Sp	Edger, drought tolerant
Carex hachijoensis 'Evergold'	Japanese Sedge	z5-9	☀	Sp	
Carex morrowii 'Ice Dance'	Sedge	z5-9	☀	Sp	White/green, Evergreen
Carex morrowii 'Silver Scepter'	Sedge	z5-8	☀	Sp	White edges
Carex muskingumensis 'Little Midge'	Palm Sedge	z5-9	☀	Sum	Edger, Yellow flowers
Festuca glauca 'Boulder Blue'	Fescue	z4-9	☀	Sum	
Festuca glauca 'Elijah Blue'	Fescue	z4-8	☀	Sum	
Hakonechloa macra 'All Gold'	Japanese ForestGrass	z5-9	☀	SumFall	Gracefully arching foliage
Lagurus ovatus	Bunny-tail Grass	annual	☀	SumFall	White fuzzy tufts
Ophiopogon	Black Mondo Grass	z6-9	☀·☀	Sum	Dark. foliage, Tiny wh.flowers
Pennisetum a. 'Little Bunny'	Fountain Grass	z5-9	☀·☀	SumFall	Fuzzy catkins
Pennisetum a.'Little Honey'	Fountain Grass	z5-8	☀·☀	SumFall	Erosion control, fuzzy catkins

Grasses 12-18"

Scientific Name	Common Name	Zone	Light	Bloom	Comments
Acorus gramineus 'Variegatus'	Sweet Flag	z5-8	☀◐	Sp	Fan shaped form, water edge
Hakonechloa macra	Japanese Forest Grass	z5-9	◐	Sum Fall	Arching foliage
Hakonechloa macra 'Aureola'	Japanese Forest Grass	z5-9	◐	Sum Fall	Gracefully arching foliage
Imperata cylindrica 'Red Baron'	Japanese Blood Grass	z5-9	☀◐		
Sesleria autumnalis	Autumn Moor Grass	z5-8	☀◐	Sum Fall	Inflor. 10-14"Taller

18-24"

Scientific Name	Common Name	Zone	Light	Bloom	Comments
Acorus calamus 'Variegatus'	Variegated Sweet Flag	z4-8	☀◐	Sum	Sweet smelling
Calamagrostis 'Avalanche'	Feather Reed Grass	z4-7	☀◐	Sum Fall	
Calamagrostis 'Overdam'	Feather Reed Grass	z4-7	☀	Sum Fall	Rosy pur inflorescence, Var.
Carex buchananii	Leatherleaf Sedge	z6-9	☀◐	Sp	Reddish bronze curly tipped
Carex elata 'Bowles Golden'	Bowles' Golden Sedge	z6-8	☀◐		Accent use
Carex muskingumensis 'Oehme'	Palm Sedge	z4-9	◐	Sum	Constant moisture, Edger
Helictotrichon s. 'Sapphire'	Blue Oat Grass	z3-9	☀◐	Sum	Steel blue, rock garden
Molina caerulea 'Moorflame'	Purple Moor Grass	z4-9	☀◐	Sum	Orange red foliage
Pennisetum a. 'Hamelin'	Fountain Grass	z5-9	☀◐	Sum Fall	Fuzzy catkins
Sporobolus heterolepis	Prairie Dropseed	z3-9	☀◐	Sum Fall	Orange foliage in fall, drought

24-36"

Scientific Name	Common Name	Zone	Light	Bloom	Comments
Chasmanthium latifolium	Northern Sea Oats	z3-8	☀◐	Sum	Moist, flat seed heads
Deschampsia caespitosa 'Bronze Veil'	Tufted Hairgrass	z4-7	☀◐	Sum	Moist
Eragrostis elliotii 'Wind Dancer'	Love Grass	z6-10	☀◐	Sum	

Grasses 24-36" ...continued

Scientific Name	Common Name	Zone	Light	Bloom	Comments
Helictotrichon sempervirens	Blue Oat Grass	z3-8	☼	Sum	Blue foliage
Leymus arenarius 'Blue Dune'	Wild Rye	z4-8	☼☀	Sum	Tolerates heat, drought
Miscanthus sinensis 'Little Kitten'	Japanese Silver Grass	z5-9	☼☀	Fall	
Panicum virgatum 'Hanse Herms'	Switch Grass	z4-9	☼☀	Sum	Foliage turns red burgundy
Pennisetum alopecuroides 'Cassian'	Fountain Grass	z5-9	☼☀	Sum Fall	Fuzzy catkins, foliage Or/Red
Pennisetum alopecuroides	Fountain Grass	z5-9	☼	Sum	Fuzzy catkins
Pennisetum alopecuroides 'Moudry'	Fountain Grass	z5-9	☼☀	Fall	Fuzzy plumes
Pennisetum a. 'Viridescens'	Fountain Grass	z5-9	☼☀	Fall	Fuzzy blackish catkins
Pennisetum orientale 'Karley Rose'	Fountain Grass	z5-9	☼	Sum Fall	Fuzzy rose catkins
Pennisetum setaceum 'Rubrum'	Fountain Grass	annual	☼☀	Sum Fall	Deep purple/red foliage
Schizachyrium scoparium 'The Blues'	Little Blue Stem	z4-10	☼	Fall	

36-48"

Scientific Name	Common Name	Zone	Light	Bloom	Comments
Calamagrostis brachytricha	Feather Reed Grass	z4-9	☼☀●	Fall	Pink blushed flower spikes
Miscanthus sinensis 'Adagio'	Japanese Silver Grass	z5-9	☼☀	Fall	
Miscanthus sinensis 'Little Zebra'	Japanese Silver Grass	z5-9	☼☀	Sum Fall	
Molina caerulea 'Moorhexe'	Purple Moor Grass	z4-9	☼☀	Sum Fall	Black purple flowers
Molina caerulea 'Strahlenquelle'	Purple Moor Grass	z4-9	☼☀	Sum Fall	18" foliage
Panicum amarum 'Dewey Blue'	Switch Grass	z4-9	☼	Sum	Sterile sandy conditions
Panicum virgatum 'Heavy Metal'	Switch Grass	z4-9	☼☀	Sum	Metal blue foliage

Grasses 36–48" ...continued

Scientific Name	Common Name	Zone	Light	Bloom	Comments
Panicum virgatum 'Rotstrahlbush'	Switch Grass	z4-8	☼	Sum	Turns red, infertile mineral soil
Panicum virgatum 'Shenandoah'	Switch Grass	z5-9	☼-☼	Sum	Infertile soil
Panicum virgatum 'Squaw'	Switch Grass	z5-9	☼-☼	Sum	
Pennisetum alopecuroides 'Red Head'	Fountain Grass	z5-9	☼-☼	Sum Fall	Fuzzy reddish catkins
Sorghastrum nutans	Indian Grass	z4-9	☼	Sum	Drought
Sorghastrum nutans 'Sioux Blue'	Indian Grass	z4-9	☼	Sum	Powder blue gray, drought
4-5'					
Calamagrostis acutiflora 'Avalanche'	Feather Reed Grass	z5-8	☼	Sum Fall	White variegated
Calamagrostis acutiflora 'Eldorado'	Feather Reed Grass	z5-8	☼	Sum Fall	Gold variegated
Calamagrostis 'Karl Foerster'	Feather Reed Grass	z5-8	☼	Sum Fall	Leaves rose purple
Miscanthus sinensis 'Dixieland'	Japanese Silver Grass	z5-9	☼-☼	Fall	
Miscanthus sinensis 'Nippon'	Japanese Silver Grass	z5-9	☼-☼	Sum	Wine inflorescences
Panicum 'Prairie Fire'	Red Switch Grass	z4-9	☼	Sum	Rosy flower panicles
Pennisetum alopecuroides 'Foxtrot'	Giant Fountain Grass	z5-9	☼-☼	Sum	Fuzzy dusty rose catkins
Spodiopogon sibiricus	Frost Grass	z5-9	☼-☼	Sum Fall	
5-7'					
Andropogon gerardii	Big Bluestem	z3-7	☼-☼	Fall	Moist to dry
Arundo donax 'Variegata'	Variegated Giant Reed	z5-6	☼-☼	Fall	
Calamagrostis acutiflora 'Overdam'	Feather Reed Grass	z5-8	☼	Sum Fall	Variegated
Fargesia rufa 'Green Panda'	Clumping Bamboo	z5-9	☼-☼	infrequently	

Grasses 5-7'...continued

Scientific Name	Common Name	Zone	Light	Bloom	Comments
Miscanthus sinensis 'Bluetenwunder'	Japanese Silver Grass	z5-9	☼	Fall	
Miscanthus sinensis 'Cabaret'	Japanese Silver Grass	z5-9	☼	Fall	Variegated
Miscanthus sinensis 'Ferner Osten'	Japanese Silver Grass	z5-9	☼	Sum Fall	
Miscanthus sinensis 'Flamingo'	Japanese Silver Grass	z5-9	☼	Sum Fall	
Miscanthus sinensis 'Graziella'	Japanese Silver Grass	z5-9	☼	Fall	
Miscanthus sinensis 'Gracillimus'	Japanese Silver Grass	z5-9	☼	Fall	
Miscanthus sinensis 'Helga Reich'	Japanese Silver Grass	z5-9	☼	Fall	
Miscanthus sinensis 'Kaskade'	Japanese Silver Grass	z5-9	☼	Sum Fall	
Miscanthus sinensis 'Malepartus'	Japanese Silver Grass	z5-9	☼	Fall	
Miscanthus sinensis 'Morning Light'	Japanese Silver Grass	z5-9	☼	Fall	Variegated
Miscanthus sinensis 'Purpurescens'	Japanese Silver Grass	z4-9	☼	Fall	
Miscanthus sinensis 'Silver Feather'	Japanese Silver Grass	z4-9	☼	Fall	
Miscanthus sinensis 'Silver Shadows'	Japanese Silver Grass	z5-9	☼	Fall	Variegated
Miscanthus sinensis 'Strictus'	Porcupine Grass	z5-9	☼	Fall	Yellow/green
Panicum virgatum 'Cloud Nine'	Switch Grass	z4-9	☼	Sum	
Panicum virgatum 'Dallas Blues'	Switch Grass	z4-9	☼	Sum	
Panicum virgatum 'Northwind'	Switch Grass	z4-9	☼	Sum Fall	
Spartina pectinata	Prairie Cord Grass	z4-9	☼	Sum Fall	
Stipa gigantea	Giant Feather Grass	z7-9	☼	Sum Fall	

Grasses 7-9'

Scientific Name	Common Name	Zone	Light	Bloom	Comments
Miscanthus s. 'Cosmopolitan'	Japanese Silver Grass	z6-9	☼ ◐	Fall	Variegated
Miscanthus s. 'Emerald Shadow'	Japanese Silver Grass	z5-9	☼ ◐	Fall	
Miscanthus s. 'Grosse Fontane'	Japanese Silver Grass	z5-8	☼ ◐	Fall	
Miscanthus s. 'Silver Arrow'	Japanese Silver Grass	z5-9	☼ ◐	Sum Fall	Variegated
Miscanthus s. 'Undine'	Japanese Silver Grass	z5-9	☼ ◐	Fall	
Miscanthus s. 'Variegatus'	Japanese Silver Grass	z5-9	☼ ◐	Fall	Variegated
Miscanthus s. 'Zebrinus'	Japanese Silver Grass	z5-9	☼	Fall	
Molina arundinacea 'Skyracer'	Tall Moor Grass	z5-7	☼ ◐	Sum Fall	Inflorescence 5' above foliage

8-12'

Scientific Name	Common Name	Zone	Light	Bloom	Comments
Cortaderia selloana 'Pumila'	Dwarf Pampas Grass	z6-10	☼	Sum Fall	Silvery cream fluffy plumes
Erianthus ravennae	Ravenna Grass	z5-9	☼ ◐	Fall	

10-14'

Scientific Name	Common Name	Zone	Light	Bloom	Comments
Cortaderia selloana	Pampas Grass	z6-9	☼	Sum Fall	8-15', Fluffy plumes
Fargesia 'Asian Wonder'	Clumping Bamboo	z5-9	☼ ◐	infrequently	

15-18'

Scientific Name	Common Name	Zone	Light	Bloom	Comments
Fargesia robusta 'Green Screen'	Bamboo	z7-8	☼	infrequently	

Hosta 0-6"

Hosta-these hosta are hardy in zone 3-9. Great for shade gardens but some will take a good amount of sun. Arranged by foliage color and height. Where multiple colors were present, the hosta is listed in the predominant color.

Bloom time - Early Summer = Esu Mid Summer = Msu Late Summer = Lsu Fragrant = Fr
Foliage variegation - Dark Center/Light Margin = D Light Center/Dark Margin = L
Flower color - Purple = P Lavender = La White = W

Cultivar or Species	Width	Light	Bloom	D	L	Flower	Fr	Comments
Green								
'Herbie'	9"	☀️🌤️	Msu	D		La		Lance shaped green leaves w/white margins
'Pandora's Box'	12"	☀️🌤️	Esu		L	La		White centers with green margin
Blue								
'Minimoon'	5"	☀️🌤️				W		Blue-green rounded leaves
'Popo'	9"	☀️🌤️	Esu			La		Blue-green cupped leaves
6-12"								
Green								
'Cherry Berry'	26"	☀️🌤️	Lsu	L		P		White leaves w/dark green margins, red scapes
'Fireworks'	12"	☀️🌤️	Msu	L		La		Deep green margins with white centers
'Ginko Craig'	20"	☀️	Lsu	D		P		Purple, Deep green leaves with white margins
'Hi Ho Silver'	16"	☀️🌤️	Msu	D		P		Lance-shaped green leaves w/wide white margins
'Saishu Jima'	20"	☀️🌤️	Lsu			P		Very narrow wavy foliage
'Tiny Tears'	21"	☀️🌤️	EsuMsu			P		
'Yakushima Mizu'	14"	☀️🌤️	Lsu			La		Narrow wavy foliage

Hosta 6-12" ...continued

Bloom time - Early Summer = Esu   Mid Summer = Msu   Late Summer = Lsu   Fragrant = Fr
Foliage variegation - Dark Center/Light Margin = D   Light Center/Dark Margin = L
Flower color - Purple = P   Lavender = La   White = W

Cultivar or Species	Width	Light	Bloom	D	L	Flower	Fr	Comments
Blue								
'Baby Bunting'	26"	☀☀	EsuMsu			La		Dense mound of blue green leaves
'Blue Mouse Ears'	12"	☀☀	Msu			La		Round blue green leaves
Yellow								
'Blonde Elf'	24"	☀☀	Esu			La		Lance shaped yellow-gold leaves
'Gold Edger'	14"	☀☀	Esu			La		Chartreuse to gold heart shaped leaves
'High Society'	12"	☀	Lsu		L	La		Narrow yellow center with wide dk. blue margins
'Just So'	20"	☀	Msu		L	La		Chartreuse-gold leaves with green margins
'Little Aurora'	20"	☀☀	Msu			La		Bright gold oval-heart shaped leaves
'Little Sunspot'	16"	☀☀	Msu		L	W		Yellow center with green margins
'Maui Buttercups'	18"	☀☀	Msu			P		Bright gold leaves deeply cupped & corrugated
12-18"								
Green								
'Diamond Tiara'	27"	☀☀	Msu Lsu	D		P		Green leaves with white, wavy margins
'Francee'	30"	☀☀	Msu Lsu	D		La		Green leaves with narrow white margins
gracillima	31"	☀☀	Lsu			P		Fall bloom, Narrow teardrop foliage
'Hanky Panky'	23"	☀☀	Msu	D		La		Dark green with pale lime margins

Hosta 12-18"...continued

Bloom time - Early Summer = Esu   Mid Summer = Msu   Late Summer = Lsu   Fragrant = Fr

Foliage variegation - Dark Center/Light Margin = D   Light Center/Dark Margin = L

Flower color - Purple = P   Lavender = La   White = W

Cultivar or Species	Width	Light	Bloom	D	L	Flower	Fr	Comments
Green...continued								
laevigata	29"	☀	Lsu			P		Fall bloom, Narrow wavy foliage
'Leather Sheen'	48"	☀	Msu			P		Lance shaped shiny dark green foliage
'Night before Christmas'	34"	☀	MsuLsu	L		La		Dark green leaves with thin white centers
'Praying Hands'	18"	☀	Lsu	D		La		Folded green leaves with thin gold margins
'Raspberry Sorbet'	34"	☀	Lsu			P		Shiny wavy green foliage/purple red scapes
'Summer Music'	20"	☀	Msu	L		La		Dk gr. margins with chartreuse lined white centers
Blue								
'Aristocrat'	22"	☀	Msu	D		La		Blue leaves with wide creamy yellow margins
'Blue Cadet'	38"	☀	Msu			La		Dense mound, blue green foliage; fast growth rate
'Hadspen Blue'	18"	☀	Msu			La		Steel blue cupped leaves
'Halcyon'	30"	☀	Msu			La		Deep blue spear shaped foliage
'Wolverine'	20"	☀	Lsu	D		La		Blue-green with wide gold margins
Yellow								
'Golden Tiara'	24"	☀	Msu	D		P		Green leaves with chartreuse-gold margins
'Grand Tiara'	30"	☀	Msu	D		P		Green with wide gold-chartreuse margins .
'Heavenly Tiara'	24"	☀	Msu	D		P		Green/gold margins change to chartreuse white

161

Hosta 12-18" ...continued

Bloom time - Early Summer = Esu   Mid Summer = Msu   Late Summer = Lsu   Fragrant = Fr

Foliage variegation - Dark Center/Light Margin = D   Light Center/Dark Margin = L

Flower color - Purple = P   Lavender = La   White = W

Cultivar or Species	Width	Light	Bloom	D	L	Flower	Fr	Comments
Yellow ...continued								
'June'	20"	☼	MsuLsu		L	La		Chartreuse centers w/wide blue-gr. jetting margins
'Stained Glass'	30"	☼	Lsu		L	La		Gold centered with green trimmed foliage
'Touch of Class'	22"	☼	Msu		L	La		Blue leaves with yellow-gold centers
'Wide Brim'	24"	☼	MsuLsu	D		La		Dark green with wide irregular yellow margins
18-24"								
Green								
'Candy Hearts'	43"	☼	Msu			La		Fast Growth
'Fortunei Hyacinthina'	55"	☼	MsuLsu			La		
'Green Fountain'	52"	☼	Lsu		L	La		Fall bloom, White interior
'Independence'	26"	☼	Msu	D		La		Dark green, white marginns speckled with green
'Invincible'	48"	☼	Lsu			La	Fr	Fall, White margins
kikutii	42"	☼	Lsu	D		La		Fall, White margins
'Minuteman'	24"	☼	EsuMsu	D		La		Dark green cupped leaves with white margins
'Patriot'	30"	☼	EsuMsu	D		La		Dark green leaves with crisp white margins
'Twilight'	30"	☼	Msu	D		La		Green with creamy-gold margins

Hosta 18-24" ...continued

Bloom time - Early Summer = Esu Mid Summer = Msu Late Summer = Lsu Fragrant = Fr

Foliage variegation - Dark Center/Light Margin = D Light Center/Dark Margin = L

Flower color - Purple = P Lavender = La White = W

Cultivar or Species	Width	Light	Bloom	D	L	Flower	Fr	Comments
Green ...continued								
ventricosa	50"	☼/☀	Msu	D		P		White margins
'Whirlwind'	30"	☼/☀	MsuLsu		L	La		Dark green margins with white/green center
Blue								
'Blue Wedgewood'	44"	☼/☀	MsuLsu			La		Ovate deep blue leaves
'Frances Williams'	30"	☼ ☀	Msu	D		W		Blue-green leaves with wide yellow margins
'Love Pat'	40"	☼/☀	Esu			W		Deep blue-green- green foliage cupped at maturity
'Zounds'	50"	☼/☀	Msu			La		Bright gold foliage
Yellow								
'August Moon'	24"	☀/☼	MsuLsu			La		Gold to chartreuse leaves
'Fragrant Bouquet'	36"	☼/☀	Msu	D		W	Fr	Light green leaves w/pale yellow margins
'Fried Bananas'	53"	☼/☀	Lsu			La	Fr	Glossy gold leaves
'Gold Standard'	30"	☼/☀	Msu		L	La		Green-gold centers with dark green margin
'Great Expectations'	24"	☼/☀	Esu Msu		L	P		Creamy yellow centers with blue-green margins
'Green Gold'	30"	☀/☼	MsuLsu	D		La		Dark green with creamy yellow border
'Guacamole'	36"	☀/☼	Lsu		L	W	Fr	Green leaves with dark green margins
'Striptease'	30"	☼/☀	MsuLsu		L	La		Narrow gold center w/very wide green margins

163

Hosta 24-36"

Bloom time - Early Summer = Esu   Mid Summer = Msu   Late Summer = Lsu   Fragrant = Fr

Foliage variegation - Dark Center/Light Margin = D   Light Center/Dark Margin = L

Flower color - Purple = P   Lavender = L   White = W

Cultivar or Species	Width	Light	Bloom	D	L	Flower	Fr	Comments
Green								
'Big John'	72"	☼☀	EsuMsu			W		Green, Largest leaves of any Hosta
'Birchwood Elegance'	77"	☼☀	EsuMsu			W		
'Dancing in the Rain'	40"	☼☀	Msu		L	La		White with blue-green margins
'Donahue Piecrust'	60"	☼☀	EsuMsu			La		Ruffled edges
'Honeybells'	50"	☼☀	Lsu			La	Fr	Fall bloom
plantaginea	57"	☼☀	Lsu			W	Fr	Fall bloom
plantaginea 'Aphrodite'	60"	☼☀	Msu			W	Fr	Double flowers
'Regal Rhubarb'	47"	☼☀	Msu Lsu			P		Vase Shaped
'Regal Ruffles'	75"	☼☀	EsuMsu			W		
'Royal Standard'	63"	☼☀	Lsu			W	Fr	Fall bloom
'Tall Boy'	62"	☼☀	MsuLsu			La		Flowers on 75" scapes
Blue								
'Abiqua Drinking Gourd'	46"		EsuMsu			W		Deeply cupped blue-green foliage
'Blue Angel'	70"	☼☀	EsuMsu			W		Deep blue foliage
'Blue Umbrellas'	72"	☼☀	EsuMsu			La		Green-blue leaves cupped downward

Hosta 24-36" ...continued

Bloom time - Early Summer = Esu   Mid Summer = Msu   Late Summer = Lsu   Fragrant = Fr

Foliage variegation - Dark Center/Light Margin = D   Light Center/Dark Margin = L

Flower color - Purple = P   Lavender = La   White = W

Cultivar or Species	Width	Light	Bloom	D	L	Flower	Fr	Comments
Blue ...continued								
'Bressingham Blue'	36"	☼	Msu			W		Blue-green foliage w/undulating margins
'Crater Lake'	40"	☼	EsuMsu			La		Blue-green cupped foliage
'Earth Angel'	40"	☼	Msu	D		La		Blue-green leaves w/wide creamy wh. margins
'Krossa Regal'	60"	☼	Msu Lsu			La		Frosted blue-green leaves vase shaped
'Northern Exposure'	42"		EsuMsu	D		W		Blue-green leaves with yellow-cream margins
'Regal Splendor'	60"	☼	Msu Lsu	D		La		Blue leaves with wavy cream to ivory margins
'Robert Frost'	30"	☼	Lsu	D		W		Blue-green leaves w/creamy margin
sieboldiana 'Elegans'	61"	☼	Msu			W		Blue-gray large rounded leaves
'SpiltMilk'	30"	☼	Msu			W		Blue-green leaves dripped w/white variegation
Yellow								
'American Icon'	36"	☼	Msu	D		La		Green leaves with wide gold edge
'Beckoning'	48"	☼	Esu		L	W		Green-gold with blue-green margins
'Gold Regal'	36"	◐☼	MsuLsu			P		Yellow-green to gold
'Holy Mole'	30"	☼	Lsu		L	W	Fr	Chartreuse with very wide dark green margins
montana 'Aureomarg.'	40"	☼	Msu	D		La		Dark green leaves w/wide irregular gold margins
'Paul's Glory'	40"	☼	Msu		L	La		Chartreuse center with blue-green margins

Hosta 24-36" ...continued

Bloom time - Early Summer = Esu Mid Summer = Msu Late Summer = Lsu Fragrant = Fr
Foliage variegation - Dark Center/Light Margin = D Light Center/Dark Margin = L
Flower color - Purple = P Lavender = La White = W

Cultivar or Species	Width	Light	Bloom	D	L	Flower	Fr	Comments
Yellow ...continued								
'Piedmont Gold'	63"	☀	Msu			La		Yellow gold leaves
'Sagae'	40"	☀	Esu Msu		L	La		Blue-green leaves with yellow to cream margins
'Singing in the Rain'	40"	☀	Msu		L	La		Blue-gr. leaves w/narrow chartreuse gold margins
'Spring Fling'	40"	☀	Late Spring	D		La		Green leaves with yellow, margins ruffled
'Sum and Substance'	48"	☀	Msu Lsu			La		Light green to chartreuse-gold margin
'Sun Power'	40"	☀☀	Msu			La		Brilliant gold leaves

Mosses

Mosses get all their nutrients from the air since they have no true roots. Mosses need shade, firmly packed acidic soil (ph between 5.0-6.0), and adequate moisture. They have no known pests and little or no disease. These little plants survive extreme moisture and temperature levels. Moss plants go dormant during extreme heat or drought and lose some of their lush green color only to be revived with the next rainfall.

Although there are hundreds of mosses only a few are available for purchase so this list is small. Where there is a presence of moss in an area it can be encouraged, or with the right shade and acidic conditions grown in the garden. *Sagina subulata* and *Sagina subulata* 'Aurea', Irish Moss and Scotch Moss, is not a true moss. *Sagina* does make a good mock alternative.

Instructions for growing mosses
1. Collect spores or handful of moss, removing as much soil as possible, into a blender.
2. Add buttermilk or yogurt, about 1 cup. Blend to mix the ingredients.
3. Spread on pot, bed area or rocks where you want moss to grow. Moss grows best in shady areas.

Scientific Name	Common Name	Comment
Dicranella scoparium	Broom Moss	Feathery
Thuidium	Fern Moss	Medium green, low growing, fern like
Dicranum	Rock Cap Moss	Medium green to dark, rock areas spiny looking, bright red spores
Hypnum imponens	Hypnum moss	Looks like green worms
Polytrichum	Haircap Moss	Sandy soil furry looking
Leucobryum	Cushion Moss	Light green, silvery appearance, sandy soil, round cushion shape

167

Vines 0-12'

The vines section does have woody selections in the list. The vines are a wonderful compliment to perennials. Whether working with trellises, fences, walls or as a ground cover, vines will be a great backdrop or add a vertical element of color to the garden.

Scientific Name	Common Name	Zone	Light	Bloom	Height	Comment
Aconitum episcopale	Climbing Monkshood	z5-8	☀	Fall	4-8'	Blue
Apios americana	Ground Nut	z4-9	☀	Sum Fall	4-18'	Brownish red
Asarina	Climbing Snapdragon	annual	☼	Sp Sum	6-8'	Pink, blue, lav.
Aster carolinianus	Climbing Aster	z6-9	☼	Fall	10-12'	Pink, purple
Cardiospermum halicacabum	Love-in-a-Puff	annual	☼		10'	White
Clematis alpina 'Constance'	Alpine Clematis	z3-9	☼☀	Sp	6-10'	Pink Purple
Clematis alpina 'Frances Rivis'	Alpine Clematis	z4-9	☼☀	Sp	7'	Single blue
Clematis 'Bees Jubilee'	Clematis	z4-9	☼☀	Sp Sum Fall	8' Pk w/carmine stripe
Clematis 'Comtesse de Bouchaud'	Clematis	z3-9	☼☀	Sum Fall	6-8'	Mauve-pink
Clematis 'Duchess of Albany'	Clematis	z4-8	☼☀	Sum Fall	8-12'	Rose-pink
Clematis 'Ernest Markham'	Clematis	z5-8	☼☀	Sum Fall	8'	Bright red
Clematis 'Etoile Violette'	Clematis	z4-9	☼☀	Sum	8-12'	Deep purple
Clematis florida 'Sieboldii'	Clematis	z7-11	☼☀	Sum Fall	10-12'	Creamy white
Clematis 'General Sikorski'	Clematis	z4-9	☼☀	Sum Fall	8-10'	Dark Lavender
Clematis 'Hagley Hybrid'	Clematis	z4-9	☼☀	Sum Fall	8'	Pink
Clematis 'Huldine'	Clematis	z4-9	☼	Sum	10'	Single white
Clematis 'Jackmanii Superba'	Clematis	z4-9	☼☀	Sum Fall	10'	Purple

Vines 0-12' ...continued

Scientific Name	Common Name	Zone	Light	Bloom	Height	Comment
Clematis macropetala 'Blue Bird'	Large Petalled Clematis	z3-8	☼	Sp	8-12'	Blue
Clematis m. 'Maidwell Hall'	Clematis	z5-9	☼◐	Sp Sum	6-8'	Blue bell shaped
Clematis m. 'Markham's Pink'	Large Petalled Clematis	z3-8	☼◐	Sp	8-12'	Pink
Clematis 'Marie Boisselot'	Clematis	z5-9	☼◐	Sum Fall	10'	White
Clematis 'Niobe'	Clematis	z4-9	☼◐	Sp Sum Fall	8-12'	Single deep red
Clematis tangutica 'Bill Mackenzie'	Clematis	z3-8	☼	Sum Fall	12-18'	Yellow orange
Clematis 'The President'	Clematis	z4-8	☼◐	Sum	10'	Purple w/silver
Clematis Vyvyan Pennell'	Clematis	z4-9	☼	Sp Sum Fall	12'	Violet blue
Clematis 'W.E. Gladstone'	Clematis	z4-9	☼◐	Sum Fall	10'	Single lavender
Dicentra scandens	Climbing Bleeding Heart	z4-9	◐●	Sum	10-12	Pale Yellow
Ipomoea alba	Moon Vine	annual	☼	Sum	8-10'	White
Ipomoea coccinea	Star Ipomoea	annual	☼	Sum Fall	10-12'	Red/orange
Ipomoea lobata	Mina Lobata	annual	☼◐	Sum	8-20'	Red fades yellow
Ipomoea tricolor 'Heavenly Blue'	Morning Glory	annual	☼	Sum Fall	10'	Blue trumpets
Lablab purpureus	Purple Hyacinth Bean	annual	☼	Sum	10'	Lavenderpurple
Lathyrus latifolius	Sweet Pea	z4-8	☼◐	Sum	6-7'	Rose purple
Lathyrus odoratus	Sweet Pea	annual	☼		6'	Fragrant/Pk/Lav
Lathyrus odoratus 'Henry Eckford'	Sweet Pea	z5-7	☼◐	Sum	6'	Fragrant/Pk/Lav
Rhodochiton atrosanguineum	Purple Bell Vine	annual	☼	Sum	10'-12'	Moist soil
Thunbergia alata	Black-Eyed Susan Vine	annual	☼◐	Sp Sum Fall	6'	Yellow orange

Vines 0-12' ...continued

Scientific Name	Common Name	Zone	Light	Bloom	Height	Comment
Tropaeolum peregrinum	Canary Creeper	annual	☼	Sum	8-12'	Yellow/feathery
Tropaeolum speciosum	Flame Nasturtium	z7-10	☼ ☀	Sum Fall	6-10'	Brilliant scarlet
12-20'						
Akebia 'Shiro Bana'	Five Leaf Akebia	z5-9	☼ ☀	Sp Sum Fall	15-20'	White/ fragrant
Clematis 'Kermesina'	Clematis	z5-9	☼	Sum	12-15'	Crimson
Clematis montana 'Freda'	Anemone Clematis	z5-9	☼ ☀	Sp	15-20'	Pink
Clematis 'Nelly Moser'	Clematis	z4-8	☼	Sp Sum Fall	15'	Pink w/carmine
Clematis 'Perle d' Azur'	Clematis	z4-8	☼ ☀	Sum Fall	6-18'	Light blue
Clematis virginiana	Virgin's Bower	z4-8	☼ ☀	Sum Fall	15-20'	Near white
Hedera helix	English Ivy	z5-11	☼ ☀ ☀		15'	Evergreen
Humulus lupulus 'Aureus'	Golden Hops	z4-8	☼	Sum Fall	20'	Greenish spikes
Ipomoea multifida	Cardinal Vine	annual	☼	Sum Fall	20'	Red
Ipomoea purpurea	Morning Glory	annual	☼	Sum Fall	20'	Various colors
Ipomoea quamoclit	Cypress Vine	annual	☀	Sum Fall	15-20'	Various colors
20-30'						
Actinidia kolomikta	Kiwi Vine	z4-8	☼ ☀	Fall	12-30'	Heart shaped
Akebia quinata 'Fruitful Combo'	Five Leaf Akebia	z4-8	☼ ☀	Sp	20-40'	
Aristolochia macrophylla	Dutchman's Pipe	z4-8	☼ ☀	Sp Sum	20-30'	Yel/brown pipes
Aristolochia tomentosa	Woolly Dutchman's Pipe	z5-8	☼ ☀	Sp Sum	20-30'	Green/yellow
Campsis radicans	Trumpet Vine	z4-10	☼ ☀	Sum Fall	30'	Orange

Vines 20-30' ...continued

Scientific Name	Common Name	Zone	Light	Bloom	Height	Comment
Celastrus scandens	American Bittersweet	z4-8	☼☀	Sum Fall	20-30'	Chartreuse
Cobaea scandens	Cup and Saucer Vine	annual	☼	Sp Sum Fall	25'	Purple bell
Hydrangea anomala 'Mirranda'	Climbing Hydrangea	z5-8	☀	Sum	20-30'	White/var foliage
Parthenocissus t. 'Fenway Park'	Golden Boston Ivy	z4-8	☀	Sum	20-30'	Yellow/or foliage
Solanum jasminoides 'Album'	Potatoe Vine	annual	☼	Sum Fall	20'	White
Vitis vinifera 'Purpurea'	Ornamental Grape	z5-9	☼☀	Sp	30'	
Wisteria frutescens	American Wisteria	z5-9	☼☀	Sp	25-30'	Lilac purple
Wisteria frutescens 'Amethyst Falls'	American Wisteria	z5-9	☼☀	Sum	15-25'	Lav/ blue, frag.
30'+						
Clematis cirrhosa	Winter Clematis	z7-9	☼☀	Fall	20'	White Bells
Clematis montana	Clematis	z4-8	☼☀●	Sum	33'	White
Clematis 'Perle d'Azur'	Clematis	z5-9	☼☀	Sum Fall	10-12'	Single, Blue
Clematis 'Serenata'	Clematis	z4-8	☼☀	Sum Fall	8-12'	Reddish purple
Clematis terniflora	Sweet Autumn Clematis	z5-8	☼☀	Fall	30'	
Hydrangea anomala ssp. *petiolaris*	Climbing Hydrangea	z4-8	☼☀	Sum	30-50'	White
Parthenoissus quinquifolia	Virginia Creeper	z3-9	☀●	Sum	40-50'	
Parthenocissus tricuspidata	Boston Ivy	z3-9	☼☀	Sum	60'	
Schizophragma hydr. 'Moonlight'	Japanese Climbing Hydr.	z6-9	☼☀●	Sum	20-30'	White

172

Section Three
Site Requirements

Soil PH-Acidic Soil

Scientific Name	Common Name	Zone	Light
Ajuga reptans	Bugle Weed	z3-9	☼ ☼ ☀
Andromeda polifolia	Bog Rosemary	z2-6	☼
Arctostaphylos uva-ursi	Bearberry	z2-6	☼ ☀
Asclepias tuberosa	Butterfly Weed	z4-8	☼
Borago officinalis	Borage	annual	☼
Calamagrostis acutiflora	Feather Reed Grass	z4-7	☼
Carex elata	Sedge	z6-8	☼ ☀
Cimicifuga racemosa	Black Cohosh	z3-7	☀
Cimicifuga ramosa	Branched Bugbane	z3-7	☀
Convallaria majalis	Lily-of-the-Valley	z2-7	☀ ✲
Cornus canadensis	Bunchberry	z2-7	☀
Cypripedium calceolus	Yellow Ladies Slipper	z3-9	☼ ☀
Digitalis grandiflora	Yellow Foxglove	z3-8	☀
Digitalis purpurea	Foxglove	z4-8	☀
Dryopteris cristata	Crested Shield Fern	z4-9	☀ ✲
Epimedium x rubrum	Red Barrenwort	z5-8	☀ ✲
Epimedium x versicolor	Barrenwort	z5-9	☀ ✲
Fragaria x ananassa	Garden Strawberry	z4-10	☼
Gaultheria procumbens	Wintergreen	z4-9	☀ ✲
Gentiana acaulis	Stemless Gentian	z3-6	☼ ☀

Soil PH-Acidic Soil ...continued

Scientific Name	Common Name	Zone	Light
Gentiana andrewsii	Bottle Gentian	z3-7	☼ ✷
Gentiana septemfida	Crested Gentian	z3-7	☼ ✷
Iris siberica	Siberian Iris	z3-9	☼ ✷
Liriope muscari	Blue Lily Turf	z6-9	☼ ● ✷
Liriope spicata	Creeping Liriope	z4-10	☼ ● ✷
Lupinus	Lupine	z3-6	☼
Mertensia virginica	Virginia Bluebells	z3-8	● ✷
Myosotis scorpioides	True Forget-me-not	z3-8	● ☼ ✷
Osmunda cinnamomea	Cinnamon Fern	z3-8	☼ ● ✷
Osmunda regalis	Royal Fern	z3-9	☼ ● ✷
Pachysandra terminalis	Japanese Spurge	z5-9	☼ ✷
Phlox stolonifera	Creeping Phlox	z2-8	☼ ✷
Physostegia virginiana	Obedient Plant	z2-9	☼ ✷
Platycodon grandiflorus	Balloon Flower	z3-7	☼ ✷
Primula auricula	Primrose	z3-7	● ☼ ✷
Primula denticulata	Drumstick Primrose	z4-7	☼
Primula japonica	Japanese Primrose	z5-7	✷
Primula veris	Cowslip	z5-9	☼ ✷
Primula vulgaris	English Primrose	z5-8	☼ ✷
Tricyrtis hirta	Toad Lily	z4-9	☼ ✷

Soil PH-Alkaline Soil

Scientific Name	Common Name	Zone	Light
Achillea filipendulina	Fern-Leaf Yarrow	z3-8	☼
Achillea millefolium	Common Yarrow	z2-9	☼
Aquilegia canadensis	Wild Columbine	z3-9	☼ ☀
Aquilegia vulgaris	Columbine	z3-8	☼ ☀
Astilbe x arendsii	Hybrid Astilbe	z4-8	☀
Astilbe chinensis	Chinese Astilbe	z4-8	☀
Bergenia ciliata	Winter Begonia	z5-8	☼ ☀
Bergenia cordifolia	Heart-Leaved Bergenia	z4-8	☀
Bergenia purpurascens	Purple Bergenia	z3-8	☼ ☀
Campanula glomerata	Clustered Bellflower	z3-8	☼ ☀
Carex dolichostachya	Birdfoot Sedge	z5-9	☀
Cerastostigma plumbaginoides	Plumbago	z5-8	☼ ☀
Chasmanthium latifolium	Northern Sea Oats	z4-7	☼
Consolida ambigua	Larkspur	annual	☼
Coreopsis tinctoria	Tickseed	annual	☼
Dianthus x allwoodii	Pinks	z4-8	☼
Dianthus barbatus	Sweet William	z3-8	☼
Dianthus deltoides	Maiden Pinks	z3-8	☼ ☀
Dicentra spectabilis	Bleeding Heart	z2-8	☼ ☀

Soil PH-Alkaline Soil ...continued

Scientific Name	Common Name	Zone	Light
Dictamnus albus	Gas Plant	z3-7	☼
Echinacea purpurea	Purple Coneflower	z3-8	☼
Echinops ritro	Globe Thistle	z3-8	☼
Eupatorium purpureum	Joe Pye Weed	z4-8	☼
Geranium sanguineum	Cranesbill	z4-8	☼
Gillenia trifoliata	Bowman's Root	z4-7	◐
Helleborus orientalis	Lenten Rose	z4-9	◐
Hemerocallis spp.	Daylily	z4-9	☼ ☼
Knautia macedonica	Knautia	z4-7	☼
Liatris spicata	Spike Gayfeather	z3-9	☼
Origanum laevigatum	Oregano	z5-9	☼
Phlox paniculata	Garden Phlox	z4-8	☼ ☼
Phlox subulata	Moss Phlox	z3-9	☼
Ruta graveolens	Rue	z4-8	☼
Salvia nemorosa	Meadow Sage	z5-7	☼
Scabiosa columbaria	Pincushion Flower	z3-9	☼
Schizachyrium scoparium	Little Bluestem	z4-10	☼

Soil Type-Clay Soil

Scientific Name	Common Name	Zone	Light	Wet
Aconitum x cammarum	Bicolor Monkshood	z4-8	☼ ☼	
Acorus calamus	Sweet Flag	z4-8	☼ ☼	x
Acorus gramineus	Dwarf Sweet Flag	z6-10	☼ ◐	x
Ajuga reptans	Bugle Weed	z3-9	☼ ◐ ☼	
Alcea rosea	Hollyhock	z3-7	☼	
Amsonia hubrichtii	Arkansas Amsonia	z6-9	☼	
Amsonia tabernaemontana	Blue Star	z4-9	☼	
Andropogon gerardi	Big Bluestem	z3-7	☼ ☼	
Anemone x hybrid	Hybrid Windflower	z5-7	☼ ☼	
Aruncus aesthusifolius	Dwarf Goat's Beard	z3-7	☼ ☼	x
Aruncus dioicus	Goat's Beard	z3-7	☼ ☼	x
Asclepias tuberosa	Butterfly Weed	z4-9	☼	
Aster novae-angliae	New England Aster	z4-8	☼	
Aster novi-belgii	New York Aster	z4-8	☼	
Aster x frikartii 'Monch'	Frikart's Aster	z5-8	☼	
Astilbe x arendsii	Hybrid Astilbe	z4-8	☼	x
Astilbe chinensis var. taquetii	Chinese Astilbe	z4-8	☼	x
Astrantia major	Great Masterwort	z5-7	☼	
Bergenia crassifolia	Leather Begonia	z4-8	☼	
Brunnera macrophylla	Siberian Bugloss	z3-8	◐ ☼	

Soil Type-Clay Soil ...continued

Scientific Name	Common Name	Zone	Light	Wet
Caltha palustris	Marsh Marigold	z3-8	☼	x
Centaurea macrocephala	Globe Centaurea	z3-7	☼	
Cimicifuga racemosa	Branched Bugbane	z3-7	☀	x
Cimicifuga simplex	Kamchatka Bugbane	z3-8	☀	x
Echinacea purpurea	Purple Coneflower	z3-8	☼	
Echinops ritro	Globe Thistle	z3-8	☼	
Eryngium yuccifolium	Sea Holly	z3-8	☼	
Filipendula ulmaria	Meadowsweet	z3-7	☀	
Gunnera manicata	Giant Rhubarb	z7-10	☼	x
Helenium autumnale	Sneezeweed	z3-8	☼	
Helianthus salicifolius	Willowleaf Sunflower	z5-9	☼	
Heliopsis helianthoides	Sunflower Heliopsis	z3-9	☼	
Hemerocallis spp.	Daylily	z4-9	☼ ☀	
Heuchera sanguinea	Coral Bells	z3-8	☀	
Humulus lupulus	Hops	z3-9	☀	
Inula ensifolia	Swordleaf Inula	z3-7	☼	x
Leucojum aestivum	Summer Snowflake	z4-8	☀	
Liatris pycnostachya	Kansas Gayfeather	z3-9	☼	
Liatris spicata	Spike Gayfeather	z3-9	☼	
Ligularia dentata	Big Leaf Ligularia	z5-8	☼ ☀	x

Soil Type-Clay Soil ...continued

Scientific Name	Common Name	Zone	Light	Wet
Ligularia stenocephala	Narrow-Spiked Ligularia	z5-9	☀	x
Lobelia cardinalis	Cardinal Flower	z2-9	☼ ☀	x
Lobelia x gerardi	Lobelia	z5-7	☀	x
Lysimachia clethroides	Gooseneck Loosestrife	z3-8	☼ ☀	x
Macleaya cordata	Plume Poppy	z3-8	☼ ☀	
Matteuccia struthiopteris	Ostrich Fern	z2-10	● ☀	x
Miscanthus sinensis	Maiden Grass	z5-9	☼	
Monarda fistulosa	Wild Bergamot	z3-7	☼	
Monarda didyma	Bee Balm	z3-7	☼ ☀	
Onoclea sensibilis	Sensitive Fern	z4-8	☀ ●	
Osmunda regalis	Royal Fern	z3-9	☼ ☀ ●	x
Panicum virgatum	Switch Grass	z4-9	☼ ☀	
Persicaria amplexicaulis 'Firetail'	Mountain Fleese	z5-9	☼ ☀	
Polemonium caeruleum	Jacob's Ladder	z2-7	☼ ☀	
Primula denticulata	Drumstick Primrose	z4-7	☼	x
Primula florindae	Florida Primrose	z6-8	☼ ☀	x
Primula japonica	Japanese Primrose	z5-7	☀	x
Primula vulgaris	English Primrose	z5-8	☀	x
Prunella grandiflora 'Loveliness'	Self Heal	z5-8	☼	
Ranunculus aconitifolius 'Flore Pleno'	Aconite Buttercup	z5-9	☀ ●	

181

Soil Type-Clay Soil ...continued

Scientific Name	Common Name	Zone	Light	Wet
Ratibida pinnata	Grayhead Coneflower	z3-7	☼	
Rheum palmatum	Ornamental Rhubarb	z4-7	☼	
Rodgersia aesculifolia	Fingerleaf Rodgersia	z5-7	☼	
Rudbeckia fulgida 'Goldsturm'	Black-eyed Susan	z3-9	☼ ☼	
Rudbeckia hirta	Black-eyed Susan	z3-7 biennial	☼	
Sanguisorba canadensis	Canadian Burnet	z3-7	☼ ☼	
Silphium perfoliatum	Cup Plant	z3-8	☼ ☼	
Solidago canadensis	Goldenrod	z3-9	☼	
Sorghastrum nutans	Indian Grass	z4-9	☼	
Spartina pectinata	Prairie Cord Grass	z4-7	☼ ☼	
Stachys macrantha	Big Betony	z2-8	☼ ☼	
Trollius europaeus	Globeflower	z4-7	☼ ☼	x
Vernonia noveboriensis	Ironweed	z5-9	☼ ☼	x
Veronica gentianoides	Gentian Speedwell	z4-7	☼	
Yucca filamentosa	Adam's Needle	z5-9	☼	

Soil Type-Sandy Loam

Scientific Name	Common Name	Zone	Light
Acaena caesiiglauca	New Zealand Bur	z4-10	☼ ☼
Acanthus spinosus	Spiny Bear's Breeches	z6-10	☼
Achillea spp.	Yarrow	z3-8	☼
Aethionema spp.	Stonecress	z4-8	☼
Anthemis tinctoria	Golden Marguerite	z3-7	☼
Antirrhinum majus	Snapdragon	annual	☼
Arenaria montana	Mountain Sandwort	z4-8	☼ ☼
Arctostaphylos uva-ursi	Bearberry	z2-6	☼ ☼
Armeria maritima	Sea Thrift	z4-8	☼
Artemisia spp.	Artemisia	z5-8	☼
Asclepias tuberosa	Butterfly Weed	z4-8	☼
Asphodeline lutea	Jacob's Rod	z6-9	☼ ☼
Aster novae-angliae	New England Aster	z4-8	☼
Baptisia australis	False Blue Indigo	z3-8	☼ ☼
Boltonia asteroides	White Boltonia	z4-8	☼
Callirhoe involucrata	Poppy Mallow	z4-7	☼
Centranthus ruber	Red Valerian	z5-10	☼
Chasmanthium latifolium	Northern Sea Oats	z4-7	☼
Cleome hassleriana	Cleome	annual	☼
Coreopsis grandiflora	Tickseed	z4-9	☼

183

Soil Type-Sandy Loam ...continued

Scientific Name	Common Name	Zone	Light
Coreopsis tinctoria	Tickseed	annual	☼
Crambe cordifolia	Colewort	z6-9	☼
Crocus sativus	Saffron Crocus	z6-9	☼
Crocus speciosus	Fall Crocus	z5-7	☼
Dianthus deltoides	Maiden Pinks	z3-8	☼ ☀
Dianthus plumarius	Cottage Pinks	z3-8	☼
Echinops ritro	Globe Thistle	z3-8	☼
Echinops sphaerocephalus	Globe Thistle	z3-8	☼
Eryngium x tripartitum	Sea Holly	z5-8	☼
Euphorbia amygdaloides	Wood Spurge	z5-8	☼ ☀
Euphorbia cyparissias	Cypress Spurge	z6-8	☼ ☀
Euphorbia myrsinites	Myrtle Euphorbia	z5-10	☼
Euphorbia polychroma	Cushion Spurge	z5-9	☼ ☀
Foeniculum vulgare	Fennel	z6-9	☼
Gaillardia x grandiflora	Blanket Flower	z2-9	☼
Gaura lindheimeri	Gaura	z5-8	☼
Helianthemum nummularium	Sunrose	z5-7	☼
Impatiens	Impatiens	annual	☀
Lavandula angustifolia	English Lavender	z5-9	☼
Limnanthes douglasii	Poached Egg Flower	annual	☼

Soil Type-Sandy Loam ...continued

Scientific Name	Common Name	Zone	Light
Limonium latifolium	Sea Lavender	z3-8	☼
Limonium sinuatum	Statice	annual	☼
Lobularia maritima	Sweet Alyssum	annual	☼
Lychnis chalcedonica	Maltese Cross	z3-7	☼
Muscari spp.	Grape Hyacinth	z4-8	☼
Nepeta x faassenii	Faassen Nepeta	z3-10	☼
Origanum vulgare	Oregano	z3-7	☼ ☼
Papaver nudicaule	Iceland Poppy	z2-7	☼ ☼
Papaver orientale	Oriental Poppy	z2-7	☼
Papaver rhoeas	Corn Poppy	annual	☼
Pelargonium	Geranium	annual	☼
Phlox subulata	Moss Phlox	z3-9	☼
Portulaca grandiflora	Moss Rose	annual	☼
Rudbeckia laciniata	Cutleaf Coneflower	z3-9	☼ ☼
Saponaria ocymoides	Soapwort	z2-7	☼
Scilla sibirica	Siberian Squill	z2-7	☼
Sedum spp.	Sedum	z4-8	☼
Sempervivum tectorum	Hens and Chicks	z3-7	☼
Verbena x hybrida	Garden Verbena	annual	☼
Yucca filamentosa	Adam's Needle	z5-10	☼

Soil Type-Sand, Dune

Dune plants are very specialized and tolerate harsh conditions but they can't withstand foot and vehicular traffic. This is but a sampling of plants that are available. The Environmental Protection Agency has a web site for plant availablity called Green Landscaping: Resources. There are separate sites for each great lake states.

Agropyron psammophilum	Great Lakes Wheat Grass
Ammophila breviligulata	Marram Grass
Arabis lyrata	Sand Cress
Arctostaphylos uva-ursi	Bearberry, Woody Ground Cover
Aristida spp.	Three Awn Grass
Artemisia campestris subsp. *caudata*	Beach Wormwood
Astragalus alpinus var. *alpinus*	Alpine Milk-Vetch
Cakile edentula	American Sea-Rocket
Calamovilfa longifolia var. *magna*	Long Leaved Reed Grass
Cirsium pitcheri	Dune Thistle
Cyperus filiculmis	Sedge
Cyperus schweinitzii	Sedge
Geaster spp.	Earthstar Fungus
Hudsonia tomentosa	False Heather
Opuntia compressa	Prickly-Pear Cactus
Oxytropis campestris var. *chartacea*	Fassett's Locoweed
Selaginella rupestris	Rock Spikemoss
Talinum rugospermum	Flameflower

Soil-Moisture-Bog

Scientific Name	Common Name	Zone	Light
Acorus calamus	Sweet Flag	z4-8	☼ ☀
Acorus japonicus	Sweet Flag	z5-8	☼ ☀
Artemisia lactiflora	White Sage	z4-9	☼
Aruncus dioicus	Goat's Beard	z3-7	☼ ☀
Asclepias incarnata	Swamp Milkweed	z3-7	☼ ☀
Aster novae-angliae	New England aster	z4-8	☼
Astilbe spp.	Hybrid Astilbe	z4-8	☀
Astilbe chinensis var. *taquetti*	Chinese Astilbe	z4-8	☼ ☀
Caltha palustris	Marsh Marigold	z3-8	☼
Carex spp.	Sedge	z5-8	☀
Colocasia affinis	Elephant Ear	z7-10	☼ ☀
Cortaderia selloana	Pampas Grass	z6-9	☼
Darmera peltata	Umbrella Plant	z5-7	☀
Dicentra spp.	Bleeding Heart	z3-7	☀
Dodecatheon meadia	Shooting Star	z4-8	☀ ●
Epilobium angustifolium	Fireweed	z2-10	☼
Equisetum hyemale	Horsetail	z4-11	☼ ● ☼
Eupatorium dubium	Joe Pye Weed	z4-8	☼ ☀
Eupatorium maculatum	Spotted Joe Pye Weed	z4-8	☼ ☀
Eupatorium purpureum	Joe Pye Weed	z4-8	☼ ☀

Soil-Moisture-Bog ...continued

Scientific Name	Common Name	Zone	Light
Filipendula spp.	Meadowsweet	z3-7	☀ ☀
Geum rivale	Water Avens	z3-7	☀ ◐
Hibiscus moscheutos	Rose Mallow	z5-9	☀ ☀
Juncus effusus 'Spiralis'	Corkscrew Rush	z5-9	☀ ☀
Iris ensata	Japanese Iris	z4-9	☀ ☀
Iris pseudacorus	Yellow Flag Iris	z5-9	☀ ☀
Iris sibirica	Siberian Iris	z3-9	☀ ☀
Iris versicolor	Blue Flag Iris	z2-8	☀ ☀
Iris virginica	Flag Iris	z5-9	☀ ☀
Lilium michauxii	Carolina Lily	z6-10	☀ ☀
Lilium michiganense	Michigan Lily	z4-8	☀ ☀
Lilium superbum	American Turk's Cap Lily	z4-8	☀ ☀
Lobelia cardinalis	Cardinal Flower	z2-9	☀
Lobelia siphilitica	Great Blue Lobelia	z4-8	☀
Lysimachia ciliata	Hairy Loosestrife	z3-8	☀ ☀
Lysimachia clethroides	Gooseneck Loosestrife	z3-8	☀
Lysimachia nummularia 'Aurea'	Creeping Jenny	z3-9	☀ ◐
Mimulus cardinalis	Red Monkey Flower	z6-9	☀ ☀
Osmunda cinnamomea	Cinnamon Fern	z3-8	☀ ◐
Osmunda regalis	Royal Fern	z3-9	☀ ◐

Soil-Moisture-Bog ...continued

Scientific Name	Common Name	Zone	Light
Peltandra virginica	Water Arum	z5-9	☼
Petasites japonicus	Japanese Butterbur	z5-9	☼ ☀
Pontederia cordata	Pickerel Weed	z4-7	☼
Primula japonica	Japanese Primrose	z5-7	☀
Primula vulgaris	English Primrose	z5-8	☀
Rodgersia aesculifolia	Fingerleaf Rodgersia	z5-7	☼
Sagittaria latifolia	Duck Potato Arrowhead	z3-11	☼
Sarracenia spp.	Pitcher Plant	z4-9	☼ ☀
Saururus cernuus	Lizard's Tail	z5-11	☼ ☀
Typha augustifolia	Narrow Leaf Cattail	z3-10	☼ ☀
Typha latifolia	North American Cattail	z3-11	☼ ☀
Verbena hastata	Blue Vervain	z3-8	☼
Veronicastrum virginicum	Culver's Root	z3-8	☼
Vernonia noveboriensis	Ironweed	z5-9	☼ ☀

Soil-Moisture-Dry Shade

Scientific Name	Common Name	Zone	Light
Alchemilla mollis	Lady's Mantle	z4-7	☼ ☼
Convallaria majalis	Lily-of-the-Valley	z2-7	☼ ☀
Dicentra eximia	Fringed Bleeding Heart	z3-9	☼
Dryopteris filix-mas	Male Fern	z5-9	☼
Epimedium spp.	Barrenwort	z5-9	☼ ☀
Epimedium pinnatum ssp. *colchicum*	Barrenwort	z5-9	☀ ☀
Euphorbia amygdaloides var. *robbiae*	Wood Spurge	z5-8	☼ ☼
Helleborus foetidus	Stinking Hellebore	z6-8	☀ ☀
Helleborus x hybridus	Hellebore	z5-9	☼ ☀
Hyacinthoides hispanica	Spanish Bluebell	z4-7	☼ ☀
Hyacinthoides non-scriptus	English Bluebell	z5-10	☀ ☀
Iris foetidissima	Stinking Gladwin	z6-9	☼ ☀
Iris foetidissima var. *citrina*	Stinking Gladwin	z6-9	☼ ☀
Lamium galeobdolon 'Herman's Pride'	Dead Nettle	z4-8	☼ ☀
Liriope muscari	Blue Lily Turf	z6-9	☼ ☀
Omphalodes verna	Blue-Eyed Mary	z6-9	☀
Ophiopogon japonicus	Dwarf Mondo Grass	z6-9	☼ ☼
Pachysandra terminalis	Japanese Spurge	z5-9	☼
Polygonatum odoratum	Fragrant Solomon's Seal	z3-9	☼ ☼

Soil-Moisture-Dry Shade ...continued

Scientific Name	Common Name	Zone	Light
Pulmonaria saccharata	Bethlehem Sage	z3-7	☀
Symphytum grandiflorum	Large-Flowered Comfrey	z3-9	☀ ☀
Tellima grandiflora	Fringe-Cup	z4-7	☀ ☀ ●
Waldsteinia ternata	Siberian Barrenwort	z3-9	☀ ☀

Soil-Moisture-Drought Tolerant

Plants that are drought tolerant often have similar characteristics that include thick & fleshy leaves/stems, light colored or glossy foliage, or fine hairs. Drought tolerant plants conserve water in areas with shortages, as well as save time and work in the garden, due to their low water requirements.

Scientific Name	Common Name	Zone	Light
Acanthus mollis	Common Bear's Breeches	z7-9	☼
Achillea filipendulina	Fern-Leaf Yarrow	z3-8	☼
Achillea millefolium	Common Yarrow	z2-9	☼
Achillea tomentosa	Woolly Yarrow	z3-7	☼
Aethionema cordifolium	Stonecress	z5-7	☼
Allium christophii	Star of Persia	z4-8	☼ ☀
Allium schubertii	Tumbleweed Onion	z5-9	☼
Anemone blanda	Grecian Windflower	z4-7	☼ ☀
Antennaria dioica 'Rosea'	Rose Pussytoes	z3-7	☼
Anthericum liliago	St. Bernard's Lily	z4-9	☼
Arabis caucasica	Wall Rock Cress	z4-7	☼
Arctostaphylos uva-ursi	Bearberry	z2-6	☼ ☀
Arenaria verna caespitosa	Sandwort	z4-8	☼ ☀
Armeria maritima	Sea Thrift	z4-8	☼
Artemisia absinthium	Wormwood	z3-9	☼
Artemisia schmidtiana	Angel's Hair	z3-8	☼
Artemisia stelleriana	Beach Wormwood	z4-8	☼

Soil-Moisture-Drought Tolerant ...continued

Scientific Name	Common Name	Zone	Light
Asclepias tuberosa	Butterfly Weed	z4-9	☼
Aster ptarmicoides	White Aster	z4-8	☼
Aurinia saxatilis	Basket-Of-Gold	z3-7	☼
Baptisia australis	False Blue Indigo	z3-8	☼ ☀
Campanula carpatica	Carpathian Harebell	z3-7	☼ ☀
Campanula divaricata	Southern Harebell	z4-9	☀
Caryopteris x clandonensis	Bluebeard	z5-9	☼
Catananche caerulea 'Bicolor'	Cupid's Dart	z4-9	☼
Centranthus ruber	Red Valerian	z5-10	☼
Centaurea montana	Bachelor's Button	z3-8	☼ ☀
Cerastium tomentosum	Snow-in-Summer	z2-7	☼
Coreopsis grandiflora	Tickseed	z4-9	☼
Coreopsis lanceolata	Lanceleaf Coreopsis	z3-8	☼
Coreopsis verticillata	Thread leaf Coreopsis	z5-9	☼
Cortaderia selloana	Pampas Grass	z6-9	☼
Dianthus barbatus	Sweet William	z3-8	☼
Echinacea purpurea	Purple Coneflower	z3-8	☼
Echinops ritro	Globe Thistle	z3-8	☼
Eremurus stenophyllus	Foxtail Lily	z5-8	☼
Erigeron flagellaris	Whiplash Daisy	z4-8	☼

193

Soil-Moisture-Drought Tolerant ...continued

Scientific Name	Common Name	Zone	Light
Eryngium amethystinum	Sea Holly	z2-8	☼
Eryngium x tripartitum	Sea Holly	z5-8	☼
Eupatorium coelestinum	Mist Flower	z5-10	☼ ☀
Euphorbia characias	Mediterranean Spurge	z6-8	☼ ☀
Euphorbia myrsinites	Myrtle Euphorbia	z5-10	☼
Festuca glauca	Blue Fescue	z4-9	☼
Gaillardia x grandiflora	Blanket Flower	z2-9	☼
Gaura lindheimeri	Gaura	z5-8	☼
Gazania	Gazania	annual	☼
Gypsophila repens	Creeping Baby's Breath	z3-7	☼
Helenium autumnale	Sneezeweed	z3-8	☼
Helianthemum nummularium	Sunrose	z5-7	☼
Helianthus salicifolius	Willowleaf Sunflower	z5-9	☼
Hemerocallis fulva 'Kwanso'	Daylily	z3-9	☼ ☀
Iberis sempervirens	Candytuft	z3-8	☼
Kniphofia uvaria	Torchlily	z5-8	☼
Lavandula angustifolia	English Lavender	z5-9	☼
Lavandula dentata	French Lavender	z7-9	☼
Lavandula stoechas	French Lavender	z7-10	☼
Liatris punctata	Blazing Star	z4-9	☼

Soil-Moisture-Drought Tolerant ...continued

Scientific Name	Common Name	Zone	Light
Liatris spicata	Gayfeather	z3-9	☼
Limonium latifolium	Sea Lavender	z3-8	☼
Linum perenne	Blue Flax	z4-8	☼ ☀
Lobularia maritima	Sweet Alyssum	annual	☼
Oenothera berlandieri	Mexican Evening Primrose	z6-8	☼
Ophiopogon japonicus	Dwarf Mondo Grass	z6-9	☼ ☀
Pachysandra terminalis	Japanese Spurge	z5-9	☀
Papaver orientale	Oriental Poppy	z2-7	☼
Pelargonium	Geranium	annual	☼
Penstemon barbatus	Common Beard Tongue	z2-8	☼
Penstemon pinifolius	Pine-Leaf Penstemon	z7-8	☼
Perovskia atriplicifolia	Russian Sage	z5-9	☼
Phlox subulata	Moss Phlox	z3-9	☼
Ratibida columnifera	Mexican Hat	z3-7	☼
Rudbeckia hirta	Black-eyed Susan	z3-7 biennial	☼
Ruta graveolens	Rue	z4-8	☼
Saponaria ocymoides	Soapwort	z2-7	☼
Santolina chamaecyparissus	Lavender Cotton	z6-8	☼
Santolina virens	Green Lavender Cotton	z7-8	☼
Sedum acre	Goldmoss Sedum	z3-8	☼

195

Soil-Moisture-Drought Tolerant ...continued

Scientific Name	Common Name	Zone	Light
Sedum maxiumum	Stonecrop	z4-10	☼ ☼
Sedum x hybrids	Stonecrop	z3-8	☼
Sedum kamtschaticum	Yellow Stonecrop	z3-8	☼
Sempervivum tectorum	Hens & Chicks	z3-7	☼
Stachys byzantina	Lamb's Ears	z4-8	☼
Teucrium chamaedrys	Germander	z4-9	☼
Thermopsis caroliniana	Southern Lupine	z3-9	☼
Thymus praecox	Creeping Thyme	z5-8	☼
Thymus pseudolanuginosus	Woolly Thyme	z5-8	☼ ☼
Thymus serphyllum	Wild Thyme	z5-8	☼ ☼
Thymus vulgaris	Garden Thyme	z4-10	☼
Vinca minor	Myrtle	z4-8	☼ ☼ ☀
Viola pedata	Bird's Foot Violet	z4-8	☼
Waldsteinia fragarioides	Barren Strawberry	z4-7	☼ ☼

Environment-Juglone Tolerant

Juglone is an allelopathic chemical, meaning it is made by one type of plant and affects the growth of another. Use this list for landscaping near *Juglans nigra* (Black Walnut), or other *Juglans spp*. Plants in this family can kill or hinder growth of plants that come in contact with their roots or leaf debris. There has been very little scientific evidence as to which plants are truly juglone resistant. These plants have been observed growing under or near black walnut trees. Some of these plants have shallow root systems that may not make direct contact with the walnut roots. Many plants can survive for years uneffected, (making the sudden illness seem like a mystery).

Scientific Name	Common Name	Zone	Light
Ajuga reptans	Bugle Weed	z3-9	☼ ☀ ☀
Alcea rosea	Hollyhock	z3-7	☼
Anemone quinquefolia	Wood Anemone	z3-7	☀
Arisaema triphyllum	Jack-in-the-Pulpit	z4-9	☀ ●
Asarum europaeum	European Wild Ginger	z4-7	☀ ☀
Astilbe spp.	Astilbe	z4-8	☀
Campanula latifolia	Great Bellflower	z3-6	☼ ☀
Chioniodoxa lucilae	Glory of the snow	z4-8	☼
Crocus spp.	Crocus	z5-8	☼
Doronicum spp.	Leopard's Bane	z4-7	☼ ☀
Dryopteris cristata	Crested Shield Fern	z3-7	☀ ☀
Eranthis hyemalis	Winter Aconite	z3-7	☼
Galanthus nivalis	Snowdrop	z3-7	☼
Galium odoratum	Sweet Woodruff	z4-7	☀
Geranium sanguineum	Cranesbill	z4-8	☼

197

Environment-Juglone Tolerant ...continued

Scientific Name	Common Name	Zone	Light
Helianthus tuberosus	Jerusalem Artichoke	z3-9	☼
Hemerocallis fulva	Orange Daylily	z3-9	☼ ☀
Heuchera x brizoides 'Pluie de Feu'	Coral Bells	z3-8	☼ ☀
Hieracium aurantiacum	Orange Hawkweed	z3-8	☼
Hosta 'Albo marginata'	White Margin Hosta	z3-9	☀ ●
Hosta fortunei	Fortune's Hosta	z3-9	☀ ●
Hosta lancifolia	Lance Leaf Hosta	z3-9	☀ ●
Hosta undulata 'Variegata'	Wavy Hosta	z3-9	☀ ●
Hyacinthoides hispanica	Spanish Bluebell	z4-7	☀ ●
Hyacinthus orientalis	Hyacinth	z5-9	☼
Hydrophyllum virginianum	Virginia Waterleaf	z4-7	☀ ●
Ipomoea 'Heavenly Blue'	Morning Glory	annual	☼
Iris siberica	Siberian Iris	z3-9	☼ ☀
Monarda didyma	Bee Balm	z3-7	☼ ☀
Monarda fistulosa	Wild Bergamot	z3-7	☼
Muscari botryoides	Grape Hyacinth	z2-8	☼ ☀
Narcissus 'Cheerfulness'	Daffodils	z4-9	☼
Narcissus 'February Gold'	Daffodils	z5-9	☼
Narcissus 'Sundial'	Daffodils	z4-9	☼

Environment-Juglone Tolerant ...continued

Scientific Name	Common Name	Zone	Light
Narcissus 'Tete a Tete'	Daffodils	z5-9	☼
Oenothera fruticosa	Common Sundrops	z4-8	☼
Onoclea sensibilis	Sensitive Fern	z3-8	☼ ◐ ●
Osmunda cinnamomea	Cinnamon Fern	z3-8	☼ ◐ ●
Phlox paniculata	Garden Phlox	z4-8	☼ ◐
Polemonium reptans	Creeping Polemonium	z3-8	◐
Polygonatum commutatum	Great Solomon's Seal	z3-7	◐
Primula x polyantha	Polyanthus Primrose	z3-8	◐ ●
Pulmonaria spp.	Leadwort	z3-8	◐ ●
Sanguinaria canadensis	Bloodroot	z3-8	◐ ●
Sanguinaria canadensis 'Multiplex'	Double Flowered Bloodroot	z3-8	◐ ●
Scilla siberica	Siberian Squill	z2-7	☼
Sedum acre	Gold Moss Stonecrop	z3-8	☼
Sedum spectabile	Stonecrop	z3-8	☼
Stachys byzantina	Lamb's Ear	z4-8	☼
Tradescantia virginiana	Spiderwort	z3-9	☼ ◐
Trillium grandiflorum	Great White Trillium	z4-9	◐ ●
Tulipa 'Cum Laude'	Tulip	z3-6	☼
Tulipa Darwin 'White Volcano'	Tulip	z3-6	☼

Environment-Juglone Tolerant ...continued

Scientific Name	Common Name	Zone	Light
Tulipa Greigii 'Toronto'	Tulip	z3-6	☼
Tulipa Parrot 'Blue Parrot'	Tulip	z3-6	☼
Uvularia grandiflora	Large Flowered Bellwort	z3-9	☀
Viola canadensis	Canada Violet	z3-8	☀ ☼
Viola sororaria	Woolly Blue Violet	z4-9	☼ ☀

Environment-Salt Tolerant

Scientific Name	Common Name	Zone	Light	Salt Tolerance
Arctostaphylos uva-ursi	Bearberry	z2-6	☼ ☀	High
Armeria maritima	Sea Thrift	z4-8	☼	High
Artemisia schmidtiana 'Silver Mound'	Wormwood	z3-7	☼	Moderate
Artemisia x 'Powis Castle'	Artemisia	z6-8	☼	Moderate
Aster divaricatus	White Wood Aster	z4-8	☼	High
Calmagrostis acutiflora 'Karl Foerster'	Reed Grass	z5-8	☼	High
Dianthus 'Little Boy Blue'	Pinks	z4-8	☼	High
Dianthus 'Spotti'	Pinks	z4-8	☼	High
Dianthus x *allwoodii* 'Helen'	Pinks	z3-8	☼	High
Festuca glauca 'Elijah Blue'	Fescue	z4-8	☼	Moderate
Helleborus orientalis	Lenten Rose	z4-9	☀	Moderate
Hemerocallis 'Stella de'Oro'	Daylily	z3-9	☼ ☀	Moderate
Hemerocallis fulva	Daylily	z3-9	☼ ☀	Moderate
Heuchera 'Palace Purple'	Coral Bells	z4-9	☼	Moderate
Hosta plantaginea	Hosta	z3-8	☀ ●	Moderate
Iberis sempervirens	Candytuft	z3-8	☼ ☀	High
Leymus arenarius	Blue Lyme Grass	z4-9	☼	High
Limomium latifolium	Sea Lavender	z3-8	☼	Moderate
Lotus corniculatus	Bird's Foot Trefoil	z3-9	☼	High
Oenothera speciosa	Showy Evening Primrose	z3-9	☼	Moderate

Environment-Salt Tolerant ...continued

Scientific Name	Common Name	Zone	Light	Salt Tolerance
Pennisetum alopecuroides	Fountain Grass	z5-9	☼ ☀	High
Schizachyrium scoparium	Little Blue Stem	z4-10	☼	High
Waldsteinia	Barren Strawberry	z4-7	☼ ☀	High
Yucca glauca	Soap Weed	z5-9	☼	Moderate

Section Four
Land Uses

Aesthetic-Architectural

With their strong form, these plants make a bold statement in the garden. Architectural plants will add a focal point to a design or unify garden elements. These distinctive structural plants bring an often exotic presence to the garden and interest from many angles. Strong shapes, both of leaves and overall growth pattern, enhance a garden. Planting style should be given careful consideration. Plants lend more depth placed at key locations or at the back of the border for a dramatic effect.

Scientific Name	Common Name	Zone	Light
Acanthus spinosus	Bear's Breeches	z6-10	☼
Allium giganteum	Giant Allium	z4-8	☼
Amaranthus tricolor 'Joseph's Coat'	Joseph's Coat	annual	☼ ☼
Angelica archangelica	Angelica	z5-7	☼
Angelica gigas	Purple Parsnip	z4-8	☼ ☼
Arisaema dracontium	Green Dragon	z4-8	☼ ◑
Armoracia rusticanna 'Variegata'	Variegated Horseradish	z3-9	☼
Arum creticum	Arum	z7-9	☼
Begonia rex	Rex Begonia	annual	☼
Begonia x tuberhybrida	Tuberous Begonia	annual	☼
Calamagrostis x acutiflora 'Avalanche'	Feather Reed Grass	z4-7	☼ ☼
Calamagrostis x acutiflora 'Overdam'	Feather Reed Grass	z4-7	☼
Canna	Canna Lily	annual	☼
Colocasia gigantea	Giant Elephant Ear	annual	☼ ☼
Colocasia esculenta 'Black Magic'	Elephant Ear	annual	☼

205

Aesthetic-Architectural ...continued

Scientific Name	Common Name	Zone	Light
Cordyline australis	Cabbage Palm	annual	☼
Cortaderia selloana	Pampas Grass	z6-9	☼
Crambe cordifolia	Colewort	z6-9	☼
Crocosmia x crocosmiiflora 'Lucifer'	Montbretia	z5-9	☼
Cynara	Cardoon	z6-10	☼
Darmera peltata	Umbrella Plant	z5-7	☼ ☀
Dracunculus vulgaris	Dragon Flower	annual	☼
Echinops bannaticus	Globe Thistle	annual	☼
Eremurus x shelford	Shelford Foxtail Lily	z5-7	☼
Eryngium giganteum	Miss Wilmot's Ghost	z4-7	☼
Eryngium yuccifolium	Rattlesnake Master	z5-9	☼
Fatsia japonica	Japanese Aralia	z7-10	☼ ☀
Fatsia japonica 'Spider's Web'	Japanese Aralia	z7-10	☼ ☀
Gladiolus x hortulanus	Gladiolus	z7-10	☼
Gunnera manicata	Giant Rhubarb	z7-10	☼
Helianthus annuus	Sunflower	annual	☼
Helleborus foetidus	Stinking Hellebore	z5-9	☼ ☀
Hosta sieboldiana 'Elegans'	Large Blue Hosta	z3-9	☀
Juncus effuses 'Curly Wurly'	Corkscrew Rush	z5-10	☼ ☀

Aesthetic-Architectural ...continued

Scientific Name	Common Name	Zone	Light	
Juncus effuses 'Unicorn'	Unicorn Rush	z5-10	☀ ☀	
Juncus effuses 'Frenzy'	Variegated Corkscrew Rush	z5-10	☀ ☀	Shallow water
Kniphofia uvaria	Torchlily	z5-8	☀	
Ligularia dentata	Bigleaf Ligularia	z5-8	☀ ●	
Ligularia stenocephala 'The Rocket'	Narrow-Spiked Ligularia	z5-9	☀ ●	
Lysichiton americanus	Skunk Cabbage	z5-7	☀ ☀ ●	Bog plant
Macleaya cordata	Plume Poppy	z3-8	☀ ☀	
Matteuccia struthiopteris	Ostrich Fern	z2-8	☀	
Musa 'Basjoo'	Hardy Banana Plant	z7-10	☀	
Musa ensete 'Rubra'	Red Banana	annual	☀	
Petasities japonicus	Japanese Butterbur	z5-9	☀ ☀	
Phormium tenax	Flax Lily	z7-11	☀	
Phormium tenax 'Purpureum'	Flax Lily	z8-11	☀	
Polystichum munitum	Sword Fern	z5-8	☀	
Rheum 'Ace of Hearts'	Ornamental Rhubarb	z5-9	☀	
Ricinus communis	Castor Bean	annual	☀	
Rodgersia aesculifolia	Fingerleaf Rodgersia	z5-9	☀ ☀	
Rodgersia pinnata	Featherleaf Rodgersia	z5-7	☀ ☀	
Sagittaria sagittifolia	Arrowhead	z6-11	☀	Marginal water plant

Aesthetic-Architectural ...continued

Scientific Name	Common Name	Zone	Light
Yucca filamentasa 'Golden Sword'	Adam's Needle	z4-10	☼
Yucca 'Color Guard'	Variegated Yucca	z5-10	☼
Zantedeschia aethiopica	Calla Lily	z7-10	☼ Marginal water plant

Aesthetic-Long Bloomers

Scientific Name	Common Name	Zone	Light	Weeks of bloom
Achillea siberica var. kamschatica	Yarrow	z5-9	☼	10
Aquilegia longissima 'Maxistar'	Long Spur Columbine	z4-8	☼ ◐	10 +
Aster x frikartii 'Monch'	Frikart's Aster	z5-8	☼	8-12
Callirhoe involucrata	Poppy Mallow	z4-8	☼	12
Coreopsis grandiflora 'Sunray'	Tickseed	z4-9	☼	12
Coreopsis verticillata 'Moonbeam'	Threadleaf Coreopsis	z5-9	☼	15 +
Corydalis lutea	Yellow Corydalis	z5-7	☼ ◐	20
Dicentra spectabilis	Bleeding Heart	z2-8	☼ ◐	10
Dicentra 'Luxuriant'	Fringed Bleeding Heart	z3-9	☼	17
Gallardia x grandiflora 'Goblin'	Blanket Flower	z3-10	☼	12
Geranium sanguineum var. striatum	Cranesbill	z4-8	☼	10
Gaura lindheimeri	Gaura	z5-8	☼	12
Gaura lindheimeri 'Siskiyou Pink'	Gaura	z5-8	☼	12
Heliopsis helianthoides 'Summer Sun'	Sunflower Heliopsis	z3-9	☼	10-13
Hemerocallis 'Happy Returns'	Daylily	z3-9	☼ ◐	18
Hemerocallis 'Stella D' Oro'	Daylily	z3-9	☼ ◐	18
Kalimeris pinnatifida	Double Japanese Aster	z5-8	☼ ◐	10 +
Leucanthemum x 'Ryan's White'	Shasta Daisy	z4-9	☼	10 +
Malva alcea 'Fastigiata'	Mallow	z4-8	☼ ◐	10

Aesthetic-Long Bloomers ...continued

Scientific Name	Common Name	Zone	Light	Weeks of Bloom
Miscanthus sinensis 'Kaskade'	Maiden Grass	z5-9	☼ ☀	10 +
Perovskia atriplicifolia	Russian Sage	z5-9	☼	12
Phlox arendsii 'Spring Pearl'	Hybrid Phlox	z4-8	☼ ☀	10
Rudbeckia fulgida 'Goldsturm'	Black-Eyed Susan	z3-8	☼	10
Rudbeckia nitida 'Herbstsonne'	Shining Coneflower	z5-9	☼	10
Salvia x *superba* 'Blue Hill'	Sage	z4-7	☼	10
Salvia x *superba* 'May Night'	Sage	z5-9	☼	12
Scabiosa columbaria 'Butterfly Blue'	Pincushion Flower	z3-9	☼ ☀	18
Sedum 'Autumn Joy'	Sedum	z3-8	☼	12 +
Tiarella 'Iron Butterfly'	Foamflower	z3-8	☀ ❋	14 +
Tradescantia virginica 'Concord Grape'	Spiderwort	z3-9	☼ ☀	12 +
Veronica 'Sunny border blue'	Speedwell	z4-8	☼ ☀	14
Veronica x 'Goodness Grows'	Speedwell	z3-8	☼	14 +

Aesthetic-Trailing Plants for Walls & Baskets

Many vines could also be included in this group and look very appropriate cascading down a wall as well as climbing up.

Scientific Name	Common Name	Zone	Light
Acaena 'Blue Haze'	New Zealand Bur	z7-9	☼
Arabis caucasica	Wall Rock Cress	z4-7	☼
Asarina	Climbing Snapdragon	annual	☼
Aubrieta deltoides	False Rock Cress	z4-7	☼☀
Campanula poscharskyana	Serbian Bellflower	z3-7	☀
Clematis 'Vyvyan Pennell'	Clematis	z4-9	☼
Cymbalaria muralis	Kenilworth Ivy	z4-8	☀
Euphorbia myrsinites	Myrtle Euphorbia	z5-10	☼
Fragaria x 'Lipstick'	Strawberry	z3-10	☼☀
Gypsophila repens	Creeping Baby's Breath	z3-7	☼
Limnanthes douglasii	Poached Egg Flower	z5-9	☼
Lithodora diffusa	Lithodora	z5-7	☼☀
Lobelia erinus	Lobelia	annual	☼☀
Lysimachia nummularia	Creeping Jenny	z3-9	☼☀●
Nemophila maculata	Five Spot	annual	☼☀
Oenothera missouriensis	Ozark Sundrops	z4-7	☼☀
Petunia Cascade Series	Petunia	annual	☼
Petunia Jamboree Series	Petunia	annual	☼

212

Aesthetic-Trailing Plants for Wall & Baskets ...continued

Scientific Name	Common Name	Zone	Light
Petunia Surfinia Series	Petunia	annual	☼
Portulaca grandiflora	Moss Rose	annual	☼
Sanvitalia procumbens	Creeping Zinnia	annual	☼
Saxifraga stolonifera	Strawberry Begonia	z7-9	☼ ☀
Schizophragma hydrangeoides 'Moonlight'	Japanese Climbing Hydrangea	z6-9	☼ ☀
Tropaeolum majus	Nasturtium	annual	☼

Aesthetic-Winter Interest

Planting with perennials that contribute to the garden during the winter months keep the garden from looking bare. Winter interest can be found in lasting foliage, emerging flowers, fruit, colorful stems, unique shapes, textures and the seed heads of past flowers.

Scientific Name	Common Name	Zone	Light	Foliage	Flower	Fruit
Acanthus spinosus	Spiny Bear's Breeches	z6-10	☼		x	
Achillea spp.	Yarrow	z3-9	☼			x
Adiantum pedatum	Maidenhair Fern	z2-8	☼☀	x		
Adonis amurensis	Amur Adonis	z4-7	☼		x	
Ajuga genevensis	Geneva Bugle Weed	z4-9	☼	x		
Ajuga reptans	Bugle Weed	z3-9	☼☀	x		
Anemone blanda	Grecian Windflower	z4-7	☼☼		x	
Arum italicum	Italian Arum	z6-9	☼☀	x		
Asarum arifolium	Arrow-Leaf Ginger	z4-8	☼☀	x		
Asarum europaeum	European Wild Ginger	z4-7	☼☀	x		
Asarum yakushimanum	Wood Spurge	z5-7	☼☼	x		
Baptisia australis	False Blue Indigo	z3-8	☼☼			x
Bergenia cordifolia	Heart-Leaf Bergenia	z4-8	☼	x		
Bergenia purpurascens	Purple Bergenia	z4-8	☼☀	x		
Bergenia x schmidtii	Hybrid Bergenia	z4-8	☼	x		
Calamagrostis brachytricha	Feather Grass	z5-9	☼☀	x		x
Calamagrostis 'Karl Foerster'	Feather Reed Grass	z5-8	☼	x		x

213

Aesthetic-Winter Interest ...continued

Scientific Name	Common Name	Zone	Light	Foliage	Flower	Fruit
Chionodoxa luciliae	Glory-of-the-Snow	z4-8	☼		x	
Clematis cirrhosa	Winter Clematis	z7-9	☼☼		x	
Cortaderia selloana	Pampas Grass	z6-10	☼	x		x
Cortaderia selloana 'Pumila'	Dwarf Pampas Grass	z6-10	☼	x		x
Crocus crysanthus	Golden Crocus	z4-7	☼		x	
Crocus laevigatus 'Fontenayi'	Crocus	z6-9	☼		x	
Crocus tommasinianus	Tommasini's Crocus	z5-9	☼		x	
Cyclamen coum	Hardy Cyclamen	z6-9	☼		x	
Deschampsia caespitosa	Tufted Hairgrass	z4-7	☼☼	x		x
Dryopteris erythrosora	Autumn Fern	z5-9	☼☼●	x		
Dryopteris marginalis	Marginal Wood Fern	z2-8	☼●	x		
Echinacea purpurea	Purple Coneflower	z3-8	☼			x
Epimedium grandiflorum	Longspur Barrenwort	z5-8	☼	x		
Epimedium perralderianum	Barrenwort	z5-8	☼●	x		
Epimedium x *rubrum*	Red Barrenwort	z5-8	☼●	x		
Eranthis cilicica	Winter Aconite	z3-7	☼☼		x	
Eranthis hyemalis	Winter Aconite	z3-7	☼		x	
Eryngium giganteum	Sea Holly	z4-7	☼			x
Eupatorium purpureum	Joe Pye Weed	z4-8	☼			x
Euphorbia amygdaloides	Wood Spurge	z5-7	☼☼	x		

Aesthetic-Winter Interest ...continued

Scientific Name	Common Name	Zone	Light	Foliage	Flower	Fruit
Euphorbia myrsinites	Myrtle Euphorbia	z5-9	☼	x		
Festuca glauca	Blue Fescue	z4-8	☼	x		
Fragaria x ananassa 'Variegata'	Strawberry	z4-10	☼	x		
Galanthus nivalis	Snowdrops	z3-7	☼		x	
Gaultheria procumbens	Wintergreen	z4-9	☼ ◐	x		x
Hedera helix	English Ivy	z5-11	☼ ◐	x		
Helleborus argutifolius	Corsican Hellebore	z6-8	☼	x	x	
Helleborus foetidus	Stinking Hellebore	z5-9	◐	x	x	
Helleborus niger	Christmas Rose	z3-8	◐	x	x	
Helleborus orientalis	Lenten Rose	z4-9	◐	x	x	
Hepatica acutiloba	Hepatica	z3-9	◐	x	x	
Hepatica americana	Round-Lobed Liverleaf	z3-7	☼ ◐		x	
Heuchera americana	American Alumroot	z4-9	☼	x		
Iberis sempervirens	Candytuft	z3-8	☼	x		
Iris danfordiae	Danford Iris	z5-9	☼	x		
Iris foetidissima	Stinking Gladwin	z6-9	◐		x	
Iris reticulata	Reticulated Iris	z5-8	☼		x	
Iris unguicularis	Algerian Iris	z7-9	☼		x	
Lamium maculatum	Spotted Nettle	z3-8	☼ ◐	x		

215

Aesthetic-Winter Interest ...continued

Scientific Name	Common Name	Zone	Light	Foliage	Flower	Fruit
Leucojum vernum	Spring Snowflake	z4-8	☼		x	
Liriope muscari	Blue Lily Turf	z6-9	☼◐●	x		
Matteuccia struthiopteris	Ostrich Fern	z2-10	◐●	x		
Miscanthus sinensis	Maiden Grass	z5-9	☼	x		x
Monarda didyma	Bee Balm	z3-7	☼◐			x
Narcissus bulbocodium	Hoop Petticoat Daffodil	z5-8	☼◐	x		
Narcissus cyclamineus	Cyclamen Daffodil	z5-7	☼		x	
Pachysandra terminalis	Japanese Spurge	z5-9	◐	x		
Phlomis fruticosa	Jerusalem Sage	z4-8	☼			x
Phlomis russeliana	Jerusalem Sage	z4-8	☼◐			x
Polystichum acrostichoides	Christmas Fern	z3-9	◐●	x		
Primula denticulata	Drumstick Primrose	z4-7	◐		x	
Primula vulgaris	English Primrose	z5-8	◐		x	
Pulmonaria angustifolia	Blue Lungwort	z2-7	◐		x	
Pulmonaria longifolia	Longleafed Lungwort	z3-8	◐		x	
Pulmonaria rubra	Red Lungwort	z4-7	◐		x	
Pulmonaria saccharata	Lungwort	z3-7	◐	x		
Puschkinia scilloides	Striped Squill	z4-9	☼		x	
Ranunculus ficaria	Lesser Celadine	z5-10	◐			x

Aesthetic-Winter Interest ...continued

Scientific Name	Common Name	Zone	Light	Foliage	Flower	Fruit
Rodgersia aesculifolia	Fingerleaf Rodgersia	z5-7	☼			x
Rodgersia pinnata	Featherleaf Rodgersia	z5-7	◐			x
Rudbeckia fulgida	Black-eyed Susan	z3-8	☼			x
Saxifraga x apiculata	Rockfoil Saxifrage	z6-9	☼	x		
Saxifraga x urbium	London Pride Saxifrage	z5-9	☼ ◐	x		
Scilla siberica	Siberian Squill	z2-7	☼		x	
Sedum 'Autumn Joy'	Autumn Joy Sedum	z3-8	☼			x
Sedum acre	Stonecrop	z3-8	☼	x		
Sedum kamtschaticum	Yellow Stonecrop	z3-8	☼	x		
Sedum spathulifolium	Stonecrop	z5-9	☼	x		
Sedum spurium	Two Row Stonecrop	z3-8	· ☼	x		
Sedum stefco	Stefanov Sedum	z5-9	☼	x		
Stachys byzantina 'Silver Carpet'	Lamb's Ears	z4-7	☼	x		
Stipa gigantea	Giant Feather Grass	z7-9	☼	x		x
Tanacetum parthenium aureum	Golden Feverfew	z4-10	☼	x		
Tellima grandiflora rubra	Fringe-Cup	z4-7	☼ ◐ ◐	x		
Teucrium chamaedrys	Germander	z4-9	☼	x		
Tiarella cordifolia	Allegheny Foamflower	z3-8	◐ ◐	x		
Tiarella wherryi	Wherry's Foamflower	z4-8	☼ ◐	x		

Aesthetic-Winter Interest ...continued

Scientific Name	Common Name	Zone	Light	Foliage	Flower	Fruit
Vinca minor	Myrtle	z4-8	☼ ☼ ☀	x		
Viola riviniana	European Dog Violet	z4-8	☼	x		
Waldsteinia ternata	Siberian Barrenwort	z3-9	☼ ☀	x		

Environmental-Crevices

Scientific Name	Common Name	Zone	Light
Acaena microphylla	New Zealand Bur	z7-9	☼
Aethionema armeneum	Turkish Stonecress	z5-7	☼
Aethionema grandiflorum	Persian Stonecress	z5-7	☼
Aethionema iberideum	Iberis Stonecress	z5-7	☼ ☀
Aethionema 'Warley Rose'	Stonecress	z4-8	☼
Alyssum montanum	Basket of Gold	z4-8	☼
Aquilegia alpina	Alpine Columbine	z3-8	☼ ☀
Arabis caucasica	Wall Cress	z4-7	☼
Aubrieta deltoidea	False Rock Cress	z4-7	☼
Aurinia saxatilis	Basket-of-Gold	z2-7	☼
Campanula poscharskyana	Serbian Bellflower	z3-7	☀
Cerastium tomentosum	Snow-in-Summer	z2-7	☼
Corydalis lutea	Yellow Corydalis	z5-7	☼ ● ☀
Corydalis cheilanthifolia	Fernleaf Corydalis	z5-8	☀
Dianthus alpinus	Alpine Pink	z3-7	☼
Dianthus deltoides	Maiden Pinks	z3-8	☼ ☀
Erinus alpinus 'Semperflorens'	Hybrid Strawberry	z5-10	☼
Galium odoratum	Sweet Woodruff	z4-7	☀
Gaultheria procumbens	Wintergreen	z4-9	● ☀
Helianthemum nummularium	Sunrose	z5-7	☼

219

Environmental-Crevices ...continued

Scientific Name	Common Name	Zone	Light
Herniaria glabra	Rupturewort	z5-8	☼ ☀
Iberis saxatilis	Rock Candytuft	z2-7	☀
Iberis sempervirens	Candytuft	z3-8	☼ ☀
Lithodora diffusa 'Heavenly Blue'	Lithodora	z5-7	☼ ☀
Lysimachia nummularia	Creeping Jenny	z3-9	☀ ☼
Matthiola maritima	Virginia Stock	annual	☼
Phlox douglasii	Iceburg Phlox	z5-7	☼
Phlox subulata	Moss Phlox	z3-9	☀ ●
Ramonda myconi	Pyrenean Violet	z5-7	☀ (wall only)
Saxifraga cotyledon	Silver Saxifrage	z5-9	☼ ☀
Saxifraga umbrosa	Saxifrage	z5-9	● ☀
Sedum acre	Goldmoss Sedum	z3-8	☼
Sedum spathulifolium 'Cape Blanco'	Broadleaf Stonecrop	z5-9	☼
Sedum spurium	Two Row Stonecrop	z3-8	☼
Thymus x citriodorus	Lemon Thyme	z6-10	☼
Thymus praecox	Creeping Thyme	z5-7	☼
Thymus serphyllum	Wild Thyme	z5-8	● ☀
Viola labradorica	Labrador Violet	z3-8	● ☀

Environmental-Erosion Control

Scientific Name	Common Name	Zone	Light
Adiantum pedatum	Maidenhair Fern	z2-8	☼ ●
Calamagrostis brachytricha	Feather Reed Grass	z4-9	☼ ☼
Calamintha nepeta	Calamint	z4-7	☼
Convallaria majalis	Lily-of-the-Valley	z2-7	☼ ●
Dryopteris marginalis	Marginal Wood Fern	z2-8	☼ ●
Eragrostis curvula	Weeping Love Grass	z7-9	☼
Eupatorium cannabinum	Hemp Agrimony	z5-8	☼
Eupatorium fistulosum	Hollow Joe Pye Weed	z4-8	☼
Eupatorium rugosum	White Snakeroot	z3-7	☼ ☼
Fragaria vesca	Wild Strawberry	z5-10	☼
Gaillardia x grandiflora	Blanket Flower	z2-9	☼
Hedera helix	English Ivy	z5-9	☼ ●
Hemerocallis flava	Daylily	z3-9	☼ ☼
Hemerocallis fulva	Daylily	z3-9	☼ ☼
Liriope muscari	Lily Turf	z6-10	☼ ●
Liriope spicata	Creeping Liriope	z4-10	☼ ●
Onoclea sensibilis	Sensitive Fern	z3-8	☼ ●
Osmunda cinnamomea	Cinnamon Fern	z3-8	☼ ●
Osmunda claytoniana	Interupted Fern	z3-8	☼ ●
Osmunda regalis	Royal Fern	z3-9	☼ ●

Environmental-Erosion Control ...continued

Scientific Name	Common Name	Zone	Light
Pachysandra terminalis	Japanese Spurge	z5-9	☀
Panicum spp.	Switch Grass	z4-9	☼ ☀
Perovskia atriplicifolia	Russian Sage	z5-9	☼
Petasities japonicus	Japanese Butterbur	z5-9	● ☀
Polygonium commutatum	Great Solomon's Seal	z3-7	☀ ●
Pteridium	Bracken Fern	z3-10	☼ ☀
Rudbeckia fulgida	Black-Eyed Susan	z3-8	☼
Rudbeckia laciniata	Cutleaf Coneflower	z3-9	☼ ☀
Rudbeckia speciosa	Dwarf Orange Coneflower	z4-8	☼ ☀
Sedum middendorfianum	Middendorf's Sedum	z4-8	☼ ☀
Sedum rupestre	Angelina Sedum	z6-8	☼
Sorghastrum nutans	Indian Grass	z4-9	☼
Spartina pectinata	Prairie Cord Grass	z4-9	☼ ☀
Tiarella cordifolia	Allegheny Foamflower	z3-8	☀ ●
Tradescantia	Spiderwort	z4-9	☼ ☀
Vinca minor	Myrtle	z4-8	☼ ☀ ●
Waldsteinia ternata	Siberian Barrenwort	z3-9	☼ ☀

Environmental-Foot Traffic

Scientific Name	Common Name	Zone	Light	Tolerance Level
Ajuga reptans 'Chocolate Chip'	Bugle Weed	z3-9	☼ ☼ ●	Moderate
Azorella trifurcata 'Nana'	Emerald Cushion	z7-10	☼ ☼	Moderate
Chamaemelum nobile	Chamomile	z4-10	☼ ☼	Light
Cymbalaria aequitriloba	Kenilworth Ivy	z6-10	☼ ●	Light
Fragaria x 'Lipstick'	Strawberry	z3-10	☼ ☼	Light
Herniaria glabra	Rupturewort	z5-9	☼ ☼	Heavy
Istomoa fluviatilis	Blue Star Creeper	z6-9	☼ ☼	Heavy
Leptinella gruveri	Miniature Brass Buttons	z7-9	☼ ☼	Heavy
Leptinella x 'Platt's Black'	Black Brass Buttons	z5-8	☼ ●	Moderate
Leptinella squalida	Green Brass Buttons	z5-9	☼ ☼	Heavy
Liriope muscari	Blue LilyTurf	z6-10	☼ ☼ ●	Heavy
Lotus corniculatus 'Plenus'	Bird's Foot Trefoil	z2-9	☼ ☼	Heavy
Lysimachia nummularia	Creeping Jenny	z3-9	☼ ☼ ●	Moderate
Mazus reptans	Mazus	z3-10	☼ ☼ ●	Moderate
Mentha requienii	Corsican Mint	z6-9	☼ ☼	Heavy
Muehlenbeckia axillaris	Creeping Wire Vine	z6-9	☼ ☼	Heavy
Ophipogon planiscapus	Black Mondo Grass	z6-9	☼ ☼	Light
Pratia pendunculata 'County Park'	Blue Star Creeper	z6-9	☼ ☼	Heavy
Sagina subulata	Pearlwort	z4-7	☼ ☼	Heavy
Sedum acre	Goldmoss Sedum	z3-8	☼ ☼	Moderate

Environmental-Foot Traffic

Scientific Name	Common Name	Zone	Light	Tolerance Level
Sedum requieni	Miniature Stonecrop	z4-8	☀	Heavy
Thymus psuedolanuginosus	Woolly Thyme	z5-8	☀	Moderate
Thymus serphyllum 'Elfin'	Wild Thyme	z5-8	☀	Heavy
Trifolium repens 'Atropurpureum'	Black Leaved Shamrock	z5-9	☀	Moderate
Veronica repens	Harebell Speedwell	5-10	☀	Moderate
Veronica surculosa	Speedwell	z4-9	☀	Moderate
Viola labradorica	Labrador Violet	z3-8	☀◐	Moderate

Environmental-Low pollen/Allergen

Simple changes in a landscape plan will help those who suffer from allergies and asthma enjoy a garden. Pollen is very frequently the cause of an asthma attack. Avoid plants with strong fragrances or odors, as they too can cause breathing difficulties. Mulching with rock or gravel instead of bark will cut down on mold and pollen spores in the garden. Fresh air and light will also reduce molds.

Low Pollen

Scientific Name	Common Name	Zone	Light	
Acanthus mollis	Common Bear's Breeches	z7-9	☼ ☀	
Aethionema spp.	Stonecress	z5-7	☼	
Agapanthus spp.	African Lily	z7-10	☼	
Ajuga spp.	Bugle Weed	z3-9	☼ ☀ ●	
Alcea spp.	Hollyhock	z3-7	☼	
Allium schoenoprasum	Chives	z3-10	☼	
Anchusa spp.	Alkanet	z3-9	☼ ☀	
Androsace spp.	Rock Jasmine	z4-6	☼	
Antennaria dioica	Pussy Toes	z4-9	☼	(females)
Antirrhinum majus	Snapdragon	annual	☼	
Aquilegia spp.	Columbine	z3-8	☼ ☀	
Arabis spp.	Rock Cress	z4-7	☼	
Armeria maritima	Sea Thrift	z4-8	☼	
Armoracia rusticana	Horseradish	z3-10	☼	

225

Environmental-Low Pollen/Allergen-Low...continued

Scientific Name	Common Name	Zone	Light
Asarum spp.	Ginger	z4-8	☼ ●
Aubrieta	Rock Cress	z4-7	☼ ☼
Baptisia australis	False Blue Indigo	z3-8	☼ ☼
Bergenia spp.	Bergenia	z4-8	☼ ☼
Bletilla striata	Hyacinth Bletilla	z5-9	☼ ☼
Brunnera macrophylla	Siberian Bugloss	z3-8	☼ ●
Caltha palustris	Marsh Marigold	z3-8	☼
Campanula	Bellflower	z3-8	☼ ☼
Centrathus ruber	Red Valerian	z5-10	☼
Chionodoxa luciliae	Glory-of-the-Snow	z4-8	☼
Clarkia	Clarkia	annual	☼
Claytonia virginica	Spring Beauty	z4-7	☼
Clintonia umbellulata	Bride's Bellflower	z5-7	☼ ☼
Coleus hybrids	Coleus	annual	☼
Colocasia spp.	Elephant's Ears	z7-10	☼ ☼
Cortaderia selloana	Pampas Grass	z6-9	☼ (female)
Crocus chrysanthus	Golden Crocus	z4-7	☼
Cyclamen	Hardy Cyclamen	z5-9	☼
Cymbalaria aequitriloba	Kenilworth Ivy	z6-10	☼ ●
Diascia	Twinspur	annual	☼

Environmental-Low Pollen/Allergen-Low ...continued

Scientific Name	Common Name	Zone	Light
Digitalis purpurea	Foxglove	z4-8	☼
Dodecatheon meadia	Shooting Star	z4-8	☼ ☀
Echinopsis ritro	Globe Thistle	z3-8	☼
Epimedium spp.	Bishop's Hat	z5-9	☼
Erythronium spp.	Dog Tooth Violet	z3-7	☼
Fragaria spp.	Strawberry	z3-10	☼ ☼
Fritillaria imperialis	Crown Imperial	z5-7	☼ ☼
Galanthus nivalis	Snowdrops	z3-7	☼
Galium odoratum	Sweet Woodruff	z4-7	☼
Gaura lindheimeri	Gaura	z5-8	☼
Gentiana spp.	Gentian	z3-7	☼ ☼
Geum chiloense	Avens	z4-8	☼
Hepatica spp.	Liverleaf	z3-7	☀ ☼
Heuchera	Coral Bells	z3-8	☼ ☼
Hosta	Plantain Lily	z3-8	☀ ☼
Hypoestes phyllostachya	Polka-Dot Plant	annual	☼
Iberis sempervirens	Candytuft	z3-8	☼ ☼
Impatiens capensis	Jewelweed	z2-8	☀ ☼
Incarvillea delavayi	Hardy Gloxinia	z5-7	☼ ☼
Leucojum spp.	Snowflake	z4-8	☼ ☼

227

Environmental-Low Pollen/Allerge-Low ...continued

Scientific Name	Common Name	Zone	Light
Lewisia spp.	Lewisia	z6-8	☼
Linaria spp.	Toadflax	z3-9	☼
Malcolmia maritima	Stock	annual	☼
Marrubium vulgare	White Horehound	z3-10	☼ ☼
Mazus reptans	Mazus	z3-10	☼ ☼
Mertensia virginica	Virginia Bluebells	z3-8	☀
Moluccella laevis	Bells of Ireland	annual	☼
Myosotis	Forget-me-Nots	z3-7	☼
Nelumbo lutea	Lotus	z6-11	☼
Nemophila	Baby Blue Eyes	annual	☼
Ocimum basilicum	Basil	annual	☼
Oenothera spp.	Evening Primrose	z4-8	☼ ☼
Paeonia	Peony	z3-8	☼ ☼
Penstemon barbatus	Bearded Tongue	z2-8	☼
Penstemon digitalis	Smooth White Penstemon	z4-8	☼
Petunia	Petunia	annual	☼
Phormium tenax	New Zealand Flax	z8-10	☼
Phyllostachys	Bamboo	z6-10	☼ ☼
Physalis alkekengi	Chinese Lantern	z3-9	☼ ☼
Pimpinella anisum	Anise	annual	☼

Environmental-Low Pollen/Allergen-Low ...continued

Scientific Name	Common Name	Zone	Light
Platycodon grandiflorus	Balloon Flower	z3-7	☼
Polemonium caeruleum	Jacob's Ladder	z2-7	☼
Polygonatum multiflorum	Solomon's Seal	z4-7	☼ ●
Pontederia cordata	Pickerel Weed	z4-10	☼ ☼
Portulaca grandiflora	Moss Rose	annual	☼
Pulmonaria	Lungwort	z3-8	☼ ☼
Sagina subulata	Pearlwort	z4-7	☼ ☼
Salvia officinalis	Sage	z4-7	☼
Sedum spectabile	Stonecrop	z3-8	☼
Sempervivum tectorum	Hens and Chicks	z3-7	☼
Shortia soldanelloides	Fringe Bells	z6-8	●
Sisyrinchium bellum	Blue-Eyed Grass	z5-8	☼ ☼
Tellima grandiflora	Fringe Cup	z4-7	☼ ● ☼
Teucrium chamaedrys	Germander	z4-9	☼
Thunbergia	Black-Eyed Susan	annual	☼
Veronica longifolia	Speedwell	z4-8	☼ ☼
Vinca minor	Myrtle	z4-8	☼ ● ☼
Viola odorata	Sweet Violet	z5-10	☼ ☼
Waldsteinia fragarioides	Barren Strawberry	z4-7	☼ ☼
Yucca filamentosa	Adam's Needle	z5-9	☼

Environmental-Low Pollen/Allergen-Medium

Scientific Name	Common Name	Zone	Light
Aconitum napellus	Monkshood	z3-6	☀
Agastache foeniculum	Anise Hyssop	z6-9	☀
Alstroemeria aurea	Peruvian Lily	z7-10	☀
Anemone x hybrida	Hybrid Windflower	z5-7	☀
Anethum graveolens	Dill	annual	☀
Arctostaphylos uva-ursi	Bearberry	z2-6	☀ ☀
Arenaria spp.	Sandwort	z4-7	☀
Aristolochia macrophylla	Dutchman's Pipe	z4-8	☀ ☀
Asclepias incarnata	Swamp Milkweed	z3-7	☀
Asclepias tuberosa	Butterfly Weed	z4-9	☀
Camassia leichtlinii	Leichtlin Quamash	z5-9	☀ ☀
Canna	Canna	z7-10	☀
Cerastium tomentosum	Snow-in-Summer	z2-7	☀
Ceratostigma plumbaginoides	Plumbago	z5-8	☀ ☀
Cimicifuga spp.	Bugbane	z3-7	☀ ☀
Colchicum autumnale	Autumn Crocus	z4-7	☀ ☀
Consolida ambigua	Larkspur	annual	☀
Crocosmia	Montbretia	z5-8	☀
Cynara	Cardoon	z7-10	☀
Delosperma spp.	Iceplant	z4-8	☀ ☀

Environmental-Low Pollen/Allergen-Medium ...continued

Scientific Name	Common Name	Zone	Light
Delphinium spp.	Delphinium	z2-7	☀
Dianthus barbatus	Sweet William	z3-8	☼
Eucomis bicolor	Pineapple flower	z8-10	☼
Fuchsia	Fuchsia	annual	☼ ☀
Geranium sanguineum	Cranesbill	z4-8	☼
Gladiolus	Gladiolus	z7-10	☼
Helianthemum nummularium	Sunrose	z5-7	☼
Hemerocallis	Daylily	z3-9	☼ ☀
Hyssopus officinalis	Hyssop	z3-11	☼ ☀
Lamium maculatum	Spotted Nettle	z3-8	☼ ☀
Lathyrus odorata	Sweet Pea	z5-7	☼ ☀
Limonium sinuatum	Statice	annual	☼
Liriope muscari	Lily Turf	z6-9	☼ ☀
Liriope spicata	Creeping Liriope	z4-10	☼ ☀
Lupinus	Lupine	z3-6	☼
Lychnis coronaria	Rose Campion	z4-7	☼
Mentha	Mint	z3-7	☼ ☀
Nicotiana	Flowering Tobacco	annual	☼
Osmunda cinnamomea	Cinnamon Fern	z3-8	☼ ☀
Passiflora spp.	Passion Flower	z7-11	☼ ☀

Environmental-Low Pollen/Allergen-Medium ...continued

Scientific Name	Common Name	Zone	Light
Phlomis fruticosa	Jerusalem Sage	z4-8	☼ ☼
Physostegia virginiana	Obedient Plant	z2-9	☼ ☼
Saponaria ocymoides	Soapwort	z2-7	☼
Sarracenia purpurea	Pitcher Plant	z4-9	☼ ☼
Satureja hortensis	Summer Savory	annual	☼
Scabiosa columbaria	Pincushion Flower	z3-9	☼ ☼
Silene armeria	Catchfly	annual	☼
Smilacina racemosa	False Solomon's Seal	z3-7	☼ ◑
Stachys byzantina	Lamb's Ear	z4-8	☼
Symphytum officinale	Comfrey	z4-7	☼ ☼
Thymus vulgaris	Garden Thyme	z4-10	☼
Torenia	Wishbone Flower	annual	◑
Tropaeolum majus	Nasturtium	annual	☼
Zinnia elegans	Zinnia	annual	☼

Environmental-Native

Incorporating plants that occur naturally offers many benefits to the ecosystem, improves our environment and connects us with nature. Native plants attract a diverse variety of birds, butterflies and other wildlife to the landscape. These plants do not need fertilizers, herbicides, pesticides or watering once established, saving time and money. Plants should be chosen according to the growing conditions of the area to be planted.

Scientific Name	Common Name	Zone	Light
Aconitum reclinatum	Monkshood	z5-8	☼ ☼
Actaea pachypoda	Baneberry	z3-7	☼ ●
Actaea rubra	Red Baneberry	z3-7	☼ ●
Agastache foeniculum	Anise Hyssop	z6-9	☼
Agastache rugosa	Purple Giant Hyssop	z5-8	☼
Amorpha canescens	Leadplant	z2-9	☼
Amsonia hubrichtii	Arkansas Amsonia	z6-9	☼ ☼
Amsonia tabermaemontana	Bluestar	z4-9	☼
Anaphalis margaritacea	Pearly Everlasting	z4-7	☼ ☼
Anemone canadensis	Meadow Anemone	z3-7	☼
Anemonella thalictroides	Rue-Anemone	z4-8	☼ ●
Antennaria neglecta	Pussytoes	z5-9	☼
Antennaria rupicola	Small Pussytoes	z4-7	☼
Aquilegia caerulea	Rocky Mountain Columbine	z3-8	☼ ☼
Aquilegia canadensis	Wild Columbine	z3-9	☼ ☼
Aquilegia chrysantha	Golden Columbine	z3-10	☼ ☼

233

Environmental-Native...continued

Scientific Name	Common Name	Zone	Light
Arctostaphylos uva-ursi	Bearberry	z2-6	☼ ☀
Arisaema draconitium	Green Dragon	z4-8	☀ ●
Arisaema triphyllum	Jack-in-the-Pulpit	z4-9	☀ ●
Artemisia ludoviciana	White Sage	z4-9	☼
Artemisia stelleriana	Beach Wormwood	z4-8	☼
Aruncus dioicus	Goatsbeard	z3-7	☼ ☀
Asarum arifolium	Arrow-Leaf Ginger	z4-8	●
Asarum canadense	Canadian Ginger	z3-7	☀ ●
Asclepias incarnata	Swamp Milkweed	z3-7	☼ ☀
Asclepias tuberosa	Butterfly Weed	z4-9	☼
Aster azureus	Skyblue Aster	z4-9	☼
Aster cordifolius	Heart-Leaf Aster	z3-8	☼
Aster divaricatus	White Wood Aster	z4-8	☼
Aster lateriflorus	Calico Aster	z5-7	☼
Aster laevis	Smooth Aster	z3-9	☼
Aster novae-angliae	New England Aster	z4-8	☼
Aster novi-belgii	New York Aster	z4-8	☼
Aster oblongifolius	Aromatic Aster	z3-8	☼
Astilbe biternata	American Astilbe	z4-8	☀
Athyrium filex-femina	Lady Fern	z4-8	☀ ●

Environmental-Native...continued

Scientific Name	Common Name	Zone	Light
Baptisia alba	Wild White Indigo	z5-8	☼
Baptisia australis	False Blue Indigo	z3-8	☼☼
Baptisia tinctoria	Yellow Wild Indigo	z5-8	☼
Boltonia asteroides	White Boltonia	z4-8	☼
Callirhoe involucrata	Poppy Mallow	z4-7	☼
Caltha palustris	Marsh Marigold	z3-8	☼
Campanula rotundifolia	Harebell	z3-9	☼☼
Caulophyllum thalictroides	Blue Cohosh	z3-7	●☼
Chelone glabra	White Turtlehead	z3-7	☼
Chelone lyonii	Turtlehead	z3-7	☼
Chelone obliqua	Turtlehead	z5-8	☼
Chimaphila maculata	Pipsissewa	z4-7	●☼☼
Chrysogonum virginianum	Goldenstar	z6-9	☼☼
Cimicifuga americana	American Bugbane	z3-7	☼
Claytonia virginica	Spring Beauty	z4-7	☼
Coreopsis auriculata	Tickseed	z4-9	☼
Coreopsis grandiflora	Tickseed	z4-9	☼
Coreopsis lanceolata	Lanceleaf Coreopsis	z3-8	☼
Coreopsis rosea	Pink Coreopsis	z4-7	☼
Coreopsis verticillata	Thread Leaf Coreopsis	z5-10	☼

Environmental-Native ...continued

Scientific Name	Common Name	Zone	Light
Cornus canadensis	Bunchberry	z2-7	☼
Dicentra cucullaria	Dutchman's Breeches	z3-7	☼
Dicentra eximia	Fringed Bleeding Heart	z3-9	☼
Dicentra formosa	Pacific Bleeding Heart	z3-9	● ☼
Dodecatheon meadia	Shooting Star	z4-8	● ☼
Dryopteris marginalis	Marginal Shield Fern	z2-8	● ☼
Echinacea pallida	Pale Coneflower	z4-8	☼
Echinacea paradoxa	Yellow Coneflower	z4-7	☼
Echinacea purpurea	Purple Coneflower	z3-8	☼
Epilobium augustifolium	Willowherb	z2-10	☼
Erigeron philadelphicus	Common Fleabane	z3-8	☼
Eryngium yuccifolium	Rattlesnake Master	z4-8	☼
Erythronium albidum	White Trout Lily	z4-8	☀
Erythronium americanum	American Trout Lily	z3-8	● ☀
Euptorium coelestinum	Mist Flower	z5-10	☼
Eupatorium maculatum	Spotted Joe Pye Weed	z3-8	☀
Eupatorium perfoliatum	Common Boneset	z3-8	☼ ☀
Eupatorium purpureum	Joe Pye Weed	z4-8	☼ ☀
Eupatorium rugosum	White Snakeroot	z3-7	☼ ☀
Filipendula rubra	Queen-of-the-Prairie	z3-7	☀

Environmental-Native ...continued

Scientific Name	Common Name	Zone	Light
Gaillardia x grandiflora	Blanket Flower	z2-9	☼
Gaultheria procumbens	Wintergreen	z4-9	◑ ☼
Gaura lindheimeri	White Gaura	z5-8	☼
Gentiana andrewsii	Bottle Gentian	z3-7	☼
Geum triflorum	Prairie Smoke	z1-7	☼
Geum triflorum var. campanulatum	Prairie Smoke	z1-7	☼
Gillenia trifoliata	Bowman's Root	z4-7	☼
Helenium autumnale	Sneezeweed	z3-8	☼
Helianthus angustifolius	Swamp Sunflower	z6-9	☼
Helianthus giganteus	Giant Sunflower	z5-9	☼
Heliopsis helianthoides	Sunflower Heliopsis	z3-9	☼
Hepatica acutiloba	Hepatica	z3-9	◑ ☼
Hepatica americana	Round-Lobed Liverleaf	z3-7	◑ ☼
Heuchera americana	American Alumroot	z4-9	☼ ◑
Heuchera micrantha	Small Flowered Alumroot	z4-7	◑
Heuchera sanguinea	Coral Bells	z3-8	◑
Heuchera villosa	Hairy Alumroot	z6-9	◑ ☼
Hibiscus moscheutos	Common Mallow	z5-9	☼ ◑
Houstonia longifolia	Summer Bluet	z3-9	☼ ◑

Environmental-Native ...continued

Scientific Name	Common Name	Zone	Light
Iris cristata	Dwarf Crested Iris	z3-8	☼
Iris fulva	Beardless Iris	z6-11	☼ ☼
Iris hexagona	Hexagonal Iris	z6-9	☼ ☼
Iris nelsonii	Louisiana Iris	z4-9	☼ ☼
Iris virginica	Blue Flag Iris	z5-9	☼
Jeffersonia dubia	Twinleaf	z5-8	☼ ●
Liatris scariosa	Devil's Bite	z3-9	☼ ☼
Liatris spicata	Spike Gayfeather	z3-9	☼
Lilium canadense	Canada Lily	z4-9	☼ ●
Lilium michauxii	Carolina Lily	z6-10	☼ ☼
Lilium philadelphicum	Wood Lily	z4-7	☼ ☼
Lilium superbum	American Turk's Cap Lily	z4-8	☼ ☼
Lobelia cardinalis	Cardinal Flower	z2-9	☼ ☼
Lobelia siphilitica	Great Blue Lobelia	z4-8	☼ ☼
Lupinus perennis	Sundial Lupine	z3-9	☼
Lysichiton americanum	Skunk Cabbage	z5-7	☼ ●
Matteuccia struthiopteris	Ostrich Fern	z2-10	● ☼
Mertensia virginica	Virginia Bluebells	z3-8	●
Monarda didyma	Bee Balm	z3-7	☼ ☼
Monarda fistulosa	Wild Bergamot	z3-7	☼

Environmental-Native...continued

Scientific Name	Common Name	Zone	Light
Oenothera fruticosa	Common Sundrops	z4-8	☼
Oenothera missouriensis	Ozark Sundrops	z4-7	☼ ☀
Oenothera perennis	Nodding Sundrops	z3-8	☼
Oenothera speciosa	Showy Evening Primrose	z3-8	☼
Onoclea sensibilis	Sensitive Fern	z3-8	☼ ☀
Opuntia humifusa	Prickly Pear Cactus	z4-10	☼
Osmunda cinnamomea	Cinnamon Fern	z3-8	☼ ●
Osmunda claytoniana	Interrupted Fern	z3-8	☼ ●
Osmunda regalis	Royal Fern	z3-9	☼ ●
Pachysandra procumbens	Allegheny Pachysandra	z5-9	●
Papaver nudicaule	Iceland Poppy	z2-7	☼
Penstemon barbatus	Common Bearded Tongue	z2-8	☼
Penstemon digitalis	Smooth White Penstemon	z4-8	☼
Penstemon hirsutus	Eastern Penstemon	z3-8	☼
Penstemon smallii	Small's Penstemon	z6-8	☼ ●
Phlox divaricata	Woodland Phlox	z3-8	☼ ●
Phlox maculata	Spotted Phlox	z3-8	☼ ●
Phlox paniculata	Garden Phlox	z4-8	☼ ●
Phlox stolonifera	Creeping Phlox	z2-8	☼ ●
Phlox subulata	Moss Phlox	z2-8	☼

Environmental-Native ...continued

Scientific Name	Common Name	Zone	Light
Physostegia virginiana	Obedient Plant	z2-9	☼
Podophyllum peltatum	Mayapple	z3-9	☼
Polemonium reptans	Creeping Polemonium	z3-8	☼
Polygonatum biflorum	Small Solomon's Seal	z3-7	●☼
Polygonatum commutatum	Great Solomon's Seal	z3-7	●☼
Polystichum acrostichoides	Christmas Fern	z3-9	☼●
Rudbeckia fulgida	Black-eyed Susan	z3-8	☼
Rudbeckia hirta	Black-eyed Susan	z3-8	☼
Rudbeckia laciniata	Cutleaf Coneflower	z3-9	☼●
Rudbeckia maxima	Giant Coneflower	z5-9	☼
Rudbeckia triloba	Three Lobed Coneflower	z3-10	☼●
Sanguisorba canadensis	Burnet	z3-7	☼
Sidalcea malviflora	Checkermallow	z5-7	☼●
Silene caroliniana	Carolina Campion	z5-8	☼●
Silene polypetala	Fringed Campion	z6-8	☼
Silene regia	Campion	z5-8	☼
Silene virginica	Fire Pink	z4-8	☼●☼
Sisyrinchium augustifolium	Blue Eyed Grass	z3-8	☼
Smilacina racemosa	False Solomon's Seal	z3-7	●☼●

Environmental-Native ...continued

Scientific Name	Common Name	Zone	Light
Solidago canadensis	Goldenrod	z3-9	☼
Spigelia marilandica	Indian Pink Pinkroot	z5-9	☼ ☀
Spiranthes odorata	Ladies Tresses	z5-8	☼
Stokesia	Stokes Aster	z5-9	☼
Stylophorum diphyllum	Celandine Poppy	z4-8	☼ ☀
Thermopsis caroliniana	Southern Lupine	z3-9	☼
Tiarella cordifolia	Allegheny Foamflower	z3-8	☼ ☀
Tradescantia ohiensis	Common Spiderwort	z4-9	☼ ☼
Tradescantia virginiana	Spiderwort	z4-9	☼ ☼
Trillium cernuum	Nodding Trillium	z2-8	☀
Trillium cuneatum	Toad Trillium	z6-9	☼ ☀
Trillium erectum	Stinking Benjamin	z4-9	☼ ● ☀
Trillium grandiflorum	Great White Trillium	z4-9	☼ ☀
Trillium luteum	Yellow Trillium	z4-7	☼ ☀
Trillium sessile	Toad Trillium	z4-7	☼ ● ☀
Uvularia grandiflora	Large Flowered Bellwort	z3-9	●
Uvularia perfoliata	Bellwort	z3-9	☼ ☀
Uvularia sessilifolia	Bellwort	z3-9	☼ ● ☀
Vancouveria hexandra	American Barrenwort	z5-7	☼ ● ☀
Veratrum viride	Indian Poke	z3-7	☼ ● ☀

Environmental-Native ...continued

Scientific Name	Common Name	Zone	Light
Vernonia noveboriensis	Ironweed	z5-9	☼ ☀
Viola labradorica	Labrador Violet	z3-8	☀ ☀
Viola pedata	Bird's Foot Violet	z4-8	☼ ☀
Waldsteinia fragarioides	Barren Strawberry	z4-7	☼ ☀
Yucca filamentosa	Adams Needle	z5-9	☼

Environmental-Naturalizing

Many native species are the best choices for naturalizing a landscape . These plants are perfect because they perform well in endemic soils and climates. Careful selection should be made to work with the ecosystem of the area. Naturalization may be used to the benefit of a landscape requiring minimal care and adding beneficial plants to the environment. This list consists of native and non-native species.

Naturalization is very effective in an unrefined setting, but some plants may become 'weeds' in small or formal settings. Limiting the palette of colors within a naturalized area is advisable as too many colors will give an unnatural effect.

Scientific Name	Common Name	Zone	Light
Achillea millefolium	Yarrow	z2-9	☼
Ajuga reptans	Bugle Weed	z3-9	☼ ☀ ●
Aquilegia spp.	Columbine	z3-8	☼ ☀
Asclepias tuberosa	Butterfly Weed	z4-9	☼
Baptisia australis	False Blue Indigo	z3-8	☀
Campanula rotundifolia	Harebell	z3-9	☼ ☀
Cerastium tomentosum	Snow-in-Summer	z2-7	☼
Convallaria majalis	Lily-of-the-Valley	z2-7	☀ ●
Coreopsis lanceolata	Lanceleaf Coreopsis	z3-8	☼
Crocus vernus	Crocus	z3-8	☼ ☀
Dicentra eximia	Fringed Bleeding Heart	z3-9	☀
Dicentra formosa	Bleeding Heart	z3-9	☀
Echinacea purpurea	Purple Coneflower	z3-8	☼
Ferns-See Fern Section- Mass column			

Environmental-Naturalizing...continued

Scientific Name	Common Name	Zone	Light
Hosta spp.	Plantain Lily	z3-8	☼ ☀
Hyacinthoides hispanica	Spanish Bluebell	z4-7	☀ ☀
Liatris spp.	Spike Gayfeather	z3-9	☼
Lobelia cardinalis	Cardinal Lobelia	z2-9	☼ ☀
Monarda didyma	Bee Balm	z3-7	☼ ☀
Narcissus	Daffodil	z4-9	☼ ☀
Penstemon grandiflorus	Large Beard Tongue	z3-9	☼
Phlox divaricata	Woodland Phlox	z3-8	☀ ☀
Phlox stolonifera	Creeping Phlox	z4-9	☀ ☀
Phlox subulata	Moss Phlox	z3-9	☼
Physostegia virginiana	Obedient Plant	z2-9	☀
Rudbeckia fulgida	Black-Eyed Susan	z3-8	☼
Tradescantia x andersoniana	Spiderwort	z4-9	☼ ☀
Veronica spp.	Speedwell	z4-8	☼
Viola spp.	Violet	z4-8	☼ ☀

Econonmical-Plants to Provide Quick Cover

Many unwanted plants can be eliminated with sustainable landscape solutions. Unwanted weedy plants grow in newly excavated empty spaces. It is very important to provide quick cover of desirable plants. Choose plants that will compliment the landscape.

Scientific Name	Common Name	Zone	Light
Acaena anserinifolia	Goose-Leaf Bur	z7-9	☼
Alchemilla mollis	Lady's Mantle	z4-7	☼ ☼
Anthemis punctata ssp. cupaniana	Dog's Fennel	z6-9	☼
Arabis caucasica	Wall Rock Cress	z4-7	☼
Aubrieta deltoids	False Rock Cress	z4-7	☼
Campanula poscharskyana	Serbian Bellflower	z3-7	☼
Euphorbia amygdaloides var. robbiae	Wood Spurge	z5-8	☼ ☼
Geranium macrorrhizum	Bigroot Geranium	z3-8	☼ ☼
Helianthemum nummularium	Sunrose	z5-7	☼
Lamium maculatum	Spotted Nettle	z3-8	☼
Monarda didyma	Bee Balm	z3-7	☼ ☼
Phlox douglasii	Alpine Phlox	z5-7	☼
Phlox subulata	Moss Phlox	z3-9	☼
Phuopsis stylosa	Crosswort	z5-8	☼
Polygonum affine	Himalayan Fleece Flower	z4-8	☼
Polygonum vacciniifolium	Vaccinium Fleece Flower	z5-7	☼
Portulaca grandiflora	Moss Rose	annual	☼

Economical-Plants to Provide Quick Cover

Scientific Name	Common Name	Zone	Light
Pulmonaria 'Bertram Anderson'	Long-Leafed Lungwort	z3-8	☼ ☀
Sanvitalia procumbens	Creeping Zinnia	annual	☼
Saxifraga stolonifera	Strawberry Begonia	z7-9	☀
Stachys byzantina	Lamb's Ears	z4-7	☼
Symphytum x uplandicum 'Variegatum'	Variegated Russian Comfrey	z4-7	☼
Tiarella cordifolia	Allegheny Foamflower	z3-8	☼ ☀
Tropaeolum majus	Nasturtium	annual	☼
Waldsteinia fragarioides	Barren Strawberry	z4-7	☼ ☀

Economical-Plants that Self Sow

Self-sowing annuals and perennials usually reseed every year. The annuals, however, are not as predictable as the perennials. These self sowers seem to come up where they please, sometimes in a distant bed. They will often come back en masse and then sometimes not at all. Reseeding in heavily mulched gardens will not be as reliable. Self seeding annuals and perennials are inexpensive and fill in the gaps in a garden.

Annuals

Scientific Name	Common Name	Light
Anethum graveolens	Dill	☼
Antirrhinum majus	Snapdragon	☼
Browallia americana	Bush Violet	☼ ☀
Bupleurum rotundifolium	Hare's Ear	☼ ☀
Calendula officinalis	Pot Marigold	☀
Centaurea cyanus	Cornflower	☼
Cleome spinosa	Spider Flower	☼
Consolida ambigua	Larkspur	☼
Consolida orientalis	Oriental Knight's Larkspur	☼ ☀
Consolida regalis	Royal Knight's-spur	☼ ☀
Coreopsis tinctoria	Tickseed	☼
Coriandrum sativum	Coriander	☀
Cosmidium burridgeanum	Burridge's Greenthread	☼
Cosmos bipinnatus	Mexican Aster	☼
Eschscholtzia californica	California Poppy	☼

Economical-Plants that Self Sow-Annuals ...continued

Scientific Name	Common Name	Light
Euphorbia marginata	Ghostweed	☼
Gilia	Globe Gilia	☼
Gypsophila elegans	Baby's Breath	☼
Ipomoea	Morning Glory	☼
Lavatera trimestris	Rose Mallow	☼
Linum grandiflorum	Scarlet Flax	☼
Lobularia maritima	Sweet Alyssum	☼
Mirabilis jalapa	Four O'Clocks	☼
Nicotiana sylvestris	Woodland Tobacco	☼
Nigella damascene	Love-in-a-Mist	☼
Papaver rhoeas	Corn Poppy	☼
Petunia hybrida	Petunia	☼
Portulaca grandiflora	Moss Rose	☼
Ricinus communis	Castor Bean	☼
Salvia farinacea	Mealy-Cup Sage	☼
Silene armeria	Catchfly	☼
Viola x wittrockiana	Pansy	☼ ☀

Economical-Plants that Self Sow-Perennials

Scientific Name	Common Name	Zone	Light
Althaea rosea	Marsh Mallow	z3-8	☼
Anchusa italica	Italian Bugloss	z3-9	☼
Anemone sylvestris	Snowdrop Anemone	z4-7	☀
Anthemis tinctoria	Golden Marguerite	z3-7	☼
Aquilegia caerulea	Rocky Mountain Columbine	z3-8	☼☀
Aquilegia canadensis	Wild Columbine	z3-9	☼☀
Aquilegia vulgaris	Columbine	z3-10	☼☀
Aster novae-angliae	New England Aster	z4-8	☼
Claytonia virginica	Spring Beauty	z4-7	☀
Coreopsis grandiflora	Tickseed	z4-9	☼
Coeopsis lanceolata	Lanceleaf Coreopsis	z3-8	☼
Corydalis lutea	Yellow Corydalis	z5-7	☀
Dianthus barbatus	Sweet William	z3-8	☼☀
Dicentra eximia	Fringed Bleeding Heart	z3-9	☀
Dicentra formosa	Western Bleeding Heart	z4-10	☼☀
Digitalis purpurea	Foxglove	z4-8	☀
Eryngium giganteum	Miss Willmott's Ghost	z4-9	☀
Foeniculum vulgare	Fennel	z6-9	☼
Geranium maculatum	Spotted Geranium	z3-8	☼☀
Heliopsis scabra	False Sunflower	z3-9	☼

Economical-Plants that Self Sow-Perennials ...continued

Scientific Name	Common Name	Zone	Light	
Helleborus orientalis	Lenten Rose	z4-9	☀	
Hesperis matronalis	Dame's Rocket	z3-9	☼	biennial
Lathyrus latifolius	Sweet Pea	z5-7	☼ ☀	
Linaria	Toadflax	z3-9	☼ ☀	
Linum perenne	Blue Flax	z5-8	☼ ☀	
Lunaria annua	Money Plant	z4-8	☼	biennial
Lychnis coronaria	Rose Campion	z4-7	☼	
Myosotis alpestris	Alpine Forget-Me-Not	z2-5	☼	
Myosotis sylvatica	Woodland Forget-Me-Not	z3-7	☀	
Papaver somniferum	Opium Poppy	z8-10	☼	
Penstemon barbatus	Common Bearded Tongue	z2-8	☼	
Penstemon digitalus	Smooth White Penstemon	z4-8	☀	
Penstemon hirsutus	Dwarf Hairy Penstemon	z4-8	☀	
Rudbeckia fulgida	Black-eyed Susan	z3-8	☼	
Verbascum chaixii	Mullein	z5-8	☼ ☀	
Verbena bonarensis	Butterfly Vervain	z6-9	☼	
Viola cornuta	Horned Violet	z6-9	☼ ☀	
Viola odorata	Sweet Violet	z5-10	☀	
Viola pedata	Bird's Foot Violet	z4-8	☼ ☀	

Deer and Rabbit Resistant

The plants represented are not usually favorites for deer and rabbits, although when very hungry will eat almost anything. Sometimes, however, fresh plantings are like the new smorgasbord in town. They all rush in to sample the new flavor in the garden. Young rabbits and fawn will try almost anything, but soon learn which plants to leave alone. Deer and rabbits generally dislike prickly, fuzzy or leathery leafed plants. They also dislike plants that are very aromatic or have caustic milky sap.

| Deer resistant plants = D | Rabbit resistant plants = R | | | | |
Scientific Name	Common Name	Zone	Light	Deer	Rabbit
Acanthus spinosus	Bear's Breeches	z6-10	☼		R
Achillea filipendulina	Fernleaf Yarrow	z3-8	☀	D	R
Achillea millefolium	Common Yarrow	z2-9			
Achillea hybrids	Common Yarrow	z3-8	☀	D	R
Achillea hybrids	Hybrid Yarrow	z3-8	☀	D	R
Aconitum carmichaelii	Azure Monkshood	z3-7	☼	D	R
Aconitum hybrids	Monkshood Hybrids	z4-8	☼	D	R
Aconitum napellus	Monkshood	z3-6	☼	D	R
Agapanthus	African Lily	z7-10	☼		R
Agastache 'Blue Fortune'	Anise Hyssop	z6-9	☼	D	
Agastache foeniculum	Anise Hyssop	z6-9	☀	D	
Ajuga reptans	Bugle Weed	z3-9	☼◐	D	R
Ajuga pyramidalis	Bugle Weed	z3-9	☼	D	R
Alcea rosea	Hollyhock	z3-7	☀		R
Alchemilla alpina	Mountain Lady's Mantle	z3-7	☼◐	D	R
Alchemilla erythropoda	Lady's Mantle	z3-7	☼	D	R

251

Deer & Rabbit Resistant ...continued

Deer resistant plants = D   Rabbit resistant plants = R

Scientific Name	Common Name	Zone	Light	Deer	Rabbit
Alchemilla mollis	Lady's Mantle	z4-7	☼	D	R
Allium schoenoprasum	Chives	z3-10	☼	D	
Althaea officinalis	Marsh Mallow	z3-8	☼		R
Amsonia hubrichtii	Arkansas Amsonia	z6-9	☼	D	
Anaphallis margaritacea	Pearly Everlasting	z4-7	☼	D	R
Anchusa azurea	Alkanet	z3-9	☼		R
Anemone blanda	Grecian Windflower	z4-7	☼	D	R
Anemone coronaria	Poppy Anemone	z6-9	☼	D	R
Anemone x hybrida	Hybrid Anemone	z5-7	☼	D	R
Anemone sylvestris	Snowdrop Anemone	z4-7	☼	D	R
Anemone tomentosa	Grapeleaf Anemone	z5-8	☼	D	R
Antennaria dioca	Pussytoes	z4-9	☼	D	
Aquilegia canadensis	Columbine	z3-9	☼	D	R
Artemisia absinthium	Wormwood	z3-9	☼	D	
Artemisia dracunculus	Tarragon	z5-9	☼	D	
Artemisia lactiflora	White Sage	z4-9	☼	D	
Artemisia ludoviciana	White Sage	z4-9	☼	D	
Artemisia schmidtiana 'Silver Mound'	Wormwood	z3-8	☼	D	
Aruncus sylvester	Goat's Beard	z3-7	☼		R
Asarum canadense	Canadian Ginger	z3-7	◐	D	
Asarum europaeum	European Ginger	z4-7	◐	D	

Deer & Rabbit Resistant ...continued

Deer resistant plants = D   Rabbit resistant plants = R

Scientific Name	Common Name	Zone	Light	Deer	Rabbit
Asclepias tuberosa	Butterfly Weed	z4-9	☼	D	
Aster spp.	Aster	z4-8	☀	D	R
Astilbe x arendsii	Astilbe	z4-9	☀	D	R
Astilbe chinensis 'Pumila'	Dwarf Chinese Astilbe	z4-8	☀	D	R
Athyrium filix-femina	Lady Fern	z3-9	☀ ●	D	R
Athyrium nipponicum 'Pictum'	Japanese Painted Fern	z4-8	☀ ●	D	R
Aurinia saxatilis	Basket-of-Gold	z3-7	☼	D	R
Bergenia cordifolia	Heart-Leaved Bergenia	z4-8	☀	D	R
Borago officinalis	Borage	annual	☼		R
Brunnera spp.	Siberian Bugloss	z3-8	☀ ●	D	R
Calamagrostis arundinacea	Feather Reed Grass	z4-8	☼	D	R
Calamintha nepeta	Calamint	z4-7	☼	D	
Caltha palustris	Marsh Marigold	z3-8	☼	D	
Campanula spp.	Bellflower	z3-8	☼ ☀	D	R
Carex	Sedge	z5-8	☼ ☀	D	
Caryopteris	Bluebeard	z6-9	☼	D	
Centaurea montana	Bachelor's Button	z3-8	☼ ☀	D	R
Cerastium tomentosum	Snow-in-Summer	z2-7	☼	D	R
Certostigma plumbaginoides	Plumbago	z5-8	☼ ☀	D	R
Chasmanthium latifolium	Northern Sea Oats	z3-8	☼ ☀	D	R

253

Deer & Rabbit Resistant ...continued

Deer resistant plants = D   Rabbit resistant plants = R

Scientific Name	Common Name	Zone	Light	Deer	Rabbit
Chelone	Turtlehead	z3-7	☼	D	
Cimicifuga americana	American Bugbane	z3-7	☼	D	
Clarkia amoena	Clarkia	annual	☼		R
Clematis spp.	Clematis	z4-8	☼	D	R
Colchicum cilicicum	Autumn Crocus	z5-7	☼		R
Convallaria majalis	Lily-of-the-Valley	z2-7	☼ ☀	D	R
Coreopsis auriculata	Mouse Ear Coreopsis	z4-9	☼	D	R
Coreopsis grandiflora	Tickseed	z4-9	☼	D	R
Coreopsis verticillata	Threadleaf Coreopsis	z5-9	☼	D	R
Cortaderia selloana	Pampas Grass	z6-9	☼	D	R
Corydalis lutea	Yellow Lutea	z5-7	☼ ☀	D	
Crinum bulbispermum	Orange River Lily	z6-10	☀		R
Crocosmia	Montbretia	z5-8	☼	D	R
Crocus spp.	Crocus	z4-9	☼	D	R
Cynara scolymus	Globe Artichoke	z8-9		D	R
Dahlia hybrids	Dahlia	z7-10	☼	D	R
Delphinium spp.	Delphinium	z2-7	☀	D	R
Dianthus barbatus	Sweet William	z3-8	☼ ☀	D	R
Dianthus plumarius	Cottage Pink	z3-8	☼	D	
Diascia spp.	Twinspur	z7-9	☼		R

Deer & Rabbit Resistant ...continued

Deer resistant plants = D   Rabbit resistant plants = R

Scientific Name	Common Name	Zone	Light	Deer	Rabbit
Dicentra spp.	Bleeding Hearts	z3-8	☼ ●	D	R
Digitalis purpurea	Foxglove	z4-8	☼ ●	D	
Dryopteris cristata	Crested Shield Fern	z4-9	☼ ●	D	R
Dryopteris erythrosora	Autumn Fern	z5-9	☼ ●	D	R
Dryopteris marginalis	Marginal Shield Fern	z2-8	☼ ●	D	R
Echinacea purpurea	Purple Coneflower	z3-8	☼	D	R
Echinops ritro	Globe Thistle	z3-8	☼	D	R
Echium vulgare	Viper's Bugloss	z2-9	☼		R
Epilobium augustifolium	Fire Weed	z2-10	☼		R
Epimedium x rubrum	Red Barrenwort	z5-8	☼ ●	D	R
Eremurus stenopyllus	Foxtail Lily	z5-8	☼	D	
Erigeron hybrids	Fleabane	z2-8	☼	D	R
Erianthus ravennae	Ravenna Grass	z5-9	☼ ●	D	R
Eryngium giganteum	Miss Wilmot's Ghost	z4-7	☼	D	R
Erythronium americanum	American Trout Lily	z3-8	☼ ●		R
Eschscholzia	California Poppy	annual	☼	D	R
Eupatorium coelestinum	Hardy Ageratum	z5-10	☼ ●	D	
Eupatorium purpureum	Joe Pye Weed	z4-8	☼ ●	D	R
Euphorbia polychroma	Spurge	z4-8	☼	D	R
Festuca glauca 'Elijah Blue'	Blue Fescue	z4-9	☼	D	R

255

Deer & Rabbit Resistant ...continued

Deer resistant plants = D   Rabbit resistant plants = R

Scientific Name	Common Name	Zone	Light	Deer	Rabbit
Filipendula vulgaris	Dropwort	z3-7	☼		R
Filipendula rubra	Queen-of-the-Prairie	z3-7	☼	D	R
Fragaria	Strawberry	z5-10	☼		R
Fritillaria imperialis	Crown Imperial	z5-7	☼☼	D	R
Gaillardia x grandiflora	Blanket Flower	z2-9	☼	D	R
Galium	Sweet Woodruff	z4-7	☼	D	R
Gentiana septemfida	Crested Gentian	z3-7	☼☼	D	
Geranium sanguineum	Cranesbill	z4-8	☼	D	R
Geum triflorum	Prairie Smoke	z1-7	☼	D	
Helenium autumnale	Sneezeweed	z3-8	☼	D	
Helianthus giganteus	Sunflower	annual	☼		R
Helichrysum bracteatum	Straw Flower	annual	☼	D	R
Helictotrichon sempervirens	Blue Oat Grass	z3-9	☼	D	R
Helleborus argutifolius var. corsicus	Corsican Hellebore	z6-8	☼☼	D	R
Helleborus orientalis	Lenten Rose	z4-9	☼	D	R
Hemerocallis	Daylily	z3-9	☼☼		R
Hesperis matronalis	Dame's Rocket	z3-8	☼	D	
Heuchera sanguinea	Coral Bells	z3-8	☼		R
Hibiscus moscheutos	Common Mallow	z5-9	☼☼	D	
Hypericum spp.	St. John's Wort	z5-9	☼	D	
Hyssopus offinalis	Hyssop	z3-11	☼☼	D	

Deer & Rabbit Resistant ...continued

Deer resistant plants = D   Rabbit resistant plants = R

Scientific Name	Common Name	Zone	Light	Deer	Rabbit
Iberis spp.	Candytuft	z3-8	☼	D	R
Impatiens spp.	Impatiens	annual	☼	D	R
Iris spp.	Iris	z3-8	☼◐	D	R
Kniphofia uvaria	Torchlily	z5-8	☼	D	R
Lamium maculatum	Spotted Nettle	z3-8	☼◐	D	R
Lavandula angustifolia	English Lavender	z5-9	◐	D	R
Lavandula stoechas	French Lavender	z7-10	◐	D	R
Lespedeza thunbergii	Thunburg Bush Clover	z4-7	◐	D	
Leucojum aestivum	Summer Snowflake	z4-8	◐		R
Liatris spicata	Spike Gayfeather	z3-9	◐	D	
Ligularia stenocephala	Spiked Ligularia	z5-9	◐☼	D	
Linaria purpurea	Toadflax	z3-9	◐	D	
Linum perenne	Blue Flax	z5-8	☼	D	
Liriope spicata	Creeping Liriope	z4-10	☼◐	D	R
Lobelia cardinalis	Cardinal Flower	z2-9	☼◐	D	R
Lunaria annua	Money Plant	z5-9 biennial	☼◐		R
Lychnis chalcedonica	Maltese Cross	z3-7	☼	D	R
Lychnis coronaria	Rose Campion	z4-7	◐	D	R
Lysimachia clethroides	Gooseneck Loosestrife	z3-8	◐		R
Malva moschata	Musk Mallow	z4-8	☼		R

Deer & Rabbit Resistant ...continued

Deer resistant plants = D   Rabbit resistant plants = R

Scientific Name	Common Name	Zone	Light	Deer	Rabbit
Marrubium vulgare	White Horehound	z3-10	☼	D	
Melissa officinalis	Lemon Balm	z4-10	☼☼	D	
Mentha suaveolens	Apple Mint	z5-10	☼	D	
Miscanthus sinensis	Maiden Grass	z5-9	☼☼	D	R
Monarda didyma	Bee Balm	z3-7	☼☼	D	R
Monarda fistulosa	Wild Bergamot	z3-7	☼	D	R
Muscari armeniacum	Grape Hyacinth	z4-8	☼☼	D	
Myosotis scorpioides	True Forget-me-Not	z3-8	☼	D	R
Narcissus	Daffodil	z4-9	☼☼	D	R
Nepeta x faassenii	Faassen Nepeta	z3-8	☼	D	R
Nicotiana sylvestris	Woodland Tobacco	annual	☼	D	R
Origanum laevigatum	Oregano	z5-9	☼	D	R
Osteospermum	African Daisy	annual	☼	D	R
Pachysandra terminalis	Japanese Spurge	z5-9	☼	D	R
Paeonia hybrids	Peony	z3-8	☼☼	D	R
Papaver orientale	Poppy	z3-7	☼	D	R
Pennisetum alopecuroides	Fountain Grass	z5-9	☼☼	D	R
Penstemon barbatus	Bearded Tongue	z2-8	☼	D	R
Perovskia atriplicifolia	Russian Sage	z5-9	☼	D	R
Phlomis fruticosa	Jerusalem Sage	z4-8	☼☼	D	R

Deer & Rabbit Resistant ...continued

Deer resistant plants = D   Rabbit resistant plants = R

Scientific Name	Common Name	Zone	Light	Deer	Rabbit
Phlox divaricata	Woodland Phlox	z3-8	☀	D	
Phlox maculata	Spotted Phlox	z3-8	☼	D	
Phlox paniculata	Garden Phlox	z4-8	☼	D	
Phlox stolonifera	Creeping Phlox	z4-9	☼	D	
Phlox subulata	Moss Phlox	z3-9	☼	D	R
Polemonium caeruleum	Jacob's Ladder	z3-7	☼	D	
Polemonium reptans	Creeping Polemonium	z3-8	☼	D	
Polyganatum multiflorum	Solomon's Seal	z4-7	☼		R
Primula vulgaris	English Primrose	z5-8	☼		R
Prunella vulgaris	Self Heal	z3-10	☼	D	
Pulmonaria angustifolia	Blue Lungwort	z2-7	● ☼	D	R
Pulmonaria longifolia	Long-Leafed Lungwort	z3-8	● ☼	D	R
Pulmonaria rubra	Red Lungwort	z4-7	☼	D	R
Pulmonaria saccharata hybrids	Bethlehem Sage	z3-7	☼	D	R
Puschkinia scilloides	Striped Squill	z4-9	☼	D	
Rheum palmatum	Ornamental Rhubarb	z4-7	☼	D	R
Rodgersia aesculifolia	Fingerleaf Rodgersia	z4-7	☼	D	R
Rudbeckia fulgida	Black Eyed Susan	z3-8	☼		R
Rudbeckia nitida	Shining Coneflower	z5-9	☼	D	
Ruta graveolens	Rue	z4-8	☼	D	

Deer & Rabbit Resistant ...continued

Deer resistant plants = D   Rabbit resistant plants = R

Scientific Name	Common Name	Zone	Light	Deer	Rabbit
Salvia officinalis	Sage	z4-7	☼	D	R
Salvia x superba	Sage	z4-7	☼	D	R
Salvia x sylvestris	Hybrid Sage	z4-7	☼	D	R
Santolina chamaecyparissus	Lavender Cotton	z6-8	☼	D	R
Santolina virens	Green Lavender Cotton	z6-8	☼	D	R
Saponaria ocymoides	Soapwort	z2-7	☼	D	
Satureya montana	Winter Savory	z5-10	☼	D	
Scabiosa causasica	Pincushion Flower	z3-7	☼	D	R
Schozostylis	Kaffir Lily	z6-9	☼		R
Scilla sibirica	Siberian Squill	z2-7	☼	D	R
Sedum kamtschaticum	Stonecrop	z3-8	☼	D	
Sedum spectabile	Showy Stonecrop Sedum	z3-8	☼	D	R
Sedum spurium	Two Row Stonecrop	z3-8	☼	D	
Sempervivum tectorum	Hen and Chicks	z3-7	☼	D	
Sisyrinchium striatum	Blue-Eyed Grass	z4-8	☼		R
Solidago	Goldenrod	z4-9	☼	D	
Stachys byzantina	Lamb's Ear	z4-8	☼☼	D	R
Stachys macrantha	Big Betony	z2-8	☼☼	D	
Stipa spp.	Feather Grass	z7-9	☼☼	D	R
Stokesia laevis	Stokes Aster	z5-9	☼☼		R
Symphytum grandiflorum	Large-Flowered Comfrey	z3-9	☼☼	D	

Deer & Rabbit Resistant ...continued

Deer resistant plants = D   Rabbit resistant plants = R

Scientific Name	Common Name	Zone	Light	Deer	Rabbit
Symphytum x rubrum	Comfrey	z3-8	☼	D	R
Tanacetum parthenium	Feverfew	z4-10	◐	D	
Tanacetum vulgare	Tansy	z5-7	☼	D	R
Teucrium chamaedrys	Germander	z4-9	☼	D	
Thalictrum aquilegifolium	Columbine Meadow-Rue	z5-7	☼	D	R
Thalictrum minus	Lesser Meadow-Rue	z3-7	☼	D	
Thalictrum rochebrunianum	Lavender Mist	z4-7	☼	D	R
Thymus pseudolanuginosus	Woolly Thyme	z5-8	☼	D	R
Thymus serphyllum	Wild Thyme	z5-8	☼	D	R
Thymus vulgaris	Garden Thyme	z5-8	☼	D	R
Tiarella cordifolia	Allegheny Foam Flower	z3-8	●	D	R
Tradescantia	Spiderwort	z4-9	☼		R
Tricyrtis hirta	Toad Lily	z4-8	☼ ●		R
Trillium grandiflorum	Great White Trillium	z4-9	☼ ●		R
Verbascum chaixii	Mullein	z5-8	☼	D	
Veronica spp.	Speedwell	z4-8	☼	D	R
Vinca minor	Myrtle	z4-8	☼ ●	D	R
Viola odorata	Sweet Violet	z5-10	☼ ◐	D	R
Waldsteinia fragarioides	Barren Strawberry	z4-7	☼	D	
Yucca filamentosa	Adam's Needle	z5-9	☼	D	
Zinnia elegans	Zinnia	annual	☼		R

Bee Resistant

The fact that **bees can not distinguish the color red** from black or grays can work to our advantage. Many people are allergic to bees or certainly want to avoid them if susceptible to a reaction. **Bees are not as attracted to red**, so planting red-hued flowers in more frequented areas of the yard or outdoor rooms will help to avoid contact.

Section Five

Plant and Flower Uses

Botanical-Aromatherapy

The essential oils of certain plants contain properties that may help affect mood or health. These plants may be dried for use in potpourri, sachets, pillows, or in a bath. Caution should be used during pregnancy with any herbal application.

Scientific Name	Common Name	Zone	Light	Benefit
Chamaemelum nobile	Chamomile	z4-10	☼	relaxing
Foeniculum vulgare	Fennel	z6-9	☼	antitoxic
Hyssopus officinalis	Hyssop	z3-11	☼ ☀	sedative
Lavandula angustifolia	English Lavender	z5-9	☼	soothing
Melissa officinalis	Lemon Balm	z4-10	☼	antidepressant
Mentha x piperita	Peppermint	z3-10	☼	invigorating
Monarda didyma	Bee Balm	z3-7	☼ ☀	uplifting
Monarda fistulosa	Bergamot	z3-7	☼ ☀	antidepressant
Ocimum basilicum	Sweet Basil	annual	☼	concentration
Origanum majorana	Sweet Marjoram	z7-10	☼	calming
Pelargonium graveolens	Rose Geranium	annual	☼	relaxing
Rosmarinus officinalis	Rosemary	z7-11	☼	invigorating
Thymus vulgaris	Garden Thyme	z4-10	☼	stimulant

Botanical-Cut Flowers & Foliage

Cut flower gardens are a great way to bring the beauty of plants indoors. This section consists of plants that are not only beautiful as a cut flower, but are long lasting. Harvest flowers in the morning when they are just opening. Vase life can be extended by re-cutting flower stems under water, adding a solution of lemon-lime soda to the vase, or using a recommended packaged cut flower additive.

Scientific Name	Common Name	Zone	Light	Flower	Foliage
Acanthus mollis	Common Bear's Breeches	z7-9	☼☀	x	
Acanthus spinosus	Spiny Bear's Breeches	z6-10	☼☀	x	
Achillea filipendulina	Fern-Leaf Yarrow	z3-8	☼	x	
Achillea millefolium	Common Yarrow	z2-9	☼	x	
Achillea ptarmica	Sneezewort	z2-9	☼	x	
Aconitum carmichaelii	Azure Monkshood	z3-7	☀☼	x	
Aconitum napellus	Monkshood	z3-6	☀	x	
Allium aflatunense	Persian Onion	z4-8	☼	x	
Allium christophii	Star of Persia	z4-8	☼☀	x	
Allium giganteum	Giant Onion	z4-8	☼	x	
Allium karataviense	Turkistan Onion	z4-8	☼	x	
Allium schubertii	Tumbleweed Onion	z5-9	☼	x	
Allium 'Beauregard'	Hybrid Onion	z4-8	☼	x	
Allium 'Globemaster'	Hybrid Onion	z4-8	☼	x	
Alstroemeria aurea	Peruvian Lily	z7-9	☼	x	
Amaranthus caudatus	Love-Lies-Bleeding	annual	☼	x	
Anaphalis margaritacea	Pearly Everlasting	z4-7	☼☀	x	

Botanical-Cut Flowers & Foliage ...continued

Scientific Name	Common Name	Zone	Light	Flower	Foliage
Anchusa azurea	Alkanet	z3-9	☼	x	
Anemone coronaria	Poppy Anemone	z6-9	☼	x	
Anemone x hybrida	Hybrid Windflower	z5-7	☼	x	
Asplenium trichomanes	Maidenhair Spleenwort	z4-8	☼ ◑		x
Artemisia lactiflora	White Sage	z4-9	☼	x	
Artemisia ludoviciana	White Sage	z4-9	☼	x	
Aster novae-angliae	New England Aster	z4-8	☼	x	
Aster novi-belgii	New York Aster	z4-8	☼	x	
Aster tataricus	Tatarian Daisy	z4-8	☼	x	
Astilbe x arendsii	Hybrid Astilbe	z4-8	◑	x	
Astilbe chinensis var. taquetii	Chinese Astilbe	z4-8	◑	x	
Astrantia major	Great Masterwort	z5-7	◑	x	
Astrantia maxima	Large Masterwort	z5-7	◑	x	
Athyrium x 'Branford Beauty'	Lady Fern	z4-8	◑ ●		x
Athyrium felix-forma	Lady Fern	z3-9	◑ ●		x
Athyrium filix-femina	Tatting Fern	z3-8	◑ ●		x
Athyrium niponicum	Japanese Painted Fern	z3-8	◑ ●		x
Baptisia alba	White Wild Indigo	z5-8	☼ ◑	x	
Baptisia australis	False Blue Indigo	z3-8	☼ ◑	x	
Baptisia sphaerocarpa	Yellow Wild Indigo	z5-8	☼ ◑	x	
Boltonia asteroides	White Boltonia	z4-8	☼	x	
Callistephus chinensis	China Aster	annual	☼	x	

267

Botanical-Cut Flowers & Foliage ...continued

Scientific Name	Common Name	Zone	Light	Flower	Foliage
Campanula lactiflora	Milky Bellflower	z5-7	☼	x	
Campanula latiloba	Delphinium Bellflower	z5-7	☼	x	
Centaurea cyanus	Cornflower	annual	☼	x	
Centaurea macrocephala	Globe Centaurea	z3-7	☼	x	
Centaurea moschata	Sweet Sultan	annual	☼	x	
Chrysanthemum coccineum	Painted Daisy	z3-7	☼	x	
Convallaria majalis	Lily-of-the-Valley	z2-7	☼ ●	x	x
Cosmos bipinnatus	Mexican Aster	annual	☼	x	
Crocosmia hybrids	Montbretia	z5-8	☼	x	x
Dahlia hybrids	Dahlia	z7-10	☼	x	
Delphinium x elatum	Hybrid Bee Delphinium	z2-7	☼ ●	x	
Dianthus barbatus	Sweet William	z3-8	☼ ●	x	
Digitalis purpurea	Foxglove	z4-8	☼ ●	x	
Dryopteris erythrosora	Autumn Fern	z5-9	☼ ●		x
Echinacea purpurea	Purple Coneflower	z3-8	☼	x	
Echinops ritro	Globe Thistle	z3-8	☼	x	
Eremurus himalaicus	Himalayan Foxtail Lily	z5-8	☼	x	
Eremurus stenophyllus	Foxtail Lily	z5-8	☼	x	
Eryngium alpinum	Alpine Sea Holly	z4-7	☼	x	
Eupatorium maculatum	Spotted Joe Pye Weed	z3-8	☼ ●	x	
Gaillardia x grandiflora	Blanket Flower	z2-9	☼	x	
Geum triflorum	Prairie Smoke	z1-7	☼	x	

Botanical-Cut Flowers & Foliage ...continued

Scientific Name	Common Name	Zone	Light	Flower	Foliage
Gladiolus	Gladiolus	z8-10	☼	x	x
Helenium autumnale	Sneezeweed	z3-8	☼	x	
Helianthus angustifolia	Swamp Sunflower	z6-9	☼	x	
Helianthus x multiflorus	Many-Flowered Sunflower	z4-8	☼	x	
Heliopsis helianthoides	Sunflower Heliopsis	z3-9	☼	x	
Helleborus niger	Christmas Rose	z3-8	◐	x	
Helleborus orientalis	Lenten Rose	z4-9	☼◐	x	
Heuchera sanguinea	Coral Bells	z3-8	☼◐	x	
Hibiscus moscheutos	Common Mallow	z5-9	☼◐	x	
Hosta	Plantain Lily	z3-8	☼◐●		x
Hypericum androsaemum	St. John's Wort	z5-7	☼◐	x	(fruit)
Iris germanica	Bearded Iris	z3-10	☼	x	x
Iris ensata	Japanese Iris	z4-9	☼◐	x	
Kniphofia spp.	Torchlily	z5-8	☼◐	x	
Leucanthemum x superbum	Shasta Daisy	z4-9	☼	x	
Liatris spicata	Gayfeather	z3-9	☼	x	
Lilium auratum	Goldband Lily	z4-9	☼◐	x	
Lilium regale	Regal Lily	z3-8	☼◐	x	
Limonium latifolium	Sea Lavender	z3-8	☼	x	
Limonium sinuatum	Statice	annual	☼	x	
Lupinus polyphyllus	Lupine	z3-6	☼◐	x	

269

Botanical-Cut Flowers & Foliage ...continued

Scientific Name	Common Name	Zone	Light	Flower	Foliage
Lycoris squamigera	Autumn Lycoris	z5-9	☼	x	
Lysimachia clethroides	Gooseneck Loosestrife	z3-8	☼	x	
Macleaya cordata	Plume Poppy	z3-8	☼☼	x	
Miscanthus sinensis	Maiden Grass	z5-9	☼☼	x	
Monarda didyma	Bee Balm	z3-7	☼☼	x	
Moluccella laevis	Bells of Ireland	annual	☼	x	
Narcissus	Daffodils	z4-9	☼☼	x	x
Nepeta x faassenii	Faassen Nepeta	z3-10	☼	x	
Nepeta sibirica	Sibirean Catnip	z3-7	☼☼	x	
Nerine bowdenii	Spider Lily	z7-9	☼	x	
Ornithogalum thyrsoides	Star of Bethlehem	z9-11	☼☼	x	
Paeonia hybrids	Peony	z3-8	☼☼	x	
Papaver nudicaule	Iceland Poppy	z2-7	☼☼	x	
Patrinia scabiosifolia	Scabious Patrinia	z5-8	☼	x	
Penstemon barbatus	Common Bearded Tongue	z2-8	☼	x	
Penstemon digitalis	Smooth White Penstemon	z4-8	☼	x	
Phlox paniculata	Garden Phlox	z4-8	☼☼	x	
Physostegia virginiana	Obedient Plant	z2-9	☼☼	x	
Platycodon grandiflorus	Balloonflower	z3-7	☼☼	x	
Polianthes tuberosa	Tuberose Bulb	z9-11	☼	x	
Polemonium foliosissimum	Jacob's Ladder	z2-7	☼	x	
Polygonatum odoratum	Fragrant Solomon's Seal	z3-9	☼☀	x	

Botanical-Cut Flowers & Foliage ...continued

Scientific Name	Common Name	Zone	Light	Flower	Foliage
Primula vialii	Vial's Primrose	z5-7	☼	x	
Rudbeckia fulgida	Black-eyed Susan	z3-8	☼	x	
Scabiosa caucasica	Pincushion Flower	z3-7	☼	x	
Stokesia laevis	Stokes Aster	z5-9	☼	x	
Thalictrum aquilegifolium	Columbine Meadow-Rue	z5-7	☼	x	
Tulipa hybrids	Tulip	z5-9	☼	x	
Veronica longifolia	Speedwell	z4-8	☼	x	
Veronicastrum virginicum	Culver's Root	z4-8	☼	x	
Xeranthemum annuum	Immortelle	annual	☼	x	
Yucca filamentosa	Adam's Needle	z5-9	☼		x
Zantedeschia aethiopica	Calla Lily	z7-10	☼	x	
Zinnia elegans	Zinnia	annual	☼	x	

271

Botanical-Dried Flowers & Fruit

Dried flower arrangements are an artistic way to use the flowers harvested from the garden. Pick flowers to be dried at their best, for optimum results. There are several ways to dry flowers. The most commonly used & easiest way is to hang freshly picked flowers upside down. Flowers can also be dried using glycerine, silica-gel, the microwave, or freeze-drying. Consult a good dried flower book for instructions on these methods.

Scientific Name	Common Name	Zone	Light	Flower	Fruit
Achillea filipendulina	Fern-Leaf Yarrow	z3-8	☼	x	
Achillea millefolium	Common Yarrow	z2-9	☼	x	
Achillea ptarmica 'The Pearl'	Sneezewort	z2-9	☼	x	
Actaea alba	White Baneberry	z3-7	☼ ◑	x	x
Actaea rubra	Red Baneberry	z3-7	☼ ◑	x	x
Alchemilla mollis	Lady's Mantle	z4-7	☼ ◑	x	
Allium acuminatum	Tapertip Onion	z4-7	☼	x	
Allium christophii	Star of Persia	z4-8	☼ ◑	x	
Allium sphaerocephalum	Drumstick Chives	z4-8	☼	x	
Amaranthus caudatus	Love-Lies-Bleeding	annual	☼	x	
Anaphalis margaritacea	Pearly Everlasting	z4-7	☼ ◑	x	
Anthemis tinictoria	Golden Marguerite	z3-7	☼	x	
Artemisia ludoviciana	White Sage	z4-9	☼	x	
Artemisia x 'Powis Castle'	Wormwood	z6-8	☼	x	
Astilbe x arendsii	Hybrid Astilbe	z4-8	◑	x	
Astilbe chinensis	Chinese Astilbe	z4-8	◑	x	
Astrantia major	Great Masterwort	z5-7	◑	x	
Baptisia australis	False Blue Indigo	z3-8	☼ ◑		x

Botanical-Dried Flowers & Fruit ...continued

Scientific Name	Common Name	Zone	Light	Flower	Fruit
Briza maxima	Quaking Grass	annual	☼	x	
Calamagrostis acutiflora	Feather Reed Grass	z5-9	☼	x	
Calamagrostis arundinacea	Reed Grass	z6-9	☼	x	
Catananche caerulea	Blue Cupid's Dart	z4-7	☼	x	
Catananche caerulea 'Major'	Blue Cupid's Dart	z4-7	☼	x	
Centaurea cyanus	Cornflower	annual	☼	x	
Centaurea macrocephala	Globe Centaurea	z3-7	☼	x	
Celosia argentea	Cockscomb	annual	☼	x	
Chamaemelum nobile	Chamomile	z4-10	☼ ☼	x	
Chasmanthium latifolium	Northern Sea Oats	z4-7	☼ ☀		x
Chrysanthemum x morifolium	Chrysanthemum	z5-9	☼	x	
Consolida ambigua	Larkspur	annual	☼	x	
Dahlia	Dahlia	z7-10	☼	x	
Delphinium x elatum	Delphinium	z2-7	☼ ☀	x	
Echinacea purpurea	Purple Coneflower	z3-8	☼	x	
Echinops ritro	Globe Thistle	z3-8	☼	x	
Eryngium alpinum	Alpine Sea Holly	z4-7	☼	x	
Gomphrena globosa	Globe Amaranth	annual	☼	x	
Gypsophilia elegans	Baby's Breath	annual	☼	x	
Gypsophilia paniculata	Baby's Breath	z3-7	☼ ☀	x	
Helichrysum italicum	Curry Plant	annual	☼	x	
Helleborus argutifolius	Corsican Hellebore	z6-8	☼ ☀	x	

273

Botanical-Dried Flowers & Fruit ...continued

Scientific Name	Common Name	Zone	Light	Flower	Fruit
Helleborus foetidus	Stinking Hellebore	z5-9	☼ ☀	x	
Helleborus niger	Christmas Rose	z3-8	☼	x	
Helleborus orientalis	Lenten Rose	z4-9	☼	x	
Humulus lupulus	Hops	z3-9	☼ ☼		x
Iris foetidissima	Stinking Gladwin	z6-9	☼ ☀		x
Knautia macedonica	Knautia	z4-7	☼	x	
Lagurus ovatus	Bunny Tails	annual	☼	x	
Lavandula angustifolia	English Lavender	z5-9	☼	x	
Liatris spicata	Gayfeather	z3-9	☼	x	
Limonium latifolium	Sea Lavender	z3-8	☼	x	
Limonium sinuatum	Statice	annual	☼	x	
Lunaria annua	Money Plant	z4-8	☼ ☀		x
Mentha x piperita	Peppermint	z3-10	☼	x	
Moluccella laevis	Bells of Ireland	annual	☼	x	
Narcissus	Daffodils	z4-9	☼ ☀	x	
Nelumbo lutea	Lotus	z6-11	☼	x	
Nigella damascene	Love-in-a-Mist	annual	☼ ☀		x
Nigella orientalis	Yellow Fennel Flower	annual	☼		x
Origanum dictamnus	Dittany of Crete	z7-11	☼	x	
Origanum vulgare	Oregano	z3-7	☼ ☀	x	
Paeonia lactiflora	Peony	z6-9	☼	x	
Papaver rhoeas	Corn Poppy	annual	☼		x

Botanical-Dried Flowers & Fruit ...continued

Scientific Name	Common Name	Zone	Light	Flower	Fruit
Papaver somniferum	Opium Poppy	z8-10	☼		x
Phlomis fruticosa	Jerusalem Sage	z4-8	☼ ☼		x
Physalis alkekengi	Chinese Lantern	z3-9	☼ ☼		x
Ranunculus acris	Meadow Buttercup	z3-7	☼	x	
Scabiosa atropurpurea	Pincushion Flower	annual	☼	x	
Solidago canadensis	Goldenrod	z3-9	☼	x	
Tanacetum parthenium	Feverfew	z4-10	☼	x	
Thalictrum aquilegifolium	Columbine Meadow-Rue	z5-7	☼	x	
Thalictrum flavum	Yellow Meadow-Rue	z5-8	☼	x	
Thalictrum rochebrunianum	Lavender Mist	z4-7	☼ ☼	x	
Thymus serphyllum	Wild Thyme	z5-8	☼	x	
Xeranthemum annuum	Immortelle	annual	☼	x	

275

Botanical-Edible-Foliage: See herb section

Flowers and herbs can provide extended value in the kitchen. When using for food, always be sure to positively identify the plant. Plants that are similar to some edibles are extremely poisonous. For example the garden pea, *Pisum sativum* is completely edible. In contrast, the sweet pea, *Lathyrus odoratus*, is entirely poisonous. Also be aware that just because a part of a plant is listed as edible, it does not make the whole plant edible. Use caution when trying new foods, as certain people may be allergic. Consume wild plants in moderation, because high doses of some plants are considered toxic. The plants listed have been used in food preparation, and are considered safe for most. Pregnant women should consult a health care practitioner before eating any flowers or herbs. Know your food source and products used by the grower and/or nursery.

Scientific Name	Common Name	Zone	Light
Agastache foeniculum	Anise Hyssop	z6-9	☼
Allium schoenoprasum	Chives	z3-10	☼
Allium tuberosum	Garlic Chives	z4-8	☼
Bellis perennis	English Daisy	z3-10	☼ ☀
Borago officinalis	Borage	annual	☼
Calendula officinalis	Pot Marigold	annual	☼ ☀
Centaurea cyanus	Cornflower	annual	☼
Chamaemelum nobile	Chamomile	z4-10	☼ (some may be allergic)
Coriandrum sativum	Cilantro	annual	☼ ☀
Crocus sativus	Saffron Crocus	z6-9	☼ (stamens)
Cucurbita	Squash	annual	☼
Dianthus caryophyllus	Clove Pinks	z8-10	☼ ☀
Dianthus plumarius	Cottage Pinks	z3-8	☼
Eruca vesicaria ssp. *sativa*	Arugula	annual	☼
Fragaria x ananassa	Garden Strawberry	z4-10	☼

Botanical-Edible Foliage: See herb section ...continued

Scientific Name	Common Name	Zone	Light	
Hemerocallis fulva 'Kwanzo'	Daylily	z3-9	☀☀	
Lavandula angustifolia	English Lavender	z5-9	☀	
Monarda didyma	Bee Balm	z3-7	☀☀	
Ocimum basilicum	Sweet Basil	annual	☀☀	
Pelargonium biennis	Scented Geraniums	annual	☀	
Phaseolus coccineus	Scarlet Runner Bean	annual	☀	
Pisum sativum	Garden Peas	annual	☀	
Raphanus sativus	Radish	annual	☀	
Rosmarinus officinalis	Rosemary	z7-11	☀	
Salvia elegans	Pineapple Sage	z8-11	☀	
Salvia officinalis	Sage	z4-7	☀	
Salvia microphylla	Cherry Sage	z9-11	☀☀	
Sanguisorba minor	Salad Burnet	z4-7	☀	
Tagetes tenuifolia	Signet Marigold	annual	☀	
Thymus x citriodorus	Lemon Thyme	z6-10	☀	
Thymus herba-barona	Caraway Thyme	z9-11	☀	
Thymus vulgaris	Garden Thyme	z4-10	☀	
Tropaeolum majus	Nasturtium	annual	☀	
Tulipa	Tulip	z4-9	☀	some may be allergic
Viola cornuta	Horned Violet	z6-9	☀☀	
Viola odorata	Sweet Violet	z5-10	☀☀	
Viola tricolor	Johnny Jump-ups	annual	☀☀	
Viola wittrockiana	Pansies	annual	☀☀	

Botanical-Fragrant

Fragrant flowers or foliage will encourage interaction in the garden. Most plants that have fragrant foliage need to be touched to give off a scent. Consider using them near walkways, on paths, or near sitting areas where they will be brushed up against or stepped on. Fragrant flowers can have a very strong scent that can be detected from a distance, or be very subtle and need to be admired closely.

Scientific Name	Common Name	Zone	Light	Flower	Foliage
Achillea filipendulina	Fern-Leaf Yarrow	z3-8	☼		x
Achillea millefolium	Common Yarrow	z2-9	☼	x	x
Acorus calamus	Sweet Flag	z4-8	☼	x	x
Adenophora lilifolia	Lilyleaf Ladybells	z3-7	☼	x	
Agastache foeniculum	Anise Hyssop	z6-9	☼		x
Allium giganteum	Giant Onion	z4-8	☼	x	x
Allium neapolitanum	Naples Onion	z5-9	☼	x	x
Allium schoenoprasum	Chives	z3-10	☼	x	x
Aloysia triphylla	Lemon Verbena	z8-11	☼		x
Althaea officinalis	Marsh Mallow	z3-8	☼		x
Anemone sylvestris	Snowdrop Anemone	z4-7	☀	x	
Anethum graveolens	Dill	annual	☼		x
Anthericum liliago	St. Bernard's Lily	z4-9	☼	x	
Arabis alpina	Alpine Rock Cress	z4-7	☼	x	
Arisaema candidissimum	White Jack-in-the-Pulpit	z7-9	☼ ☀		x
Artemisia arbrotanum	Southernwood	z5-8	☼		x
Borago officinalis	Borage	annual	☼	x	x
Calamintha nepeta	Calamint	z4-7	☼	x	x

Botanical-Fragrant ...continued

Scientific Name	Common Name	Zone	Light	Flower	Foliage
Calendula officinalis	Pot Marigold	annual	☼	x	
Campanula lactiflora	Milky Bellflower	z5-7	☼	x	
Cardiocrinum giganteum	Giant Lily	z7-9	☼	x	
Centaurea moschata	Sweet Sultan	annual	☼	x	
Chamaemelum nobile	Chamomile	z4-10	☼	x	x
Convallaria majalis	Lily-of-the-Valley	z2-7	●	x	
Corydalis lutea	Yellow Corydalis	z5-7	● ☼	x	
Cosmos atrosanguineus	Chocolate Cosmos	annual	☼	x	
Crinum bulbispermum	Orange River Lily	z6-10	☼	x	
Crocus angustifolius	Crocus	z4-9	☼	x	
Crocus chrysanthus	Golden Crocus	z4-7	☼	x	
Crocus longiflorus	Crocus	z4-9	☼	x	
Cyclamen hederifolium	Cyclamen	z5-10	☼	x	Some Strains
Cyclamen purpurescens	Cyclamen	z5-9	☼	x	
Cyclamen repandum	Ivy Leafed Cyclamen	z6-9	☼	x	
Dianthus caryophyllus	Clove Pinks	z8-10	☼	x	
Dianthus gratianopolitanus	Cheddar Pinks	z3-8	☼	x	
Dianthus plumarius	Cottage Pinks	z3-8	☼	x	
Dictamnus albus	Gas Plant	z3-7	☼	x	
Echinacea purpurea	Purple Coneflower	z3-8	☼	x	
Epimedium x 'Niveum'	Bishop's Hat	z5-9	●	x	
Eupatorium maculatum	Spotted Joe Pye Weed	z3-8	☼	x	x

Botanical-Fragrant ...continued

Scientific Name	Common Name	Zone	Light	Flower	Foliage
Filipendula vulgaris	Dropwort	z3-7	☼	x	x
Filipendula ulmaria	Meadowsweet	z3-7	☼	x	x
Foeniculum vulgare	Fennel	z6-9	☼		x
Fritillaria imperialis	Crown Imperial	z5-7	☼	x	
Galanthus nivalis	Snowdrops	z3-7	☼	x	
Galium odoratum	Sweet Woodruff	z4-7	☼	x	
Galtonia candicans	Summer Hyacinth	z6-9	☼	x	
Gaultheria procumbens	Wintergreen	z4-9	☼ ●		x
Gladiolus alatus	Gladiolus	z8-10	☼	x	
Gladiolus tristis	Gladiolus	z7-10	☼	x	
Heliotropium peruvianum	Heliotrope	annual	☼	x	
Hemerocallis flava	Lemon Daylily	z4-9	☼	x	
Hesperis matronalis	Dame's Rocket	z3-8 biennial	☼	x	
Hosta plantaginea	Fragrant Plantain Lily	z3-10	☼	x	
Hyacinthoides hispanica	Spanish Bluebell	z4-7	☼ ●	x	
Hyacinthoides non-scripta	English Bluebell	z5-10	☼	x	
Hyacinthus orientalis	Hyacinth	z5-9	☼	x	
Iris graminea	Plum Scented Iris	z3-9	☼	x	
Iris pallida	Sweet Iris	z4-9	☼	x	
Iris reticulata	Reticulated Iris	z5-8	☼	x	
Iris unguicularis	Algerian Iris	z7-9	☼	x	
Lablab purpureus	Hyacinth Bean	annual	☼		x

Botanical-Fragrant ...continued

Scientific Name	Common Name	Zone	Light	Flower	Foliage
Lathyrus odoratus	Sweet Pea	z5-7	☼	x	
Lavandula angustifolia	English Lavender	z5-9	☼	x	x
Lavandula latifolia	English Spike Lavender	z7-10	☼	x	x
Lavandula stoechas	French Lavender	z7-10	☼	x	x
Leucojum aestivum	Summer Snowflake	z4-8	☼	x	
Leucojum vernum	Spring Snowflake	z4-8	☼	x	
Lilium auratum	Goldband Lily	z4-9	☼	x	
Lilium candidum	Madonna Lily	z4-9	☼	x	
Lilium henryi	Henry Lily	z4-7	☼	x	
Lilium regale	Regal Lily	z3-8	☼	x	
Lilium 'Star Gazer'	Star Gazer Lily	z6-9	☼	x	
Lupinus polyphyllus	Lupine	z3-6	☼	x	
Melissa officinalis	Lemon Balm	z4-10	☼		x
Mentha x piperita	Peppermint	z3-10	☼		x
Mentha pulegium	Pennyroyal	z5-10	☼		x
Mentha suaveolens	Apple Mint	z5-10	☼	x	
Monarda didyma	Bee Balm	z3-7	☼	x	x
Monarda fistulosa	Wild Bergamot	z3-7	☼	x	x
Muscari armeniacum	Grape Hyacinth	z4-8	☼	x	
Muscari botryoides	Grape Hyacinth	z2-8	☼	x	
Myosotis sylvatica	Woodland Forget-me-not	z3-7	☼	x	
Myrrhis odorata	Sweet Cicily	z4-10	☼	x	x

281

Botanical-Fragrant ...continued

Scientific Name	Common Name	Zone	Light	Flower	Foliage
Narcissus jonquilla	Jonquilla Daffodils	z4-9	☼	x	
Nepeta x faassenii	Faassen Nepeta	z4-7	☼	x	
Nicotiana alata	Flowering Tobacco	annual	☼	x	
Nicotiana sylvestris	Nicotiana	annual	☼	x	
Oenothera biennis	Evening Primrose	annual	☼	x	
Oenothera caespitosa	Tufted Evening Primrose	z4-9	☼	x	
Oenothera missouriensis	Ozark Sundrops	z5-9	☼	x	
Origanum marjorana	Sweet Marjoram	z7-10	☼	x	x
Origanum vulgare	Oregano	z3-7	☀	x	x
Paeonia lactiflora	Chinese Peony	z6-9	☀	x	
Paeonia officinalis	Common Peony	z3-8	☀	x	
Papaver nudicaule	Iceland Poppy	z2-7	☼	x	
Pelargonium fragrans	Nutmeg Geranium	annual	☀		x
Pelargonium graveolens	Rose Geranium	annual	☼		x
Pelargonium odoratissimum	Apple Geranium	annual	☼		x
Pelargonium quercifolium	Oak-Leafed Geranium	annual	☼		x
Pelargonium tomentosum	Peppermint Geranium	annual	☀		x
Perovskia atriplicifolia	Russian Sage	z5-9	☼		x
Phlox divaricata	Woodland Phlox	z3-8	☀	x	x
Phlox maculata	Spotted Phlox	z3-8	☀	x	
Phlox paniculata	Garden Phlox	z4-8	☼	x	
Polygonatum odoratum	Fragrant Solomon's Seal	z3-9	☼	x	

Botanical-Fragrant ...continued

Scientific Name	Common Name	Zone	Light	Flower	Foliage
Primula aricula	Primrose	z3-7	◐☀	x	
Primula bulleyana	Primrose	z6-9	☼	x	
Primula denticulata	Drumstick Primrose	z4-7	☼	x	
Primula eliator	Oxlip	z5-9	☀	x	
Primula japonica	Japanese Primrose	z5-7	◐☀	x	
Primula pulverulenta	Primrose	z6-9	☼◐	x	
Primula veris	Cowslip	z5-9	◐☀	x	
Primula vulgaris	English Primrose	z5-8	◐☀	x	
Rosmarinus officinalis	Rosemary	z7-11	☼		x
Ruta graveolens	Rue	z4-8	☼	x	x
Scabiosa atropurpurea	Pincushin Flower	annual	☼	x	
Spiranthes odorata	Ladies Tresses	z5-8	☀	x	
Thymus x citriodorus	Lemon Thyme	z6-10	☼		x
Thymus praecox	Creeping Thyme	z5-8	☼		x
Thymus pseudolanuginosus	Woolly Thyme	z5-8	◐☀		x
Thymus serphyllum	Wild Thyme	z5-8	◐☀		x
Thymus vulgaris	Garden Thyme	z4-10	☼		x
Tiarella 'Iron Butterfly'	Foamflower	z3-8	◐☀	x	
Tiarella 'Pink Bouquet'	Foamflower	z3-8	◐☀	x	
Tiarella wherryi	Wherry's Foamflower	z4-8	◐☀	x	
Trillium luteum	Yellow Trillium	z4-7	◐☀	x	
Tropaeolum majus	Nasturtium	annual	☼	x	

Botanical-Fragrant ...continued

Scientific Name	Common Name	Zone	Light	Flower	Foliage
Tulipa 'Angelique'	Tulip	z5-9	☼	x	
Tulipa 'Apricot Beauty'	Tulip	z5-9	☼	x	
Tulipa 'Ballerina'	Tulip	z5-9	☼	x	
Tulipa 'Daydream'	Tulip	z5-9	☼	x	
Tulipa 'Holland's Glory'	Tulip	z5-9	☼	x	
Tulipa 'Prince of Austria'	Tulip	z5-9	☼	x	
Tulipa sylvestris	Tulip	z5-9	☼	x	
Verbena x hybrida 'Defiance'	Garden Verbena	annual	☼	x	
Viola cornuta	Horned Violet	z6-9	☀	x	
Viola odorata	Sweet Violet	z5-10	☀	x	

Botanical-Herbs

Herbs are plants valued for culinary uses, medicinal properties or scent. Most herbs used in cooking are considered safe for most. Some can be toxic in large quantities or be dangerous to pregnant women and those with heart conditions. **Those checked as poisonous should not be used under certain circumstances (pregnancy, heart condition, etc...), or are poisonous.** Always be sure to accurately identify any herb to be ingested, because some herbs have similar looking plants that are poisonous.

Scientific Name	Common Name	Zone	Light	Cooking	Can be poisonous
Achillea ageratum	English Mace	z6-10	☼	x	
Achillea millefolium	Common Yarrow	z2-9	☼	x	x
Aconitum napellus	Monkshood	z3-6	◐		x
Agastache foeniculum	Anise Hyssop	z6-9	☼	x	
Ajuga reptans	Bugle Weed	z3-9	☼		
Alchemilla alpina	Mountain Lady's Mantle	z3-7	●		
Alchemilla mollis	Lady's Mantle	z4-7	◐		
Allium sativum	Garlic	z4-10	☼	x	
Allium schoenoprasum	Chives	z3-10	☼	x	
Aloe vera	Aloe Vera	z8-11	☼		x
Aloysia triphylla	Lemon Verbena	z8-11	☼	x	
Althaea officinalis	Marsh-Mallow	z3-8	☼	x	
Anethum graveolens	Dill	annual	☼	x	
Angelica archangelica	Angelica	z5-7	◐	x	x
Anthriscus cerefolium	Chervil	annual	◐	x	
Armoracia rusticana	Horseradish	z3-10	☼	x	x
Arnica montana	Leopards Bane	z4-9	◐	x	x

Botanical-Herbs ...continued

Scientific Name	Common Name	Zone	Light	Cooking	Can be Poisoness
Artemisia absinthium	Wormwood	z3-9	☀		x
Artemisia dracunculus	Tarragon	z3-9	☀ ☀	x	
Atriplex hortensis	Orach	annual	☀	x	
Ballota nigra	Black Horehound	z4-10	☀ ☀		
Borago officinalis	Borage	annual	☀	x	x
Calamintha nepeta	Calamint	z4-7	☀	x	
Calandula officinalis	Pot Marigold	annual	☀	x	
Carum carvi	Caraway	z3-8	☀	x	
Cedronella carariensis	Balm of Gilead	z8-11	☀		
Centranthus ruber	Red Valerian	z5-10	☀		x
Chamaemelum nobile	Chamomile	z4-10	☀ ☀	x	x
Cichorium intybus	Chicory	z3-10	☀	x	x
Convallaria majalis	Lily-of-the-Valley	z2-7	☀ ◑		x
Coriandrum sativum	Cilantro	annual	☀	x	
Dianthus deltoides	Maiden Pinks	z3-8	☀	x	
Dianthus gratianopolitanus	Cheddar Pinks	z3-8	☀	x	
Dianthus plumarius	Cottage Pinks	z3-8	☀	x	
Digitalis purpurea	Foxglove	z4-8	☀		x
Echium vulgare	Vipers Bugloss	z2-9	☀		
Equisteum arvense	Horsetail	z4-9	☀		x
Eruca vesicaria ssp. sativa	Arugula	annual	☀	x	

Botanical - Herbs ...continued

Scientific Name	Common Name	Zone	Light	Cooking	Can Be Poisonous
Filipendula ulmaria	Meadowsweet	z3-7	☼	x	
Foeniculum vulgare	Fennel	z6-9	☼	x	
Fragaria vesca	Wild Strawberry	z5-10	☼	x	
Galium odoratum	Sweet Woodruff	z4-7	☼		x
Glycyrrhiza glabra	Liquorice	z7-10	☼		x
Helichrysum italicum	Curry Plant	annual	☼		
Hesperis matronalis	Dame's Rocket	z3-8	☼		
Humulus lupulus	Hops	z3-9	☼		x
Hyoscymus niger	Henbane	annual	☼		x
Hypericum perforatum	St. John's Wort	z3-7	☼		x
Hyssopus officinalis	Hyssop	z3-11	☼	x	x
Iris germanica var. florentina	Orrisroot	z4-10	☼		x
Lavandula angustifolia	English Lavender	z5-9	☼	x	
Levisticum officinale	Lovage	z3-10	☼	x	x
Malva sylvestris	Mallow	z4-8	☼	x	
Marrubium vulgare	White Horehound	z3-10	☼		
Melissa officinalis	Lemon Balm	z4-10	☼	x	
Mentha x piperita	Peppermint	z3-10	☼	x	x
Mentha pulegium	Pennyroyal	z5-10	☼	x	x
Mentha suaveolens	Apple Mint	z5-10	☼	x	x
Monarda didyma	Bee Balm	z3-7	☼	x	x

Botanical-Herbs ...continued

Scientific Name	Common Name	Zone	Light	Cooking	Can Be Poisonous
Myrrhis odorata	Sweet Cicely	z4-10	☼	x	x
Nepeta cataria	Catnip	z2-7	☼	x	
Ocimum basilicum	Sweet Basil	annual	☼	x	
Oenothera biennis	Evening Primrose	biennial	☼	x	
Origanum majorana	Sweet Marjoram	z7-10	☼	x	
Origanum vulgare	Oregano	z3-7	☼	x	
Papaver rhoeas	Corn Poppy	annual	☼	x	x
Pelargonium biennis	Scented Geranium	annual	☼	x	x
Petroselinum crispum	Curled Parsley	z5-9	☼	x	x
Petroselinum c.var. neapolitanum	Flat-Leaved Parsley	z5-9	☼	x	x
Phlomis fruticosa	Jerusalem Sage	z4-8	☼	x	
Polemonium caeruleum	Jacob's Ladder	z2-7	☼		
Polygonatum multiflorum	Solomon's Seal	z4-7	☼		x
Primula veris	Cowslip	z5-9	☼	x	x
Primula vulgaris	English Primrose	z5-8	☼	x	x
Prunella vulgaris	Self Heal	z3-10	☼		
Pulmonaria saccharata	Bethlehem Sage	z3-7	☼		
Rosmarinus officinalis	Rosemary	z7-11	☼	x	x
Rumex acetosa	Sorrel	z3-9	☼	x	x
Ruta graveolens	Rue	z4-8	☼		x

Botanical—Herbs ...continued

Scientific Name	Common Name	Zone	Light	Cooking	Can Be Poisonous
Salvia elegans	Pineapple Sage	z8-11	☼	x	x
Salvia officinalis	Sage	z4-7	☼	x	x
Sanguisorba minor	Salad Burnet	z4-7	☼ ☀	x	x
Santolina chamaecyparissus	Lavender Cotton	z6-8	☼		
Saponaria officinalis	Bouncing Bet	z2-8	☼		x
Satureja hortensis	Summer Savory	annual	☼	x	
Satureja montana	Winter Savory	z5-10	☼	x	
Sempervivum tectorum	Hens and Chicks	z3-7	☼		
Stachys officinalis	Betony	z4-8	☼ ☀		x
Symphytum officinale	Comfrey	z4-7	☼ ☀		x
Tanacetum balsamita	Alecost	z5-10	☀	x	
Tanacetum cinerariifolium	Pyrethrum	z6-10	☼		x
Tanacetum parthenium	Feverfew	z4-10	☼		x
Tanacetum vulgare	Tansy	z3-10	☼ ☀		x
Taraxacum officinale	Dandelion	z3-10	☼ ☀	x	x
Teucrium scorodonia	Wood Sage	z6-10	☼ ☀	x	
Thymus x citriodorus	Lemon Thyme	z6-10	☼	x	x
Thymus pseudolanuginosus	Woolly Thyme	z5-8	☼ ☀	x	x
Thymus pulegioides	Mother-of-Thyme	z4-9	☼	x	x
Thymus vulgaris	Garden Thyme	z4-10	☼	x	x
Tropaeolum majus	Nasturtium	annual	☼	x	x

289

Botanical-Herbs ...continued

Scientific Name	Common Name	Zone	Light	Cooking	Can Be Poisonous
Urtica dioica	Stinging Nettle	z3-8	☀	x	x
Valeriana officinalis	Valerian	z4-9	☀		x
Verbena officinalis	Vervain	z4-10	☀☀		x
Viola odorata	Sweet Violet	z5-10	☀☀	x	
Viola tricolor	Johnny Jump-ups	annual	☀☀	x	

Botanical-Medicinal

Medicinal plants have been valued for centuries, and many are still used to produce modern medicine. **Most of these plants are considered poisonous, and should not be used as home remedies.** Use this list as an educational reference, or in a garden for use by medical students, pharmacists, or doctors.

Scientific Name	Common Name	Zone	Light	Property or Benefit
Achillea millefolium	Common Yarrow	z2-9	☼	fevers
Aconitum napellus	Monkshood	z3-6	☀	local analgesic
Acorus calamus	Sweet Flag	z4-8	☼	antibiotic
Alchemilla mollis	Lady's Mantle	z4-7	☼☀	menopausal discomfort
Allium sativum	Garlic	z4-10	☼	reduce blood pressure/cholesterol
Aloe vera	Aloe Vera	z8-11	☼	promotes healing
Anethum graveolens	Dill	annual	☼	upset stomach/insomnia
Arctostaphylos uva-ursi	Bearberry	z2-6	☼	antiseptic/diuretic
Armoracia rusticana	Horseradish	z3-10	☼	diuretic/gout/rheumatism
Calendula officinalis	Pot Marigold	annual	☀	promotes healing
Chamaemelum nobile	Chamomile	z4-10	☼☀	antiseptic/anti-inflammatory
Cimicifuga racemosa	Black Cohosh	z3-7	☀	premenstrual & menopausal symptoms
Colchicum autumnale	Autumn Crocus	z4-7	☼	gout
Convallaria majalis	Lily-of-the-Valley	z2-7	☀●	cardiac drug
Digitalis purpurea	Foxglove	z4-8	☀	cardiac drug
Echinacea purpurea	Purple Coneflower	z3-8	☼	respiratory & urinary infection
Filipendula ulmaria	Meadowsweet	z3-7	☀	acidic stomach
Foeniculum vulgare	Fennel	z6-9	☼	dyspepsia

291

Botanical-Medicinal ...continued

Scientific Name	Common Name	Zone	Light	Property or Benefit
Hypericum perforatum	St. John's Wort	z3-7	●	depression/sleep
Lavandula angustifolia	English Lavender	z5-9	☼	anxiety/restlessness
Marrubium vulgare	White Horehound	z3-10	☼	cough medicine
Melissa officinalis	Lemon Balm	z4-10	●	headaches
Mentha x piperita	Peppermint	z3-10	☼	gastro-intestinal spasms
Oenothera biennis	Evening Primrose	z3-8	☼	many uses
Papaver somniferum	Opium Poppy	z8-10	☼	morphine/codeine
Plantago psyllium	Psyllium	annual	☼	laxative may lower cholesterol
Podophyllum peltatum	Mayapple	z5-8	●	warts
Prunella vulgaris	Self Heal	z3-10	☼	sore throats/healing
Rosmarinus officinalis	Rosemary	z7-11	☼	rheumatism
Ruta graveolens	Rue	z4-8	☼	sedative
Salvia officinalis	Sage	z4-7	☼	excessive perspiration
Sempervivum tectorum	Hens & Chicks	z3-7	☼	astringent
Symphytum officinale	Comfrey	z4-7	●	promotes healing
Tanacetum parthenium	Feverfew	z4-10	☼	migranes
Thymus vulgaris	Garden Thyme	z4-10	☼	bronchitis/cough
Valeriana officinalis	Valerian	z4-9	☼	sleep aid

Nature-Attracts Butterflies & Butterfly Larvae

Butterflies can be attracted to your garden by providing flowers that produce nectar. The plants for the larval (caterpillar) stage are a more critical need and necessary for repopulation. Most butterflies use a variety of flowers as nectar sources. Many trees and shrubs are also needed. Provide plants that serve the needs of all life stages.

Butterflies need a place to lay eggs, food plants for the larva (caterpillar), a place to form a chrysalis, and nectar sources for the adult butterfly. The caterpillars that turn into butterflies also need certain plants to feed upon and are often not the same plants! Many caterpillars only rely on one or two species of plants.

Most adult butterflies live 10-20 days. Some live no longer than three or four days, while others, such as over wintering monarchs, may live six months. Find out which butterflies are native to your area and plan for their needs.

Nectar-producing plants should be grown in open, sunny areas, as adults of most species rarely feed on plants in the shade. The flowers have nectar in narrow tubes or spurs, reached by the long tongue of the butterflies. These are plants for butterfly nectar and host for caterpillars (larval plants).

Scientific Name	Common Name	Zone	Light	Nectar	Larval
Achillea 'Cerise Queen'	Yarrow	z3-9	☼	x	
Agastache foeniculum	Anise Hyssop	z6-9	☼	x	
Agastache rugosa	Anise Hyssop	z5-8	☼	x	
Alcea rosea	Hollyhock	z3-7	☼		x
Amorpha canescens	Lead Plant	z2-9	☼	x	x
Anaphalis margaritacea	Pearly Everlasting	z4-7	☼ ☀		x
Anethum graveolens	Dill	annual	☼		x
Antennaria dioica	Pussytoes	z4-9	☼		x
Anthemis cupaniana	Marquerite Daisy	z5-7	☼	x	
Anthemis marschalliana	Marshall Chamomile	z5-7	☼ ☀	x	

293

Nature-Attracts Butterflies & Butterfly Larvae ...continued

Scientific Name	Common Name	Zone	Light	Nectar	Larval
Anthemis tinctoria	Golden Marguerite	z3-7	☼	x	
Antirrhinum majus	Snapdragon	annual	☼		x
Arctium	Burdock	z2-10	☀		x
Artemisia ludoviciana	White Sage	z4-9	☀		x
Asclepias incarnata	Milkweed Silkweed	z3-7	☼	x	
Asclepias syriaca	Milkweed	z3-9	☼		x
Asclepias tuberosa	Butterfly Weed	z4-9	☼	x	
Asclepias verticillata	Butterfly Weed	z3-10	☼	x	
Aster azureus	Sky Blue Aster	z4-9	☼		x
Aster carolinianus	Climbing Aster	z6-9	☼	x	
Aster laevis	Smooth Aster	z3-9	☼	x	
Aster oblongifolius	Aster	z3-8	☼	x	
Aster novae-angliae	New England Aster	z4-8	☼	x	
Baptisia australis	False Blue Indigo	z3-8	☀	x	
Calendula officinalis	Pot Marigold	annual	☀	x	
Carum carvi	Caraway	z3-8	☼		x
Centaurea cyanus	Cornflower	annual	☼	x	
Ceratostigma	Plumbago	z5-8	☀		x
Chelone glabra	Turtlehead	z3-7	☀		x
Cleome hasslerana	Cleome	annual	☼	x	
Coreopsis auriculata	Tickseed	z4-9	☼	x	
Coreopsis tinctoria	Tickseed	annual	☼	x	

Nature-Attracts Butterflies & Butterfly Larvae ...continued

Scientific Name	Common Name	Zone	Light	Nectar	Larval
Cosmos bipinnatus	Mexican Aster	annual	☼	x	
Dalea purpurea	Prairie Clover	z3-8	☼		x
Daucus carota	Carrots	annual	☼		x
Echinacea purpurea	Purple Coneflower	z3-8	☼	x	
Echium plantagineum	Viper's bugloss	annual	☼	x	
Echium vulgare	Vipers Bugloss	z2-9	☼	x	
Erigeron philadelphicus	Common Fleabane	z3-8	☼		x
Eupatorium purpureum	Joe Pye Weed	z4-8	☼	x	
Filipendula rubra	Meadowsweet	z3-7	☼		x
Foeniculum vulgare	Fennel	z6-9	☼		x
Gaillardia x grandiflora	Blanket Flower	z2-9	☼	x	
Gilia achilleifolia	Scarlet Gilia	annual	☼	x	
Helianthus giganteus	Giant Sunflower	z5-9	☼		x
Heliopsis helianthoides	Sunflower Heliopsis	z3-9	☼	x	
Hesperis matronalis	Dame's Rocket	z3-8 biennial	☼	x	
Heuchera sanguinea	Coral Bells	z3-8	☼	x	
Hibiscus moscheutos	Common Mallow	z5-9	☼		x
Humulus lupulus	Hops	z3-9	☼		x
Hypericum spp.	St. John's Wort	z5-9	☼	x	
Hypoestes phyllostachya	Polka-Dot Plant	annual	☼	x	
Hyssopus offinalis	Hyssop	z3-11	☼	x	
Kniphofia spp.	Red Hot Poker	z5-8	☼	x	

Nature-Attracts Butterflies & Butterfly Larvae ...continued

Scientific Name	Common Name	Zone	Light	Nectar	Larval
Lantana	Lantana	annual	☼	x	
Lavandula angustifolia	English Lavender	z5-9	☼	x	
Lavandula stoechas	French Lavender	z7-10	☼	x	
Linaria	Toadflax	z3-9	☼	x	
Liriope muscari 'Big Blue'	Blue Lily Turf	z6-9	☼ ☼ ●	x	
Lobelia cardinalis	Cardinal Flower	z2-9	☼ ●	x	
Lobularia maritima	Sweet Alyssum	annual	☼ ●	x	
Lupinus perennis	Sundial Lupine	z3-9	☼	x	x
Malcomia maritima	Stock	annual	☼	x	
Mimulus	Monkey Flower	annual	☼ ☼ ●		x
Monarda spp.	Bee Balm	z3-7	☼ ●	x	
Nepeta cataria	Catnip	z2-7	☼ ●	x	
Nicotiana spp.	Flowering Tobacco	annual	☼ ●	x	
Ophiopogon japonicus	Dwarf Mondo Grass	z6-9	☼ ●	x	
Origanum laevigatum 'Hopley's'	Hople's Purple Oregano	annual	☼	x	
Penstemon barbatus	Common Bearded Tongue	z2-8	☼	x	x
Penstemon digitalis	Smooth White Penstemon	z4-8	☼ ●	x	x
Penstemon hirsutus	Bearded Tongue	z3-8	☼	x	x
Penstemon hybrids	Bearded Tongue	z4-8	☼	x	x
Pentas lanceolata	Egyptian Star Cluster	annual	☼ ●	x	
Pentas carnea	Star Clusters	annual	☼ ●	x	

Nature-Attracts Butterflies & Butterfly Larvae ...continued

Scientific Name	Common Name	Zone	Light	Nectar	Larval
Perovskia atriplicifolia	Russian Sage	z5-9	☼	x	
Petroselinium crispum	Curled Parsley	z5-9	☼		x
Petroselinium c.var. neapolitanum	Flat-Leafed Parsley	z5-9	☼		x
Physostegia virginiana	Obedient Plant	z2-9	☼	x	
Polemonium coeruleum	Jacob's Ladder	z2-7	☼	x	
Rudbeckia fulgida	Black-eyed Susan	z3-8	☼	x	
Rudbeckia hirta	Black-eyed Susan	z3-7 biennial	☼	x	
Rumex	Rhubarb	z3-7	☼		x
Salvia azurea	Sage	z5-9	☼	x	
Salvia pratensis	Meadow Sage	z3-7	☼	x	
Salvia x sylvestris	Hybrid Sage	z4-7	☼	x	
Scabiosa 'Butterfly Blue'	Pincushion Flower	z3-9	☼	x	
Sedum spectabile	Stonecrop	z3-8	☼	x	
Sidalcea malviflora	Checkermallow	z5-7	☼		x
Silene regia	Campion	z5-8	☼	x	
Silphium laciniatum	Compass Plant	z3-7	☼	x	
Solidago rugosa	Goldenrod	z3-8	☼	x	
Stachys officinalis	Betony	z4-8	☼	x	
Stokesia laevis	Stokes Aster	z5-9	☼	x	
Tagetes	Marigold	annual	☼		x
Thymus spp.	Thyme	z5-8	☼	x	

Nature-Attracts Butterflies & Butterfly Larvae ...continued

Scientific Name	Common Name	Zone	Light	Nectar	Larval
Tithonia rotundifolia	Mexican Sunflower	annual	☼	x	
Urtica dioica	Stinging Nettle	z3-8	☼		x
Verbascum phoeniceum	Purple Mullien	z6-8	☼	x	
Verbena bonariensis	Butterfly Vervain	z6-9	☼	x	
Vernonia fasciculata	Ironweed	z5-9	☼	x	
Veronica alpina 'Goodness Grows'	Speedwell	z3-8	☼	x	
Veronica austriaca	Austrian Speedwell	z4-7	☼	x	
Viola labradorica	Labrador Violet	z3-8	☼◑		x
Viola pedata	Bird's Foot Violet	z4-8	☼◑		x
Zinnia elegans	Zinnia	annual	☼	x	x

Nature-Food for Song Birds

Perennials are a important food source for song birds. Fruit and seeds from trees and shrubs are an important winter food source as well. Consider providing escape cover, shade, nesting areas and water source for local song birds. Check a bird book for birds that frequent the area.

Scientific Name	Common Name	Zone	Light
Agastache foeniculum	Lavander Hyssop	z6-9	☼
Ageratum houstonianum	Floss Flower	annual	☼
Antirrhinum majus	Snapdragon	annual	☼
Asclepias syriaca	Milkweed	z3-9	☼
Asclepias tuberosa	Butterfly Weed	z4-9	☼
Aster spp.	Aster	z4-8	☼
Bouteloua gracilis	Blue Grama	z3-10	☼
Campanula rotundifolia	Harebell	z3-9	☼ ☀
Centaurea cyanus	Bachelor's Button	annual	☼
Celosia	Cockscomb	annual	☼
Chelone glabra	Turtlehead	z3-7	☀
Cleome spinosa	Cleome	annual	☼
Consolida ambigua	Larkspur	annual	☼
Coreopsis grandiflora	Lance Tickseed	z4-9	☼
Coreopsis lanceolata	Lanceleaf Coropsis	z3-8	☼
Cosmos	Cosmos	annual	☼
Echinacea purpurea	Purple Coneflower	z3-8	☼
Epilobium augustrifolium	Fireweed	z2-10	☼

Nature-Food for Song Birds

Scientific Name	Common Name	Zone	Light
Helianthus annuus	Sunflower	annual	☀
Iris versicolor	Blue Flag Iris	z2-8	☀ ☀
Lespedeza capitata	Round Headed Bush Clover	z4-8	☀ ☀
Liatris aspera	Rough Blazing Star	z3-8	☀
Liatris spicata	Blazingstar	z3-9	☀
Lilium superbum	Turk's Cap Lily	z4-8	☀ ☀
Lobelia siphilitica	Great Blue Lobelia	z4-8	☀ ☀
Mertensia virginica	Virginia Bluebells	z3-8	● ☀
Mirabilis jalapa	Four O'Clocks	annual	☀
Monarda	Bee Balm	z3-7	☀ ☀
Pennisetum glaucum	Proso Millet	annual	☀
Penstemon spectabilis	Penstemon	z6-10	☀
Phlox divaricata	Woodland Phlox	z3-8	● ☀
Rudbeckia hirta var. *pulcherrima*	Gloriosa Daisy	biennial	☀ ☀
Scabiosa caucasica	Pincushion Flower	z3-7	☀
Sedum spectabile	Stonecrop	z3-8	☀
Silphium laciniatum	Compass Plant	z3-8	☀
Solidago	Goldenrod	z4-9	☀
Tiarella cordifolia	Foamflower	z3-8	☀ ●
Tithonia rotundifolia	Mexican Sunflower	annual	☀

Nature-Food for Hummingbirds

Attracting hummingbirds requires more than just nectar filled flowers. The garden should create an entire habitat for the birds. A fresh source of water for drinking and bathing must be available. Create both sun and shade areas for the hummingbirds, providing places to perch in shade. Nesting materials include small bits of leaves, mosses and other organic material. Hummingbirds must feed 3-5 times per hour and will need a good source of consistent food. When flowers are not blooming a feeder should be provided. Bright red is the best color for a feeder. Feeders should be filled with 1 part sugar to 4 parts water thoroughly dissolved. **Do not use food coloring and <u>never use honey</u>.** Keep feeders clean and filled.

Scientific Name	Common Name	Zone	Light
Ajuga reptans	Bugle Weed	z3-9	☼ ☼ ●
Alcea rosea	Hollyhock	z3-7	☼
Antirrhinum majus	Snapdragon	annual	☼
Aquilegia	Columbine	z3-8	☼ ☼
Asclepias tuberosa	Butterfly Weed	z4-9	☼
Campanula	Bellflower	z3-8	☼ ☼
Canna	Canna	z7-10	☼
Castilleja	Paintbrush	z4-8 biennial, semi-parasitic	☼
Clarkia amoena	Clarkia	annual	☼
Cleome hasslerana	Cleome	annual	☼
Cosmos bipinnatus	Mexican Aster	annual	☼
Delphinium spp.	Delphinium	z2-7	☼ ☼
Dianthus	Pinks	z4-8	☼ ☼
Dianthus barbatus	Sweet William	z3-8	☼ ☼

Nature-Food for Hummingbirds ...continued

Scientific Name	Common Name	Zone	Light
Dicentra	Bleeding Heart	z3-7	☀
Digitalis grandiflora	Yellow Foxglove	z3-8	☀
Digitalis lutea	Straw Foxglove	z3-8	☀
Digitalis x mertonensis	Strawberry Foxglove	z3-8	☀
Digitalis purpurea	Foxglove	z4-8	☀
Fuchsia	Fuchsia	annual	☀
Gladiolus	Gladiolus	z7-10	☼
Hemerocalis	Daylily	z4-9	●☀
Hesperis matronalis	Dame's Rocket	z3-8 (biennial)	☼
Heuchera sanguinea	Coral Bells	z3-8	☀
Heuchera sanguinea 'Snow Angel'	Coral Bell	z3-9	☀
Hibiscus moscheutos	Common Mallow	z5-9	☀
Hosta spp.	Plantain Lily	z3-8	☀
Impatiens spp.	Impatiens	annual	☀
Ipomoea purpurea	Tall Morning Glory	annual	☼
Iris cristata	Crested Dwarf Iris	z3-8	☀
Iris ensata	Japanese Iris	z4-9	☀
Iris 'Bearded hybrids'	Bearded Iris	z3-10	☼
Iris pallida	Sweet Iris	z4-9	☼
Iris sibirica	Siberian Iris	z3-9	☀
Kniphofia uvaria	Red Hot Poker	z5-8	☼
Lantana	Lantana	annual	☼

Nature-Food for Hummingbirds ...continued

Scientific Name	Common Name	Zone	Light
Lavandula angustifolia	English Lavender	z5-9	☼
Liatris punctata	Blazing Star	z4-9	☼
Liatris spicata	Spike Gayfeather	z3-9	☼
Lilium auratum	Goldband Lily	z4-9	☼ ☀
Lilium bulbiferum	Fire Lily	z2-8	☼ ☀
Lilium candidum	Madonna Lily	z4-9	
Lilium formosanum	Formosa Lily	z5-8	☼
Lilium henryi	Henry Lily	z4-7	☼ ☼
Lilium martagon	Turk's Cap	z3-7	☼ ☼ ☀
Lilium philadelphicum	Wood Lily	z4-7	☼ ☀
Lilium pumilum	Coral Lily	z3-7	☼
Lilium regale	Regal Lily	z3-8	☼
Lilium speciosum	Speciosum Lily	z4-8	☼ ☼
Lilium tigrinum	Tiger Lily	z3-9	☼
Linum grandiflorum 'Rubrum'	Flax	annual	☼
Lobelia cardinalis	Cardinal Flower	z2-9	☼
Lobelia siphilitica	Great Blue Lobelia	z4-8	☼ ☼
Lupinus hybrids	Lupine	z3-6	☼ ☼
Lychnis coronaria	Rose Campion	z4-7	☼
Mimulus	Monkey Flower	annual	☼ ☀
Monarda didyma	Bee Balm	z3-7	☼ ☼
Monarda fistulosa	Wild Bergamot	z3-7	☼

Nature-Food for Hummingbirds ...continued

Scientific Name	Common Name	Zone	Light
Nepeta cataria	Catnip	z2-7	☼-☼
Nicotiana alata	Tobacco Plant	annual	☼
Penstemon barbatus	Common Bearded Tongue	z2-8	☼
Penstemon digitalis	Smooth White Penstemon	z4-8	☼
Petunia	Petunia	annual	☼
Phlox maculata	Spotted Phlox	z3-8	☼
Phlox paniculata	Garden Phlox	z4-8	☼-☼
Physostegia virginiana	Obedient Plant	z2-9	☼
Platycodon grandiflorus	Balloonflower	z3-7	☼-☼
Polygonatum commutatum	Great Solomon's Seal	z3-7	☼-●
Primula vulgaris	English Primrose	z5-8	☼-●
Pulmonaria angustifolia	Blue Lungwort	z2-7	●-●
Pulmonaria longifolia	Long-Leafed Lungwort	z3-8	●-●
Pulmonaria saccharata	Bethlehem Sage	z3-7	●-●
Rosemarinus officinalis	Rosemary	z7-11	☼
Salvia greggii	Texas Sage (Red)	annual	☼
Silene virginica	Fire Pink	z4-7	☼
Tropaeolum majus	Nasturtium	annual	☼
Verbena	Vervain	annual	☼
Yucca filimentosa	Adam's Needle	z5-9	☼
Zinnia	Zinnia	annual	☼

Nature-Plants for Honeybees

Bees tend to be attracted to plants that are bluer in hue. **Bees can not distinguish red.** Some plants on this list may have red cultivars and this would not be a good choice to attract bees. Perfumes and flower fragrance also attract bees.

Scientific Name	Common Name	Zone	Light
Achillea x 'Coronation Gold'	Yarrow	z3-9	☼
Achillea filipendulina	Fern-Leaf Yarrow	z3-8	☼
Achillea grandifolia	White Yarrow	z5-8	☼
Achillea millefolium	Common Yarrow	z2-9	☼
Achillea x 'Moonshine'	Yarrow	z3-7	☼
Agastache foeniculum	Anise Hyssop	z6-9	☼
Allium sphaerocephalum	Drumstick Chives	z4-8	☼
Ammi majus	False Queen Anne's Lace	z3-9	☼
Anchusa officinalis	Bugloss	z3-8	☼
Antennaria dioica rosea	Rose Pussytoes	z3-7	☼
Anthemis nobilis	Chamomile	z5-9	☼
Antirrhinum majus	Snapdragon	annual	☼
Aruncus dioicus	Goat's Beard	z3-7	☼-☼
Asclepias syriaca	Milkweed	z3-9	☼
Asclepias tuberosa	Butterfly Weed	z4-9	☼
Aster cordifolius	Heart-Leaf Aster	z3-8	☼
Aster divaricatus	White Wood Aster	z4-8	☼
Aster ericoides	Heath Aster	z5-8	☼
Aster x frikartii	Aster	z5-8	☼
Aster lateriflorus	Calico Aster	z5-7	☼

Nature-Plants for Honeybees ...continued

Scientific Name	Common Name	Zone	Light
Aster novae-angliae	New England Aster	z4-8	☼
Aster novi-belgii	New York Aster	z4-8	☼
Borago officinalis	Borage	annual	☼
Campanula garganica	Gargano Bellflower	z5-7	☼ ☀
Campanula glomerata	Clustered Bellflower	z3-8	☼ ☀
Campanula lactiflora	Milky Bellflower	z5-7	☼
Centaurea montana	Bachelor's Button	z3-8	☼ ☀
Chrysanthemum nipponicum	Nippon Daisy	z5-9	☼
Cichorium endivia	Chicory	z4-11	☼
Convallaria majalis	Lily of the Valley	z2-7	☼ ☀
Coreopsis lanceolata	Lanceleaf Coreopsis	z3-8	☼
Digitalis purpurea	Foxglove	z4-8	☀
Echinacea purpurea	Purple Coneflower	z3-8	☼
Epilobium augustifolium	Fireweed	z2-10	☼
Erigeron philadelphicus	Common Fleabane	z3-8	☼
Erigeron pulchellus	Poor Robin's Plantain	z3-7	☼
Eupatorium purpureum	Joe Pye Weed	z4-8	☼ ☀
Eupatorium rugosum	White Snakeroot	z3-7	☼
Fagopyrum esculentum	Buckwheat	annual	☼
Filipendula rubra	Queen-of-the-Prairie	z3-7	☀
Foeniculum vulgare	Fennel	z6-9	☼
Fragaria vesca	Wild Strawberries	z5-10	☼

Nature-Plants for Honeybees ...continued

Scientific Name	Common Name	Zone	Light
Fuchsia	Fuchsia	annual	☼☼
Gaillardia x grandiflora	Blanket Flower	z2-9	☼
Lamium maculatum	Spotted Nettle	z3-8	☼☼
Lavandula augustifolia	English Lavender	z5-9	☼
Leucanthemum x superbum	Shasta Daisy	z4-9	☼
Mentha	Mint	z3-7	☼☼
Monarda fistulosa	Wild Bergamot	z3-7	☼
Nepeta x faassenii	Faassen Nepeta	z4-7	☼
Ocimum basilicum	Sweet Basil	annual	☼☼
Origanum majorana	Sweet Marjoram	z7-10	☼
Origanum vulgare	Oregano	z3-7	☼☼
Perovskia atriplicifolia	Russian Sage	z5-9	☼
Potentilla fruticosa	Shrubby Cinquefoil	z3-7	☼
Pulmonaria angustifolia	Blue Lungwort	z2-7	●☼
Pulmonaria longifolia	Long-Leafed Lungwort	z3-8	●☼
Pulmonaria saccharata	Bethlehem Sage	z3-7	●☼
Pulsatilla	Pasque Flower	z5-7	☼☼
Rosmarinus officinalis	Rosemary	z7-11	☼
Rudbeckia fulgida	Black-eyed Susan	z3-8	☼
Salvia azurea	Sage	z5-9	☼
Salvia officinalis	Sage	z4-7	☼
Salvia pratensis	Meadow Sage	z3-7	☼

307

Nature-Plants for Honeybees

Scientific Name	Common Name	Zone	Light
Salvia x sylvestris	Hybrid Sage	z4-7	☼
Satureja montana	Winter Savory	z5-8	☼ ☼
Scabiosa	Pincushion Flower	z3-7	☼
Sedum acre var. aurea 'Goldmoss'	Mossy Stonecrop	z3-8	☼
Sisyrinchium angustifolium	Blue-Eyed Grass	z3-8	☼ ☼
Solidago canadensis	Goldenrod	z3-9	☼
Stevia rebaudiana	Stevia	annual	
Symphytum officinale	Comfrey	z4-7	☼ ☼
Teucrium chamaedrys	Germander	z4-9	☼ ☼
Thymus serphyllum	Wild Thyme	z5-8	☼ ☼
Thymus vulgaris	Garden Thyme	z4-10	☼
Trifolium pratense	Red Clover	z3-8	☼
Tropaeolum majus	Nasturtium	annual	☼
Verbascum chaixii	Mullein	z5-8	☼
Veronica spp.	Speedwell	z4-8	☼

Section Six

Theme Gardens

Theme Gardens-Biblical

Scientific Name	Common Name	Zone	Light
Allium cepa	Spring Onion	z4-11	☼
Allium sativum	Garlic	z7-10	☼
Anemone coronaria	Poppy Anemone	z6-9	☼
Anethum graveolens	Dill	annual	☼
Anthemis tinictora	Golden Marguerite	z3-7	☼
Artemisia abrotanum	Southernwood	z5-8	☼
Artemisia lactiflora	White Sage	z4-9	☼
Aremisia ludoviciana ssp. *albula*	White Sage	z4-9	☼
Artemisia vulgaris	Mugwort	z4-10	☼
Centaurea macrocephala	Globe Centaurea	z3-7	☼
Centaurea montana	Bachelor's Button	z3-8	☼ ☀
Cichorium intybus	Chicory	z3-10	☼ ☀
Coriandrum sativum	Cilantro	annual	☼
Crocus sativum	Saffron Crocus	z6-9	☼
Cyperus papyrus	Papyrus	z9-10	☼ ☀
Eruca vesicaria ssp. *sativa*	Arugula	annual	☼
Foeniculum vulgare	Fennel	z6-9	☼
Hyacinthus orientalis	Hyacinth	z5-9	☼
Hyssopus officinalis	Hyssop	z3-11	☼ ☀
Iris pseudacorus	Yellow Flag Iris	z5-9	☼ ☀

311

Theme Gardens-Biblical ...continued

Scientific Name	Common Name	Zone	Light
Iris versicolor	Blue Flag Iris	z2-8	☼ ◐
Juncus effuses	Common Rush	z5-9	☼ ◐
Lilium candidum	Madonna Lily	z4-9	☼ ◐
Linum perenne	Flax	z5-8	☼ ◐
Malva moschata	Musk Mallow	z4-8	☼
Mentha spicata	Spearmint	z3-10	☼ ◐
Mentha suaveolens	Apple Mint	z5-10	☼ ◐
Narcissus	Daffodil	z4-9	☼ ◐
Nigella sativa	Black Cumin	z7-10	☼
Origanum vulgare	Oregano	z3-7	☼ ◐
Ornithogalum umbellatum	Star-of-Bethlehem	z4-9	☼ ◐
Papaver alpinum	Alpine Poppy	z4-6	☼
Papaver orientale	Oriental Poppy	z2-7	☼
Papaver rhoeas	Corn Poppy	annual	☼
Ruta graveolens	Rue	z4-8	☼
Salvia officinalis	Sage	z4-7	☼
Thymus vulgaris	Garden Thyme	z4-10	☼
Tulipa	Tulip	z4-9	☼
Typha domingensis	Cattail	z3-10	☼ ◐
Viola odorata	Sweet Violet	z5-10	☼ ◐

Theme Gardens-Children's

Many themes can be used for a children's garden. Depending on how big an area there is to plant, several themes may be incorporated. Some possibilities are; plants for birds, butterflies, miniature mazes, sunflower house, an alphabet garden, tepees, historical, ponds, sound, touch, smell, taste, rainbow or storybook gardens. We want to enchant, encourage and spur on enthusiastic young gardeners with fanciful and unusual plants to inspire curiosity.

Scientific Name	Common Name	Zone	Light	Comments
Agastache cana	Mosquito Plant	z6-9	☼	Smells like bubblegum
Arachis hypogaea	Peanut Plant	z8-10	☼	
Allium 'Globemaster'	Hybrid Onion	z4-8	☼	Giant globes
Allium giganteum	Giant Onion	z4-8	☼	
Allium schubertii	Tumbleweed Onion	z5-9	☼	Unusual flower
Alocasia calodora	Persian Palm	z10-11	☼◐	
Aloysia triphylla	Lemon Verbena	z8-11	☼	Strong lemon scent
Amorphophallus konjac	Voodoo Lily	z6-10	☼●	Unusual flower
Anethum graveolens	Dill	annual	☼	Dill pickle smell
Arisarum proboscideum	Mouse Plant	z5-9	☼●	Blooms look like a hiding mouse
Artemisia 'Silver Mound'	Satiny Wormwood	z4-9	☼	
Asclepias	Milkweed	z4-7	☼	
Briza maxima	Quaking Oat Grass	annual	☼	
Campanula punctata 'Cherry Bells'	Bellflower	z5-9	☼◐	
Campanula x symphiandra	Bellflower	z3-8	☼◐	
Chasmanthium latifolium	Northern Sea Oats	z4-7	☼	Flat seedheads

Theme Gardens-Children's ...continued

Scientific Name	Common Name	Zone	Light	Comments
Colocasia	Elephant Ear	z7-10	☀	Large leaf
Cortaderia selloana 'Pumila'	Dwarf Pampas Grass	z6-10	☼	
Cynara cardunculus	Cardoon	z7-10	☼	
Dicentra spectabilis	Bleeding Heart	z4-8	☀	Fold heart see lady in a bathtub
Dichelostemma ida-maia	Fire Cracker Flower	z5-8	☼	
Echinops ritro	Globe Thistle	z3-8	☼	
Equisteum hyemale	Rush Horsetail	z3-11	☼	
Eryngium bourgatii	Mediterranean Sea Holly	z5-8	☼	
Eryngium planum 'Blaukappe'	Flat Sea Holly	z5-8	☼	
Eryngium planum	Flat Sea Holly	z5-8	☼	
Fragaria vesca	Wild Strawberry	z5-10	☀	
Gunnera manicata	Giant Rhubarb	z7-10	☼	Enormous leaves
Helianthus annuus	Sunflower	annual	☼	
Humulus lupulus 'Aureus'	Golden Hops	z5-7	☼	
Impatiens capensis	Jewelweed	z2-8	☀ ◐	Seeds pop when touched
Ipomoea purpurea	Tall Morning Glory	annual	☼	
Ipomoea alba	Moon Vine	annual	☼	
Juncus effusus 'Curly Wurly'	Corkscrew Rush	z5-9	☼	
Juncus effusus 'Spiralis'	Corkscrew Rush	z5-9	☼	

Theme Gardens-Children's ...continued

Scientific Name	Common Name	Zone	Light	Comments
Juncus effusus 'Unicorn'	Corkscrew Rush	z5-9	☼ ☼	
Lablab purpureus	Purple Hyacinth Bean	annual	☼	
Lagurus ovatus	Bunny-tail Grass	annual	☼	
Lathyrus odoratus	Sweet Pea	z5-7	☼ ☼	
Lavandula angustifolia	Lavender	z5-9	☼	
Lunaria annua	Money Plant	z4-8	☼ ☼	Papery seeds
Lycoris radiata	Spider Lily	z7-10	☼	
Mentha x piperita f. citrata 'Chocolate'	Chocolate Mint	z3-7	☼ ☼	
Mimosa nuttallii	Sensitive Briar	z6-9	☼	Leaves fold when touched
Mimosa pudica	Sensitive Plant	z9-10	☼	Leaves fold when touched
Miscanthus sinensis	Maiden Grass	z5-9	☼ ☼	
Molina caerulea 'Variegata'	Purple Moorgrass	z4-9	☼ ☼	
Musa basjoo	Hardy Banana	z7-10	☼	
Nigella damascena	Love-in-a-Mist	annual	☼ ☼	
Ophiopogon	Mondo Grass	z6-9	☼ ☼	
Pennisetum orientale 'Tall Tails'	Giant Fountain Grass	z6-10	☼ ☼	
Physalis alkekengi	Chinese Lantern	z3-9	☼ ☼	
Platycodon grandiflorus	Balloon Flower	z3-7	☼ ☼	Flowers like a balloon
Pulsatilla vulgaris	Pasque Flower	z5-7	☼ ☼	Fuzzy seed heads

315

Theme Gardens-Children's ...continued

Scientific Name	Common Name	Zone	Light	Comments
Salvia argentea	Silver Sage	z5-8	☼	Velvety foliage
Sarracenia purpurea	Pitcher Plant	z4-9	☼ ☀	Carniverous plant, eats insects
Sempervivum tectorum	Hens and Chicks	z3-7	☼	
Stachys byzantina	Lamb's Ear	z4-8	☼	
Stipa tenuissima	Feather Grass	z7-10	☼	
Strelitzia reginae	Bird of Paradise	z10-12	☼ ☀	Looks like a bird
Tropaeolum majus	Nasturtium	annual	☼	
Zantedeschia aethiopica	Calla Lily	z7-10	☼	

Theme Gardens-Evening

An evening garden can be a great way for people to get more enjoyment out of their outdoor areas. This list is comprised of plants that really stand out in the evening, some of which only bloom or emit fragrance at night. The possibilities are great as to what other plants can be used. Perennials to be considered are those with white or light colored flowers, variegated leaves or fragrance.

Scientific Name	Common Name	Zone	Light	Comments
Allium tuberosum	Garlic Chives	z4-8	☼	Aggressively seeds
Artemisia spp.	Artemisia	z5-8	☼	All varieties w/ silver foliage
Callirhoe alcaeoides 'Logan Calhoun'	Poppy Mallow	z4-9	☼	
Cerastium tomentosum	Snow-in-Summer	z2-7	☼	
Clematis armandi	Clematis	z8-11	☀	Fragrant
Gladiolus tristis	Gladiolus	z7-10	☼	Scent is released at night
Hakonechloa macra 'Alba Striata'	Japanese Forest Grass	z5-7	☀ ●	
Heliotropium arborescens	Heliotrope	annual	☼ ☀	Scented at night
Hemerocallis citrina	Daylily	z3-8	☀	Very fragrant/Nocturnal
Hesperis matronalis	Dame's Rocket	z3-8	☼	Evening fragrance/biennial
Hosta spp.	Hosta	z3-9	☀ ●	Fragrant/White variegated types
Iberis sempervirens	Candytuft	z3-8	☀	
Ipomoea alba	Moon Vine	annual	☼	Fragrant/Nocturnal flowering
Leucanthemum x superbum	Shasta Daisy	z4-9	☼	
Lobularia maritima	Sweet Alyssum	annual	☼	Fragrant
Lysimachia clethroides	Gooseneck Loosestrife	z3-8	☼	

317

Theme Gardens-Evening...continued

Scientific Name	Common Name	Zone	Light	Comments
Miscanthus sinensis 'Dixieland'	Japanese Silver Grass	z5-9	☼ ☀	
Nicotiana alata	Nicotiana	annual	☼	Intense fragrance at night
Nicotiana sylvestris	Nicotiana	annual	☼	Intense fragrance at night
Oenothera caespitosa	Tufted Evening Primrose	z4-9	☼	Fragrant/Opens late in the day
Oenothera missouriensis	Ozark Sundrops	z4-7	☼ ☀	Fragrant/Opens late in the day
Paeonia spp.	Peony	z3-8	☼ ☀	Fragrant/White colored cultivars
Penstemon tubaeflorus	White Plains Penstemon	z4-7	☼	
Petunia	Petunia	annual	☼	Fragrant/White colored cultivars
Sedum 'Frosty Morn'	Sedum	z4-8	☼ ☀	
Valeriana officinalis	Valeriana	z4-9	☼	Fragrant/Aggressively seeds
Zantedeschia aethiopica	Calla Lily	z7-10	☼	
Zephyranthes candida	White Rain Lily	z7-10	☼ ☀	

Theme Gardens-Japanese

Scientific Name	Common Name	Zone	Light	
Acorus gramineus	Sweet Flag	z5-8	☼	
Adiantum pedatum	Maidenhair Fern	z2-8	☼ ☀	
Asplenium trichomanes	Maidenhair Spleenwort	z2-9	☼ ☀	
Aster tataricus	Tatarian Daisy	z4-8	☼	
Athyrium nipponicum	Japanese Painted Fern	z4-8	☼ ☀	
Chrysanthemum x morifolium	Chrysanthemum	z5-9	☼	
Dianthus superbus	Fringed Pink	z3-9	☼	
Equisetum hyemale	Rush Horsetail	z4-11	☼ ☀	
Fargesia nitida	Fountain Bamboo	z5-9	☼ ☀	Clumping
Iris ensata	Japanese Iris	z4-9	☼	
Liriope muscari	Blue Lily Turf	z6-9	☼ ☀	
Liriope spicata	Creeping Liriope	z4-10	☼ ☀	
Lycoris radiata	Spider Lily	z7-10	☼	
Miscanthus sinensis	Japanese Silver Grass	z5-9	☼ ☀	
Moss-See Moss List				
Nelumbo nucifera	Sacred Lotus	z4-11	☼	
Ophiopogon japonicus	Dwarf Mondo Grass	z6-9	☼ ☀	
Paeonia lactiflora	Peony	z4-9	☼	
Petasites japonicus	Japanese Butterbur	z5-9	☼ ☀	
Phyllostachys aureosulcata	Yellow Groove Bamboo	z5-10	☼ ☀	Needs Containment

Theme Gardens-Japanese...continued

Scientific Name	Common Name	Zone	Light
Phyllostachys nigra	Black Bamboo	z6-10	☼ ☀ Needs Containment
Phyllostachys nuda	Snow Bamboo	z5-10	☼ ☀ Needs Containment
Platycodon grandiflorus	Balloon Flower	z3-7	☼ ☀

Theme Gardens-Knot

Knot gardens are special feature gardens designed in a formal pattern or framework usually divided into groups of four. These gardens provide impact, interest, shape and form. The interest in a Knot garden comes in part from contrasting foliage colors. Knot gardens have been in use since medieval times with a variety of aromatic & culinary herbs. Traditional knot gardens follow designs of Lindisearne, Kells, Tudor, Oriental, Love and Celtic knots. Plants used for the knot portion of the garden are boxwoods, barberries, germander, hyssop and lavender cotton.

Scientific Name	Common Name	Zone	Light
Acanthus spinosus	Bear's Breeches	z6-9	☼
Allium sphaerocephalum	Chives	z4-8	☼
Artemisia absinthium 'Frigida'	Wormwood	z3-9	☼
Artemisia absinthium 'Lambrook Silver'	Wormwood	z3-9	☼
Artemisia absinthium	Wormwood	z3-9	☼
Artemisia lactiflora	White Sage	z4-9	☼
Artemisia ludoviciana 'Valerie Finnis'	White Sage	z4-10	☼
Artemisia ludoviciana	White Sage	z4-9	☼
Artemisia schmidtiana	Silver Mound Artemisia	z3-8	☼
Artemisia x 'Powis Castle'	Wormwood	z6-8	☼
Chamaemelum nobelis	Chamomile	z4-10	☼
Dianthus alpinus	Alpine Pink	z3-7	☼
Dianthus barbatus	Sweet William	z3-8	☼
Dianthus deltoides	Maiden Pinks	z3-8	☼

Theme Gardens-Knot ...continued

Scientific Name	Common Name	Zone	Light
Dianthus gratianopolitanus	Cheddar Pinks	z3-8	☼
Dianthus x allwoodii	Pinks	z4-8	☼
Gaultheria procumbens	Wintergreen	z4-9	☼ ●
Hyssopus offininalis	Hyssop	z3-11	☼ ☼
Iberis sempervirens	Candytuft	z3-8	☼ ☼
Lavandula angustifolia	English Lavender	z5-9	☼
Malcomia maritima	Virginia Stock	annual	☼
Malva alcea	Mallow	z4-8	☼ ☼
Mentha pulegium	Penny Royal	z5-10	☼
Ocimum basilicum 'Marseille'	Basil	annual	☼
Ocimum basilicum 'Minett'	Basil	annual	☼
Ocimum basilicum 'Minimum'	Basil	annual	☼
Ocimum basilicum 'Spicy Globe'	Basil	annual	☼
Origanum laevicatum 'Herrenhausen'	Oregano	z6-7	☼
Origanum majorana	Sweet Marjoram	z7-10	☼
Origanum vulgare 'Album'	Oregano	z3-7	☼ ☼
Origanum vulgare 'Aureum'	Oregano	z6-7	☼ ☼
Origanum vulgare 'Compactum Aureum'	Oregano	z6-7	☼ ☼
Origanum vulgare 'Dark Leaf'	Dark Leaf Oregano	z3-7	☼ ☼

Theme Gardens-Knot ...continued

Scientific Name	Common Name	Zone	Light
Origanum vulgare 'Variegata'	Oregano	z3-7	☼ ☼
Origanum vulgare	Oregano	z3-7	☼ ☼
Petroselinium c. var. *neapolitanum*	Flat-Leaved Parsley	z5-9	☼
Petroselinium crispum	Curled Parsley	z5-9	☼
Raphanus sativus	Radishes	annual	☼
Rosmarinus officinalis	Rosemary	z7-11	☼
Ruta graveolens	Rue	z4-8	☼
Salvia officinalis	Common Sage	z4-7	☼
Santolina chamaecyparissus	Lavender Cotton	z6-9	☼
Sedum ellacombianum	Sedum	z3-8	☼
Sedum requieni	Miniature Stonecrop	z4-8	☼ ☼
Sedum spurium	Two Row Stonecrop	z3-8	☼
Tagetes signata 'Gem Series'	Tiny Marigolds	annual	☼
Teucrium chamaedrys	Germander	z4-9	☼
Teucrium scorodonia	Wood Sage	z6-10	☼
Thymus x citriodorus	Lemon Thyme	z6-10	☼
Thymus vulgaris	Garden Thyme	z4-10	☼
Thymus serphyllum 'Elfin'	Wild Thyme	z5-8	☼ ☼
Torenia	Wishbone Flower	annual	☼
Trifolium pratense	Red Clover	z3-8	☼

Theme Gardens-Knot ...continued

Scientific Name	Common Name	Zone	Light
Veronica alpina	Alpine Speedwell	z3-8	☀
Veronica austriaca	Austrian Speedwell	z4-7	☀
Viola	Pansy	annual	☀ ☀

Theme Gardens-Rock

Scientific Name	Common Name	Zone	Light
Aethionema 'Warley Rose'	Stonecress	z4-8	☼
Aethionema armeneum	Turkish Stonecress	z5-7	☼
Aethionema grandiflorum	Persian Stonecress	z5-7	☼
Aethionema iberideum	Iberis Stonecress	z5-7	☼ ☀
Alyssum serphyllifolium	Mountain Alyssum	z4-7	☼
Aurinia saxatile	Basket-of-Gold	z3-7	☼
Androsace carnea	Rock Jasmine	z4-7	☼
Androsace lanuginosa	Rock Jasmine	z4-5	☼
Anemone blanda	Grecian Windflower	z4-7	☼ ☀
Aquilegia alpina	Alpine Columbine	z3-8	☼ ☀
Aquilegia flabellata 'Alba'	Fan Columbine	z3-9	☀
Arabis alpina	Alpine Rock Cress	z4-7	☼
Arabis blepharophylla	Fringed Rock Cress	z5-7	☼
Arabis caucasica	Wall Rock Cress	z4-7	☼
Arenaria montana	Mountain Sandwort	z4-8	☼ ☀
Arenaria purpurascens	Pink Sandwort	z4-7	☼
Armeria maritima	Sea Thrift	z4-8	☼
Aruncus aesthusifolius	Dwarf Goat's Beard	z3-7	☼ ☀
Asarum europaeum	European Wild Ginger	z4-8	☀ ☀

325

Theme Garden-Rock ...continued

Scientific Name	Common Name	Zone	Light
Aubrieta deltoidea	False Rock Cress	z4-7	☼ ☀
Aubrieta deltoidea 'Whitewall Gem'	False Rock Cress	z4-7	☼ ☀
Campanula carpatica	Carpathian Bellflower	z3-7	☼ ☀
Campanula poscharskyana	Serbian Bellflower	z3-7	☀
Cerastium tomentosum	Snow-in-Summer	z2-7	☼
Corydalis lutea	Yellow Corydalis	z5-7	☼ ● ☀
Cyclamen coum	Hardy Cyclamen	z6-9	☀
Delosperma nubigena	Ice Plant	z4-8	☼ ☀
Dianthus alpina	Alpine Pink	z3-7	☼
Dianthus deltoides	Maiden Pinks	z3-8	☼ ☀
Dianthus gratianopolitanus	Cheddar Pinks	z3-8	☼
Draba aizoides	Yellow Whitlow Grass	z3-7	☼
Draba sibirica	Whitlow Grass	z3-7	☼
Epimedium x youngianum 'Niveum'	Bishop's Hat	z5-9	☀
Erinus alpinus	Alpine Liverwort	z4-7	☼ ☀
Euphorbia myrsinites	Myrtle Euphorbia	z5-10	☼
Gentiana acaulis	Stemless Gentian	z3-6	☼ ☀
Gentiana septemfida	Crested Gentian	z3-7	☼ ☀
Geranium cinereum 'Ballerina'	Grayleaf Cranesbill	z4-9	☼ ☀
Geranium dalmaticum	Dalmatian Cranesbill	z4-7	☼

Theme Garden-Rock ...continued

Scientific Name	Common Name	Zone	Light
Geranium sanguineum var. *striatum*	Cranesbill	z4-8	☼
Globularia cordifolia	Heartleaf Globe Daisy	z4-9	☼ ☀
Gypsophila repens	Creeping Baby's Breath	z3-7	☼
Lewisia cotyledon	Lewisia	z6-9	☼
Narcissus bulbocodium	Hoop Petticoat Daffodil	z5-8	☼ ☀
Petrorhagia saxifraga	Tunic Flower	z5-8	☼
Phlox douglasii	Phlox	z3-8	☼
Phlox subulata	Moss Phlox	z3-9	☼
Pulsatilla vulgaris	Common Pasque Flower	z5-7	☼ ☀
Saponaria ocymoides	Soapwort	z2-7	☼
Saponaria x 'Bressingham Hybrid'	Soapwort	z2-7	☼
Saxifraga x *arendsii*	Arend's Saxifrage	z4-7	☀
Saxifraga oppositifolia	Saxifrage	z2-6	☀
Saxifraga paniculata	Aizoon Saxifrage	z3-6	☀
Sedum acre	Goldmoss Sedum	z3-8	☼
Sedum kamtschaticum	Stonecrop	z3-8	☼
Sedum reflexum	Stonecrop	z3-8	☼
Sempervivum spp.	Hens & Chicks	z3-7	☼
Silene schafta	Schafta Campion	z4-8	☼

Theme Garden-Rock ...continued

Scientific Name	Common Name	Zone	Light
Thymus praecox	Creeping Thyme	z5-8	☼
Thymus serphyllum	Wild Thyme	z5-8	☼
Veronica pectinata	Comb Speedwell	z2-7	☼ ☼

Theme Garden-Sensory or Healing

Sensory gardens are designed to be interactive and can be theraputic. They contain plants which entice the visitor to touch, smell, taste and view the garden. Some plants can even draw your ear to listen, such as the knocking of a bamboo grove or rustling grasses on a breezy day. Making plants easily accessible to visitors is another design consideration for a sensory garden.

Raised beds, vertical elements, and wide paths will provide access for those who are unable to bend, or are in a wheelchair. Not all fragrant perennials are listed here, please consult fragrant list for additional plant material.

Scientific Name	Common Name	Zone	Light	Sense
Aloysia triphylla	Lemon Verbena	z8-11	☼	Taste Smell
Artemisia 'Silver Mound'	Satiny Wormwood	z4-9	☼	Touch
Festuca glauca	Blue Fescue	z4-8	☼	Touch
Briza maxima	Quaking Oat Grass	annual	☼	Sound
Chasmanthium latifolium	Northern Sea Oats	z4-7	☼	Sound
Anethum graveolens	Dill	annual	☼	Taste Smell
Echinops ritro	Globe Thistle	z3-8	☼	Touch
Equisteum hyemale	Horsetail	z3-11	☼ ❋	Touch
Eryngium giganteum	Miss Willmott's Ghost	z4-7	☼	Touch
Fragaria vesca	Wild Strawberry	z5-10	☼ ❋	Taste
Hakonechloa macra	Japanese Forest Grass	z5-9	❋	Touch
Lagurus ovatus	Bunny-tail Grass	annual	☼	Touch
Mimosa nuttallii	Sensitive Briar	z6-9	☼	Touch

329

Theme Gardens-Sensory or Healing...continued

Scientific Name	Common Name	Zone	Light	Sense
Mimosa pudica	Sensitive Plant	z9-10	☼	Touch
Tropaeolum majus	Nasturtium	annual	☼	Taste
Pennisetum alopecuroides	Fountain Grass	z5-9	☼ ☀	Touch
Salvia argentea	Silver Sage	z5-8	☼	Touch
Salvia officinalis	Sage	z4-7	☼	Touch Taste Smell
Sempervivum tectorum	Hens & Chicks	z3-7	☼	Touch
Stachys byzantina	Lamb's Ear	z4-8	☼	Touch
Stipa gigantean	Giant Feather Grass	z7-9	☼ ☀	Sound

Theme Gardens-Tropical Looking

These plants will provide bold colors with lush contrasting foliage. Some are hardy and others may be grown as annuals or brought indoors for the winter.

Scientific Name	Common Name	Zone	Light
Actinidia kolomikta	Kiwi Vine	z4-8	☼ ☽
Belamcanda chinensis	Blackberry Lily	z4-10	☼ ☼
Belamcanda chinensis 'Nana'	Blackberry Lily	z4-10	☼ ☼
Belamcanda flabellata 'Halo Yellow'	Blackberry Lily	z5-10	☼ ☼
Colocasia gigantean	Giant Elephant Ear	z7-10	☼ ☼
Colocasia esculenta 'Black Magic'	Elephant Ear	z7-10	☼
Canna spp.	Canna	z7-10	☼
Coleus	Coleus	annual	☽
Cortaderia selloana	Pampas Grass	z6-9	☼
Crocosmia spp.	Montbretia	z5-8	☼
Darmera peltata	Umbrella Plant	z5-7	☼ ☽
Datura wrightii	Devil's Trumpet	annual	☼
Eryngium yuccafolium	Rattlesnake Master	z5-9	☼
Euphorbia amygdaloides var. robbiae	Wood Spurge	z5-8	☼ ☽
Euphorbia characias 'Ember Queen'	Cypress Spurge	z6-8	☼ ☼
Euphorbia characias 'John Tomelson'	Cypress Spurge	z6-8	☼ ☼
Euphorbia x 'Blackbird'	Cypress Spurge	z5-9	☼ ☽
Gunnera manicata	Giant Rhubarb	z7-10	☼

Theme Gardens-Tropical Looking...continued

Scientific Name	Common Name	Zone	Light
Hakonechloa macra 'Aureola'	Japanese Forest Grass	z5-9	☼
Hedichium 'Assam Orange'	Ginger Lily	z7-10	☼
Hedichium coccineum	White Ginger Lily	z8-10	☼
Hibiscus moscheutos	Common Mallow	z5-9	☼
Ipomoea lobata	Mina Lobata	annual	☼
Ipomoea multifida	Cardinal Vine	annual	☼
Kniphofia spp.	Torchlily	z5-8	☼
Ligularia tussilaginea 'Aureo Maculata'	Leopard Plant	z7-10	☼
Lilium auratum	Goldband Lily	z4-9	☼
Lilium auratum var. *platyphyllum*	Goldband Lily	z4-9	☼
Lilium candidum	Madonna Lily	z4-9	☼
Lycoris radiata	Spider Lily	z7-10	☼
Matteuccia struthiopteris	Ostrich Fern	z2-10	●☼
Miscanthus sinensis 'Cosmopolitan'	Japanese Silver Grass	z6-9	☼
Miscanthus sinensis 'Silver Feather'	Japanese Silver Grass	z4-9	☼
Miscanthus sinensis 'Variegatus'	Japanese Silver Grass	z5-9	☼
Musa basjoo	Hardy Banana	z7-10	☼
Nelumbo nucifera	Sacred Lotus	z4-11	☼
Osmunda regalis	Royal Fern	z3-10	●☼
Passiflora spp.	Passion Flower	z7-11	☼

Theme Gardens-Tropical Looking...continued

Scientific Name	Common Name	Zone	Light	
Petasites japonicus	Japanese Butterbur	z5-9	☀ ☀	
Phormium tenax	New Zealand Flax	z8-10	☼	
Phyllostachys aureosulcata	Yellow Groove Bamboo	z5-10	☼ ☀	Needs Containment
Phyllostachys nigra	Black Bamboo	z6-10	☼ ☀	Needs Containment
Phyllostachys nuda	Snow Bamboo	z5-10	☼ ☀	Needs Containment
Rheum palmatum	Ornamental Rhubarb	z4-7	☀	
Ricinis communis	Caster Oil Plant	annual	☼	Very Poisionous
Rodgersia aesculifolia	Fingerleaf Rodgersia	z5-7	☼	
Rodgersia pinnata 'Superba'	Featherleaf Rodgersia	z5-8	☀	
Rodgersia podophylla	Rodgersia	z5-8	☼	
Rodgersia sambucifolia	Rodgersia	z5-8	☼	
Tricyrtis affinis 'Tricolor'	Toad Lily	z5-9	● ☀	
Tricyrtis x 'Lightning Strike'	Toad Lily	z4-9	● ☀	
Yucca filamentosa	Adam's Needle	z4-10	☼	
Zantedeschia aethiopica	Calla Lily	z7-10	☼	

333

334

Glossary of Terms Used in This Book

335

Glossary of Terms used in this book

acidic soil-having a soil ph between 5.0-6.5

alkaline soil-having a soil ph of 6.5 and higher

annual-plant that grows one year or season, and then dies

bearded-having long 'hairs', in the flower , such as Iris germanica

bract-much smaller leaf, from the axil of which a flower or stalk begins

bulb-mass of overlapping fleshy leaves consisting of scales on a short stem base enclosing one or more buds capable of developing new plants, such as *Tulipa*

biennial-growing vegetatively the first year, flowering and fruiting the second, then dying

catkin-resembling kitten's tail , such as *Pennisetum spp.*

clustered-leaves or flowers closely arranged or grouped

cordate–heart–shaped

corm-enlarged bulb-like base of a stem, not differentiated into scales, as in *Crocus*

downy-having soft fine 'hairs'

ephemeral-plant flowers for a season, such as annuals

fall-petal bends downward, as in the *Iris*

foliage-leaves

glaucous-having a powdery whitish waxy coating that easily rubs off

glossy-shining, lustrous

habit-general outline or shape of a plant

hairy-pubescent, but with longer 'hairs', as in the bearded iris

head-pollinating portion of the plant which consists of ray or disc flowers

herbaceous-plant which has no persistent, woody tissue

hybrid-unique result of a cross between two or more plants

337

Glossary of Terms used in this book

infertile soil-soil without nutrients

inflorescence-flowers grouped into one flowerhead

linear-long and narrow leaves, as in long-leaf lungwort

midrib-center vein of a leaf

monocarpic-plant which flowers and fruits and then dies, some may live several years before flowering

native-inherent or original to an area

orb-sphere

panicle-branched flower cluster with lower flowers open first

perennial-herbaceous plant which returns every year

picotee edge- having a margin of different color

plume-a feathery flowerhead

procumbent-lying along the ground without rooting

prostrate-prone on the ground

pubescent-covered with short soft 'hairs', as in *Stachys*

scape-a leafless flower stalk commencing from the plant base

spike-shorter spire

spire -elongated flower grouping arising from the main axis

spore-reproductive body produced by plants such as ferns and mosses

stamen-pollen-bearing male reproductive organ of a flower

sterile-unable to produce seed

umbel-inflorescence spreading from a single point of the flower stalk, such as *Eupatorium maculatum*

undulate-wavy form of leaf

variegated-having distinct markings of different colors

Sources for Plant Material

Sources for Plant Material

Arrowhead Alpines
1310 N. Gregory Rd.
Fowlerville, MI 48836
517-223-8750
www.arrowhead-alpines.com
mail order
dwarf conifers, rock garden
and alpine plants

Brent and Becky's Bulbs
7463 Heath Trail
Gloucester, VA 23061
877-661-2852
www.brentandbeckysbulbs.com
mail order
bulbs

Bluestone Perennials, Inc.
7211 Middle Ridge Rd.
Madison, OH 44057
800-852-5243
www.bluestoneperennials.com
wholesale, retail, mail order
perennials, shrubs, temperennials

Hortech
14109 Cleveland Drive
Nunica, Michigan
616-842-1392
wholesale
perennials, grasses, rooftop plants

Heronswood Nursery
7530 NE 288th St.
Kingston, WA 98346
360-297-4172
www.heronswood.com
mail order
rare and unusual plants

ItSaul Plants
1280 Union Hill Rd.
Alpharetta, GA 30004
Toll Free: 888-448-7285
Phone: 678-297-7823
Fax: 678-297-7825
wholesale nursery

Jonkers Garden
897 Lincoln Ave.
Holland, MI 49423
616-392-7234
www.jonkersgarden.com
retail
perennials, annuals

Klyn Nurseries, Inc.
3322 South Ridge Rd.
P.O. Box 343
Perry, OH 44081
800-860-8104
wholesale
trees, shrubs, perennials, bamboo
and bog plants

341

Sources for Plant Material

Koraleski Flowers
5001 Monroe St.
Toledo, OH 43623
419-472-1650
retail
perennials, annuals, roses

Niche Gardens
1111 Dawson Road
Chapel Hill, NC 27516
919-967-0078
www.nichegardens.com
mail order, retail
perennials

North Creek Nurseries, Inc.
388 North Creek Rd.
Landenberg, PA 19350
610-225-0100
wholesale, mail order
perennials, annuals, shrubs

Plant Delights Nursery
9241 Sauls Rd.
Raleigh, NC 27603
919-772-4794
www.plantdelights.com
mail order
rare and unusual

Prairie Nursery
P.O. Box 306
Westfield, WI 53964
www.prairienursery.com
mail order and retail
prairie plants, seeds

Sunny Border
1709 Kensington Road
Box483
Kensington, CT 06037
800-732-1627
wholesale and retail
locations throughout the northeast
perennials, annuals, temperennials

Walters Gardens
96th Ave. and Business I-196
P.O. Box 137
Zeeland, MI 49464
888-925-8377
wholesale
perennials

White Flower Farms
P.O. Box 50
Litchfield, CT 06759
800-503-9624
www.whiteflowerfarm.com
mail order
perennials, bulbs, annuals

Bibliography

344

Bibliography

Armitage, Allan M. 2000. *Armitage's Garden Perennials*. Timber Press, Inc. Portland, OR.

Armitage, Allan M. 1989. *Herbaceous Perennial Plants*. Stipes Publishing, L.L.C. Champaign, IL.

Bloom, Allan. 1980. *Alpines for Your Garden*, Floraprint U.S.A., Chicago, IL

Brickell, Christopher, and Elvin McDonald. 1993. *The American Horticultural Society Encyclopedia of Gardening*, New York: Dorling Kindersley

Brickell, Christopher, and Judit Zuk. 1996. *The American Horticultural Society A-Z Encyclopedia of Garden Plants*. New York: Dorling Kindersley

Bull, John and Farrand, Jr., John. 1990. *The Audubon Society Field Guide to North American Birds*. Knopf, Alfred, NY, NY

Cullina, William. 2000. *The New England Wild Flower Society Guide to Growing and Propagating Wildflowers of the United States and Canada*. Houghton Mifflin Company, New York, NY.

Darke, Rick. 1999. *The Color Encyclopedia of Ornamental Grasses*. Timber Press, Inc. Portland, OR.

DiSabato-Aust, Tracy. 2003. *The Well-Designed Mixed Garden*. Timber Press, Inc. Portland, OR.

DiSabato-Aust, Tracy. 1998. *The Well Tended Garden*. Timber Press, Inc. Portland, OR.

Duthie, Pam. 2000. *Continuous Bloom*. Ball Publishing. Batavia, IL.

Evison, Raymond. 1998. *Clematis*. Timber Press, Inv. Portland, OR.

Foster, F. Gordon. 1984. *Ferns To Know And Grow*. Timber Press, Inc. Portland, OR.

Halpin, Anne with Bartolomei, Robert. 1997. *Rock Gardens*, *The New York Botanical Garden*, Clarkson Potter, New York, NY

Hawke, Richard. 1999. Clematis: the queen of vines, *In Flowering Vine*, Karen Davis Cutler, ed. Brooklyn, NY: Brooklyn Botanic Garden

345

346

Bibliography

Hinkley, Daniel J. 1999. *The Explorers Garden*. Timber Press, Inc. Portland, OR.

Hudak, Joseph. 1976. *Gardening with Perennials*. Timber Press, Inc. Portland, OR.

Innes, Clive. 1995. *Alpines, The Illustrated Dictionary*. Timber Press, Inc. Portland, OR.

McVicar, Jessica. 1994. *The Complete Herb Book*. Kyle Cathie Limited, London.

Mickel, John. 1994. *Ferns for American Gardens*. Macmillan Publishing Company, New York, NY

Nielsen, Mogens C. 1999. *Michigan Butterflies & Skippers*, MSU Extension, Michigan State University, East Lansing

Niering, William A. and Olmstead, Nancy C. and Thieret, John W. 2001. *National Audubon Society Field Guide to North American Wildflowers Eastern Region*. Alfred A. Knopf, Inc.

Oudolf, Piet. 2000. *Designing with Plants*. Timber Press, Inc. Portland, OR.

Raworth, Jenny. 1993. *Dried Flowers for all Seasons*. Reader's Digest Association, Inc. Pleasantville, NY.

Rice, Graham. 1999 *Discovering Annuals*, Timber Press, Inc. Portland, OR.

Schenk, George. 1997. *Moss Gardening*. Timber Press, Inc. Portland, OR.

Still, Steven. 1994. *Manual of Herbaceous Ornamental Plants*, 4th ed. Stipes Publishing L.L.C., Champaign, IL.

Tekiela, Stan. 2000. *Wildflowers of Michigan Field Guide*. Adventure Publications, Inc. Cambridge, Minnesota

Thomas Leo Ogren. 2000. *Allergy-Free Gardening*. Ten Speed Press. Berkeley, CA.

Verey, Rosemary. 1988. *The Garden in Winter*. Timber Press, Inc. Portland, OR.

Verey, Rosemary. 1981. *The Scented Garden*. Van Nostrand Reinhold Co. New York, NY.

Wilder, Louise Beebe. 1974. *The Fragrant Garden*. Dover Publications, Inc. New York, NY.

Zillis, Mark R. 2000. *The Hosta Handbook*. Q & Z Nursery Inc. Rochelle, IL

ISBN 978-1-58874-682-5